Ipswich Churches Ancient & Modern

by

Roy Tricker

BRECHINSET PUBLICATIONS

BRECHINSET PUBLICATIONS
7-11 King Street, Ipswich, Suffolk, England IP1 1EG

ISBN 0–9507064–1–8

Typeset by
Brechinset,
7-11 King Street, Ipswich, Suffolk IP1 1EG

Printed in Great Britain by
Alderman Printing & Bookbinding Co. Ltd.,
Russell Road, Ipswich, Suffolk IP1 2BN

Contents

To my wife

JENNY

who is extremely patient

and my father-in-law

BILL

for his encouragement

Acknowledgements

The major text-book for a work such as this has been the fabric of the churches themselves and my gratitude is expressed firstly to those who built them and maintained them over the centuries.

Much material has been gleaned from the *Ipswich Journal* and D. E. Davy's notes on microfilm, and also a host of other documents in the Suffolk Record Office. I am grateful to the staff there for the use of their facilities.

I also owe a great debt of gratitude to the following individuals:

The Bishop of St. Edmundsbury and Ipswich for kindly writing the Foreword.

George Pipe, for useful details about the bells.

Simon Pulham and John Budgen, for a wealth of information about the organs.

Cynthia Brown, for sharing with me some of her vast resources of dates of newspaper references to church restorations.

Birkin Haward, for advising me on the 19th century glass in the churches.

Peter Northeast, for valuable information from mediaeval wills.

Also several of the Ipswich clergy and their people for useful assistance and information.

My thanks finally to Val Brechin for turning masses of poorly produced typescript into an attractive book.

The Publishers are particularly grateful to King Design for their assistance in this publication.

Foreword

The Church Guides produced by Roy Tricker are widely appreciated and I am glad to commend this book on the Anglican churches in Ipswich.

Despite the problem of churches being locked to protect them from vandals, the number of those visiting them grows. Not all are drawn simply by their interest in architecture or in history, neither are those who come confined to people who are themselves members of Christian congregations.

Today there is a search for reality beyond human thought and for the fulfilment of needs not capable of being met by the gods of a materialistic society. It is here that many of our church buildings can speak louder than words and provide help in a world where confusion abounds. May they long continue to minister to us in this way.

John St. Edm. & Ipswich

Notes to the Reader

This brief description of the Anglican churches of Ipswich does not set out to be a detailed treatise on the history and architecture of the buildings or the development of the parishes. It is simply a short catalogue of items of interest connected with these buildings which may be of use to amateurs who, like myself, enjoy the beauty and antiquity to be seen both inside and outside these shrines, which were built for the glory of God.

Several of the churches have to be kept locked when not in use for services. This is an unfortunate necessity but the clergy are usually pleased to welcome visitors and will gladly arrange for the doors to be opened up, particularly if given prior notice. Even if one is unsuccessful in gaining entry, there is usually much which is worth seeing and enjoying on the exterior of the building.

Most of the churches are still in regular use for the purpose for which they were built, but five have outlived their usefulness for worship. One is now in the care of the Redundant Churches Fund and four are maintained and preserved by the Ipswich Historic Churches Trust, which was formed in 1979 to tend them and to find useful purposes for them. Ipswich is fortunate therefore that none of its ancient churches will be lost.

It is quite possible for anybody to enjoy old churches with very little background knowledge. The main problems are mastering the art of dating architecture by identifying the styles, and being able to differentiate between original work and modern restoration. The best method of doing this is by practice and these notes attempt to describe features such as doorways and windows and to make clear which parts were restored in earlier centuries.

The churches of Rushmere, Westerfield and Whitton originally served villages outside the town, so their descriptions have been appended at the end of the mediaeval section.

R.T.

General Introduction

The view across the town of Ipswich, from whichever direction we choose to enter it, is punctuated with towers and spires. Although they now have strong rivals for the skyline in the shape of tall office blocks which have been built during recent years, these towers still hold their own as they have done for centuries. Many have overlooked Ipswich for hundreds of years and several of the bells inside them have sounded for many generations. Many rang out for Victoria's Jubilee, some hailed the victory at Trafalgar and some may have sounded the victory of the British fleet over the Spanish Armada.

These towers mark a small part of one of England's greatest treasures, her rich heritage of mediaeval churches. Twelve churches of mediaeval foundation remain in Ipswich, which have survived the weather and storms of hundreds of years. They have been carefully tended, beautified and restored by loving hands and were erected long before the days of cranes and cement-mixers. These buildings were built for the glory of God and for His worship. They still incorporate fine examples of the mediaeval craftsman's art in wood and stone and their walls are saturated with the atmosphere which is brought about by the continuous prayer and devotion of many generations of Ipswich people who have used them over the centuries.

There are more than 10,000 mediaeval churches in this country and every one is of interest and worth visiting. Enjoying these buildings is a fascinating and rewarding pastime and very little knowledge is required in order to appreciate the wealth of beauty and antiquity which they contain. In nearly every town or village the church is by far the oldest building and may have stood for a thousand years. Ipswich is no exception to this. Although when compared with the shoals of magnificent mediaeval churches to be found in such places as Norwich, York and London, the dozen which we have in

Ipswich may seem modest, they do have, however, a tremendous amount of interest and beauty which more than rewards examination.

Like all mediaeval churches, each of these buildings is unique, with its own design and atmosphere and each must be studied for its own sake. Churches are very much like people – each has its own individual character, composed of many facets, which its creator and the years have moulded.

The oldest work in these churches dates from Saxon times and craftsmanship of most of the architectural periods can be seen in them. Unfortunately much beautiful work has been lost or destroyed over the centuries, particularly during the mid-17th century when the Puritans ordered a wholesale destruction of everything thought to be 'superstitious'. In the light of this we can be thankful that so much has been preserved for us to enjoy today.

This brief survey attempts to catalogue most of the details worthy of note, also giving particulars about items which are not accessible, such as bells and plate. There are also notes about the post-mediaeval churches which were built during the 19th and 20th centuries. Unfortunately space does not permit mention of the many Nonconformist churches in the town, some of which are also worth seeing, especially the Unitarian Meeting House which is a period-piece and of tremendous interest.

The Mediaeval Churches
(their features and treasures)

The twelve ancient churches of Ipswich have undergone many changes and restorations since their foundation. Additions and alterations have been made throughout their history, at various times during the mediaeval period, and during the last century. They have been beautified and parts have been rebuilt or 'improved', in mediaeval times as wealth increased, the population grew and new fashions in architecture came into being. There was a national wave of church restoration during Victorian times. Some have mixed feelings about this, but it must be remembered that in the years preceding this period the fabric of many church buildings had been neglected, furnishings were often allowed to rot and, although we have to suffer the syncretism of their own interpretation of mediaeval architecture with the authentic mediaeval work, we do owe a great debt to our Victorian forefathers for the fact that they cared for the churches and spent money to improve them and preserve them.

Building Materials

Like most of our East Anglian churches the ancient churches of Ipswich are built mainly of **flint,** with dressed stone for the quoins, windows and doorways. Occasionally we see stone blocks incorporated in the flintwork, for example, in the tower of St. Stephen's. The flint in these churches is predominantly whole stones, although examples of knapped (split) flintwork do occur (e.g. St. Clement's). A picturesque feature to be found on the walls of these churches is the use of flint-panelling, or flushwork. This is the use of flint and stone for decoration and is employed in the buttresses, parapets and around the base of some parts of the churches, particularly in the porches and towers. The porch of St. Margaret's and the 19th century flushwork on the tower of St. Lawrence are good examples, as is also the clerestory of St. Clement's.

In the walls of St. Nicholas Church are blocks of **septaria** which deserves mention here because this is the local building material and can be seen in many of the village churches to the east of Ipswich. It is a brownish material which was obtained near the coast from Orfordness to the Naze.

The other building material to be seen in the Ipswich churches is **brick.** This can be seen at its best in the tower of St. Mary at the Elms, which dates from the Tudor period when brick was introduced for building houses and was also employed in churches. Some of the best examples are to be found in Essex and there are also several brick-built church towers in the Ipswich area, which date from the 15th and 16th centuries. Brick was also used at later times to restore the walls of some churches, e.g. St. Lawrence and St. Stephen and for building the 18th century porch at St. Nicholas.

Design and Structure

Most of the Ipswich churches have north and south **aisles** and in some cases either one or both of these aisles continue eastwards to form chapels. Three churches have mediaeval transepts – St. Margaret's, St. Mary at the Quay and St. Mary at the Elms.

At one time every Ipswich church had a south **porch.** St. Matthew's and St. Lawrence have now lost theirs and the south-west tower of St. Mary-le-Tower serves the purpose of a porch.

Towers are at the west end of the churches, with two exceptions. At St. Helen's the old western tower was taken down and at St. Mary-le-Tower the mediaeval tower stood at the western end of the south aisle. The mediaeval towers are square and spireless, the spires of St. Mary-le-Tower and St. Helen's being of 19th century date. The towers of St. Matthew and St. Mary Stoke are the only two without buttresses – the rest have diagonal buttresses, with the exceptions of St. Lawrence which has angle buttresses, and St. Mary at the Elms which has polygonal buttresses of brick. The parapets of all the mediaeval towers (with the single exception of St. Clement's) are embattled. Five have stepped battlements and six have pinnacles at the corners, although the pinnacles at St. Margaret's have been taken down in recent years. Many of these parapets were restored or rebuilt during the last century, but the restorers tried faithfully to re-create the former mediaeval parapets (with the ghastly exception of St. Mary Stoke). Flushwork can be seen in the masonry of six of the parapets. The majority of the twelve towers have spiral staircases at the north-east or south-east corners. In five of the ten mediaeval towers this extends to the ringing chamber and in the others it reaches either to the bell chamber or to the parapet.

Arcades in the churches date from the Decorated and Perpendicular periods. The piers are built of stone and the arcade of St. Stephen's is built of Purbeck marble. Piers are either octagonal or quatrefoil in section and are crowned with moulded capitals. The capitals at St. Nicholas are particularly fine examples.

The **windows** are mainly in the Perpendicular style and are usually of three-lights. Many have been carefully restored or replaced during the last century. These windows are, on the whole, very worthy and have pleasing tracery. Particularly good examples can be seen in St. Lawrence and St. Stephen. In St. Margaret's and St. Nicholas the windows have 'Y' tracery, a feature of the early Decorated style. Three of the churches have fine Perpendicular clere-stories – St. Clement's, St. Mary at the Quay and St. Margaret's (which is noted for its superb carved stonework.)

At one time three of the churches had a pair of dormer windows near the division of nave and chancel. Only one of these now remains, at St. Nicholas, which contains some of the original barge-boards used.

Many of the **doorways** are extremely noteworthy and several of these are in the Perpendicular style, with a square hood-mould over the arch and various carvings in the spandrels. These hood-moulds rest upon corbels, of which the crowned lion is a very common feature. The west doorways of St. Nicholas and St. Mary at the Quay are good examples. These both have friezes of shields above them. The west doorway of St. Peter's is superb and merits careful examination, there are many motifs carved in the moulding of the arch, including shields, heads, fleurons, crowns and thistles. See also the north doorways of St. Matthew's and St. Lawrence.

One of the most interesting doorways in the town is the south doorway of St. Mary at the Elms. This is the only Norman doorway in Ipswich and is very fine. In fact, apart from the Saxon stone fragments at St. Nicholas, this doorway is the only piece of Romanesque stonework in Ipswich.

There are a fair number of **niches** to be seen and many of these still retain their canopies. Those flanking the west doorway of St. Peter's are among the finest. There is a pair which has groined vaulting with tiny heads on the western buttresses of St. Stephen's tower and, inside the church, another has fan-vaulting. A large niche in the north aisle of St. Nicholas and those in the porches of St. Helen's and St. Margaret's are also noteworthy.

Some churches retain their **piscinas**, which can be seen either in the south wall of the sanctuary (e.g. St. Mary at the Quay) or towards the eastern ends of the aisles (e.g. St. Clement's). Perhaps the most curious is the piscina drain in the north pier of the chancel arch at St. Matthew's.

Several, but by no means all, of the Ipswich churches possess their mediaeval **fonts**. Those that remain are (with one exception) octagonal, built of stone and date from the 15th century. The finest of these can be seen at St. Matthew's, which somehow escaped Cromwell's 'purge'. This is particularly surprising because the panels of the bowl depict the five Joyful Mysteries of the Rosary. The other font bowls usually follow the East Anglian tradition, depicting angels alternating with either the symbols of the Evangelists or with lions. There are usually lions around the stem, although angels can be seen at St. Matthew's and wodewoses (wild, hairy men) at St. Clement's. The prize exception to this pattern of mediaeval fonts can be seen at St. Peter's and is of great interest and antiquity. Here the massive bowl is square and is built of black Tournai marble. It is believed that only seven such fonts exist in England. This font dates from the late 12th century and stands upon a 15th century stem.

Other stone remains which are especially worthy of note are the **Saxon carvings** in St. Nicholas Church. These three fragments, which date back to the 11th century, are described in greater detail in the notes on St. Nicholas Church.

Woodwork

A considerable amount of ancient woodwork remains in the Ipswich churches. Wood has not the endurance which stone possesses and Cromwell's iconoclasts found it a great deal easier to destroy.

A few mediaeval **doors** remain, of which the south door of St. Mary at the Elms is probably the oldest. Many authorities reckon that this door is contemporary with its doorway, which is Norman. Another fine old door, although now very much the worse for wear, is the south door of St. Mary at the Quay.

Although many of the church **roofs** have been rebuilt during Victorian times, Ipswich does possess some magnificent mediaeval examples. There are splendid double hammer-beam roofs at St. Margaret's and St. Mary at the Quay, and single hammer-beam roofs remain in the chancels of St. Matthew's and St. Stephen's, also in the former nave (now the north aisle) of St. Mary Stoke. Ancient work can also be seen in the aisle roofs of St. Margaret's,

St. Mary at the Quay and St. Mary at the Elms and mediaeval timbers are incorporated in restored roofs of other churches.

The mediaeval **furnishings** remaining in the Ipswich churches are very scanty. A few painted screen panels can be seen in St. Matthew's, there is mediaeval work in the priests' stalls at St. Stephen's and also in St. Mary-le-Tower.

Some of the churches have retained specimens of 17th and 18th century woodwork. There are fine Jacobean **pulpits** at St. Mary-le-Tower, St. Nicholas and another (which is now at Elmsett) once stood in St. Mary at the Quay. There are 17th century Holy Tables at St. Lawrence and St. Margaret's, and Stuart Communion **rails** at St. Nicholas, where there is also woodwork from box pews now used as panelling round the walls. St. Clement's has a 17th century oak **screen** which is now at the east end of the north aisle and some fine seats of this period in the sanctuary. Other 17th and 18th century additions to the churches include the clock at St. Margaret's, the porch at St. Nicholas and the cupola on the tower of St. Mary at the Quay, which has now been taken down.

Five of the churches display the **Royal Arms** of King Charles II, the best examples being at St. Margaret's and St. Clement's. The only other set of Royal Arms are those of King Henry VIII on the east wall of St. Peter's. Two churches (St. Margaret's and St. Stephen's) possess the **Prince of Wales' Feathers,** which probably date from the Restoration period (c. 1660).

Before the Victorian restorations, the churches contained far more 17th and 18th century woodwork than we see in them today, and it is clear that some of this was of considerable merit. The manuscript notes of David Elisha Davy, taken as a result of his visits to the churches between c.1811 and 1850, provide us with a fair account of their furnishings during this period, of which this woodwork is a feature.

In all the churches the altar table was railed off with wooden balustrades and behind it rose an altar-piece which, in several churches, was beautifully painted. At the centre of the altar-piece was usually a 'glory' (rays of light emanating from the IHS symbol of Christ or the Dove of the Holy Spirit) which, in some cases was surrounded by clouds. Either side of this could be seen the Lord's Prayer, the Apostles' Creed and Commandments (e.g. at St. Peter and St. Lawrence), a text of Scripture (as at St. Mary at the Quay and St. Lawrence), or paintings of Biblical events (as at St. Clement's). Where there was no 'glory', the Lord's Prayer, Creed and Commandments were there or nearby. The altar-pieces of St. Lawrence and St. Peter's terminated in fine pediments. Several of the altar-pieces were made of mahogany, as were some of the pulpits. In the times before the Oxford Movement the preaching of the Word was of paramount importance and in the churches of St. Clement and St. Helen, the pulpit stood in a central position, in front of the altar.

At this time the churches were usually seated with box pews and Davy comments that these, in most Ipswich churches, were neatly and uniformly arranged, and that those in St. Helen's were painted white. Most of the churches were equipped with galleries at the west end and sometimes at the sides also. St. Lawrence had a gallery at the west end of the chancel, which carried the organ.

Monuments

A number of the churches possess some interesting monuments to people of the past who have been associated with them, including several 16th and 17th century examples. The majority of our church monuments are wall-plaques, which have inscriptions often worth reading. Several are in Latin and one, in St. Clement's, also uses Greek. There are also many 17th and 18th century ledger slabs.

Several Ipswich monuments have **effigies** of the people they commemorate. Usually the husband and wife kneel, facing each other, with the children either behind or beneath them, also kneeling. Those children who died before their parents carry a skull and those who died in infancy are wrapped in swaddling clothes. Some of the more noteworthy of these monuments include those in the chancel of St. Matthew's, the Leman monument at St. Stephen's and the Acton monument at St. Mary at the Elms.

There is a **table tomb** to Henry Tooley (1551) in the north transept of St. Mary at the Quay and the huge slab from a similar tomb, of Edmund Withipoll, can be seen in the north transept wall of St. Margaret's Church.

Ipswich is quite rich in **brasses** and the matrices of several lost brasses can also be seen. The huge Flemish brass of Thomas Pownder is perhaps the best known. It has now been removed, together with another brass, from St. Mary at the Quay to Christchurch Mansion. Other brasses remain at St. Mary-le-Tower, St. Clement's, St. Nicholas and St. Peter's (this brass is now at Christchurch Mansion), and there are brass inscriptions at St. Lawrence and St. Stephen's.

Bells and Plate

Ipswich is quite an oasis for the church bell enthusiast. In the twelve mediaeval churches there are a total of 66 bells and nine churches have rings of five or more bells. There are nine pre-Reformation bells, including a complete ring of five at St. Lawrence, which is one of two such peals in the country. Of the post-Reformation bells worthy of note, fifteen are the work of the famous Miles Graye, of Colchester, who cast bells from 1605-1646. Sixteen bells were made by John Darbie, the local bell-founder, who worked from 1658-1691. A complete peal of Darbie's bells hangs in the tower of St. Clement's. Six of the remaining 18th century bells are the work of Pleasant and Gardiner, who were both Sudbury bell-founders.

Nearly every church possesses **plate** of some antiquity. Five of the churches have Elizabethan chalices amongst their plate. In many cases chalices of this period were the old mediaeval chalices which were melted down and remade in a shape more convenient to the Elizabethan church. Every mediaeval church in Ipswich, with two exceptions, possesses some 17th or 18th century plate.

Nineteenth Century Restoration

A tremendous amount of restoration work was carried out on the churches during the 19th century and all twelve buildings were affected to a greater or lesser extent and a great deal of visible workmanship is the result of these restorations.

Two local architects, whose names have so far avoided much recognition in the 'standard works' about the area, but who were responsible for designing a large amount of 19th century work, were Frederick Barnes and E. F. Bisshopp. Although they were not shining lights in the story of the Gothic Revival, their work is generally very worthy and in the spirit of the Revival. They quite often used the Decorated style of architecture because it was generally thought by Victorian architects, in the spirit of the Ecclesiological Movement which steered the Gothic Revival, to be the purest expression of mediaeval architecture.

Barnes was responsible for the chancel at St. Clement's (1860) and for much of the 1875 additions to St. Helen's, also (in conjunction with H. Gaye) for the sumptuous rebuilding of the tower of St. Lawrence, which is so much a part of the Ipswich skyline. He restored several Suffolk churches and designed a few new ones (e.g. Melton and St. Mary Magdalene, Colchester). He was responsible for the rebuilding of Whitton Church, and also designed the United Reformed Churches in Portman Road and Tacket Street, together with the distinctive railway stations at Needham Market and Stowmarket.

Bisshopp made his appearance a little later in the 19th century. His work can be seen at St. Mary at the Elms, St. Nicholas and St. Matthew. He was a versatile architect and gave Holy Trinity its neo-Classical chancel and designed St. Michael's.

A better-known architect was Richard Makilwaine Phipson, who was the Norwich Diocesan Surveyor, living first in Ipswich, then at Norwich. He restored many Suffolk and Norfolk churches and his most monumental work in Ipswich was his handsome rebuild of St. Mary-le-Tower, the town's Civic Church. He was also involved in the restoration of St. Lawrence and the old part of St. Mary Stoke.

George Gilbert Scott restored two Ipswich churches within a year of each other. He widened the north aisle of St. Matthew's in 1877, which was rather subdued in contrast to his work at St. Peter's where in 1878, the aisles were lengthened and the organ chamber, chancel arch and east window were rebuilt to his designs.

Between 1870-72 St. Mary Stoke gained a new nave, chancel and south porch, designed by William Butterfield, one of the Gothic Revival's greatest architects, who created some of the best known Victorian churches in the country. The original church became the north aisle and chapel and Butterfield's spacious but unprepossessing nave and chancel has worthily accommodated the increased congregations.

As with a great percentage of English churches, many new roofs, stained glass windows and other furnishings were installed during this century. Some of the work was very tastefully designed, while other specimens leave much to be desired. Six churches received new fonts at this time, of which none are particularly noteworthy.

A notable firm of Ipswich church woodcarvers was that of Henry Ringham who, mainly during the 1850s and 60s, was responsible for several benches, pulpits, etc., in the Ipswich area. His workshop was on the eastern side of the town and his name is perpetuated in Ringham Road. Mention of his work will often appear in the notes on individual churches.

The lost Churches of Ipswich

According to the Domesday Survey, there were seven churches standing in Ipswich in the year 1086. Of these only four remain today and they have been rebuilt during subsequent years. We do know that several Ipswich churches perished during a great storm in 1287, which is recorded in Stowe's Annals.

There were also five Religious Houses in the town during mediaeval times. These also had their churches, some of which may have been very fine. These were destroyed at the Dissolution of the Monasteries in the 16th century. In addition to these, records exist of twelve mediaeval churches which are now lost, although in some cases there is reason to believe that later churches were built on, or near, the site and some materials from the lost buildings may have been re-used in them.

Religious Communities in Mediaeval Ipswich

The five Religious Houses held considerable importance and many of the parish churches in the town were annexed or appropriated to them.

The Priory of St. Peter and St. Paul

This was a community of Augustinian Canons. It was founded in 1130 and stood in St. Peter's parish, probably immediately to the north of St. Peter's churchyard and maybe extended some distance to the east of it. It was suppressed in 1527 in order to make room for Wolsey's College. The churches of St. Mary at the Quay, St. Matthew, St. Nicholas, St. Peter and the lost churches of St. Edmund de Pountney, St. Augustine and St. Mildred, were all appropriated to this priory.

The Dominican Friary (Blackfriars)

The friars came to Ipswich in 1263 and founded this community to the north of the church of St. Mary at the Quay. The original house was built in Foundation Street, but it extended to cover the area between Orwell Place and Star Lane. After the Dissolution a charitable institution known as Christ's Hospital was established in the old monastic buildings. These were demolished in 1848. We know that the church here was aisleless and was built in the Decorated style.

The Priory of the Holy Trinity

This was another Augustinian House, founded in 1162. It stood at the northern end of the town and owned most of the present Christchurch Park. It has been suggested that the ponds in the park were once the priory fishponds. The original site of the buildings is reckoned to be between Christchurch Mansion and St. Margaret's Church. The town churches appropriated to this priory were St. Lawrence, St. Margaret, St. Mary at the Elms and St. Mary-le-Tower.

The Carmelite Friary (Whitefriars)

This house was founded in 1278 and was gradually enlarged over a period of about 120 years. It stood to the south of the Buttermarket and extended from Queen Street to St. Stephen's Lane.

The Franciscan Friary (Greyfriars)

The Franciscans founded their House in Ipswich in 1297. It stood in the parish of St. Nicholas and the grounds extended westwards of St. Nicholas Church. They reached the banks of the River Gipping (i.e. the natural banks before its course was diverted at a later time). Some ancient stonework from this friary can be seen in the modern Greyfriars precinct.

Mediaeval Churches which have disappeared

All Saints. This church stood near Handford Bridge. It fell into disuse and its parish was united with St. Matthew's before 1383. In St. Nicholas Church is a dedication stone which is believed to have come from this church.

St. George. This building was situated on the west side of St. George's Street. It fell into disuse after the Reformation and was used for a long time as a barn. It was finally destroyed by fire in 1764. Thomas Bilney, the martyr, preached here during the Reformation. He was later arrested by Wolsey in 1527.

St. Mildred. This church stood on Cornhill. When it ceased to be used as a church it was incorporated into the original Town Hall, which was demolished in 1812.

Our Lady of Grace. This was a chapel, situated at the top of Lady Lane. It contained the famous image of Our Lady of Ipswich and was a great place of pilgrimage during mediaeval times. In 1534 Thomas Cromwell caused the image to be conveyed to London and it was burned at Smithfield. The careful research of Mr. Stanley Smith has revealed, however, that the image may have survived and could now be in a church at Nettuno, on the west coast of Italy.

St. John the Baptist in Cauldwell. This church stood somewhere on the Woodbridge Road, but its exact site is unknown.

St. James' Chapel was attached to the Hospital of St. James, which stood at the eastern end of the town, in the parish of St. Helen's.

St. Saviour. This church fell into disuse very early and the church of St. Mary at the Elms was later built on the same site. It is believed that the fine Norman doorway at St. Mary's came from this church.

St. Michael's, like St. Saviour's, was dismantled many years ago. It stood on, or near, St. Nicholas Church, which almost certainly replaced it. The interesting Anglo-Saxon sculptures of St. Michael and the dragon and of the Apostles, now in St. Nicholas Church (q.v.) are thought to have come from St. Michael's.

St. Augustine. This church stood on the Stoke side of the river. We know that it was still in use in 1482, but all traces of it have now disappeared.

St. Edmund de Pountney. This church was situated near the south-west corner of Rosemary Lane, which links Lower Brook Street with Foundation Street. Foundation Street was originally called St. Edmund de Pountney Lane.

St. Gregory. The only information which we have about this church is that it was appropriated to Woodbridge Priory.

St. Osterbolt. This church was mentioned in 1293 and it seems to have stood somewhere near St. Clement's. It has been suggested that perhaps St. Clement's replaced it.

William Dowsing's visit to the Ipswich churches and his destruction in them:

William Dowsing was the "Parliamentary visitor for demolishing the superstitious pictures and ornaments of churches, etc., within the County of Suffolk". He was appointed under a warrant from the Earl of Manchester to 'visit' the churches of his area and to order the demolition of everything which was deemed by the Puritans to be in any way 'superstitious'. Such things included representations of Our Lord or the Saints in painting, wood or stone-carving, also angels, crucifixes, crosses, and certain inscriptions. As a result, the Ipswich churches had many beautiful things wantonly destroyed in the dubious name of 'true' Christianity. Dowsing's misguided zeal can still be seen in many places, where carvings have been hacked to an unrecognisable state, particularly on our fonts. This 'Church Official' from the period of time when the Church of England reached its lowest ebb has recorded the details of his sacrilege in a 'Journal', from which I quote the items relating to the Ipswich churches he visited on 29th and 30th January 1643.

"Ipswich, Stoke Mary's. Crosses in Wood, and 2 Cherubims painted; and one Inscription in Brass with 'ora pro nobis' &c.

"At Peter's, was on the Porch, the Crown of Thorns, the Spunge and Nails, and the Trinity in Stone; and the Rails were there, which I gave order to Break in pieces.

"Mary's at the Key. I brake down 6 superstitious Pictures.

"St. Mary Elmes. There was 4 iron Crosses on the Steeple; which they promised to take down that day, or the next.

"Nicholas. We brake 6 superstitious Pictures; and took up 2 Brass Inscriptions, of 'ora pro nobis'; and gave order for another, 'cujus anima propitietur Deus'; and there was the Crown of Thorns.

"Matthew's. We brake down 35 superstitious Pictures, 3 Angels with Stars on their breasts, and Crosses.

"Mary's at the Tower. We took up 6 Brass Inscriptions, with 'ora pro nobis', and 'ora pro animabus', and 'cunjus animae propitietur Deus'; and 'pray for the soul', in English; and I gave order to take down 5 iron Crosses, and one of Wood on the Steeple.

"Margarett's. There was 12 Apostles in Stone taken down; and between 20 and 30 superstitious Pictures to be taken down, which a (godly man) a churchwarden promised to do.

"Steven's. There was a popish Inscription in Brass, 'pray for the Soul'.

"Lawrence. There was 2 popish Inscriptions, one with beads, and written 'ora pro nobis'.

"Clement's. They four Days before had beaten up divers superstitious Inscriptions.

"At Elen's. Nothing. " (This referred to St. Helen's Church.)

Ipswich had a very strong Cromwellian following and it is more than likely that much destruction was wrought in Ipswich before Dowsing's visit (as in the case of St. Clement's), so that Dowsing just put the finishing touches to the work already done in some churches. It is clear that the above account is by no means the sum total of the destruction. It is certainly possible that the 'godly' churchwarden of St. Margaret's also inspired the dreadful mutilation of the font, which was doubtless done before Dowsing's visit.

It must also be remembered that a great deal of destruction had taken place during the previous century. An account survives of destruction at St. Lawrence in 1547, "in obedience to the King's command", which reads:

"Item we have in our Churche and chancell IX glas wyndows of fayned storyse contrary to the king's majesties injouncions whiche we have bargayned for to be glaced w^t^ whyght glas ffor the wiche we haue payd and must paye for the said glass . . . . XIj."

So, during the two periods we have lost many treasures in glass, wood, stone, brass and paintwork, treasures which the Victorians, trying as they faithfully and painstakingly did in many cases, could never replace.

St. Helen's Church, etched by Henry Davy in 1841, showing the mediaeval tower and brick transept

St. Nicholas' Church, etched by Henry Davy in 1840, before the rebuilding of the tower

St. Mary at the Elms, etched by Henry Davy in 1841, before the new chancel was erected in 1883

St. Mary at Stoke, etched by Henry Davy in 1839, before the addition of the new nave and chancel in 1870-2

St. Lawrence tower, rebuilt by Barnes & Gaye in 1882

St. Matthew, monument to Anthony Penning and family

St. Matthew, 15th century font

All Hallows, (Munro Cautley, 1939)

St. Matthew, south aisle – knapped flints and dressed stone, flushwork on the buttresses and hood-moulds with corbel heads framing the windows

St. Margaret, 19th century stall-carving, showing the Pelican feeding her young with her own blood – an emblem of the Blessed Sacrament

St. Mary-le-Tower. Carvings on Corporation Pews, showing a sea-horse on the bench end and a lion holding a ship (part of the town crest) on the bookrest

The simple and devotional interior of St. Mary at the Elms,
showing F. F. Bisshopp's chancel arch (1883)

pre-19th century Churches

St. Clement

This large and dignified church stands on the eastern side of the town, a short distance from the river and docks. It has always been associated with mariners and merchants and was known as the 'sailor's church'. No doubt these merchants provided much of the wherewithal for the building and beautification of this church, which dates mainly from the 14th and 15th centuries.

St. Clement's stands well, in its tree-shaded churchyard. Modern traffic development has enabled this church to be seen to much greater advantage and the views of it from the south are most attractive, with its elegant tower pointing above the houses.

Several people who have had connections with the sea have been associated with this church. It is the burial-place of Thomas Eldred, who accompanied Cavendish on his voyage round the world, also of Sir Thomas Slade, who designed the 'Victory'.

The building consists of nave with north and south aisles, chancel, south porch and western tower.

Exterior

It is worth pausing to admire from a distance the fine proportions of this building and to appreciate its good Perpendicular craftsmanship as a whole. The fabric dates mainly from the late 14th and early 15th centuries, with the exception of the chancel, which was built in 1860. The aisles are lit by sets of three-light Perpendicular windows, and are strengthened and enhanced by elegant buttresses. Above these can be seen the magnificent 15th century clerestory which consists of twelve two-light Perpendicular windows each side set amidst elegant flushwork panelling. The walls are faced with knapped flints, which have been split to expose their dark cores.

The chancel was built in 1860 to the designs of Frederick Barnes, using the Decorated style. It is well designed and complements the rest of the building. The five-light east window with its intricate tracery is particularly noteworthy.

The handsome western tower rises about 77 ft., is supported by thin buttresses and is crowned with tiny spiky pinnacles. A staircase turret in the north-east corner reaches to the level of the ringing chamber. The west window, of two-lights, is in the Decorated style and beneath it is a plain west doorway. In the west face can be seen a square aperture, similar to a 'Norfolk sound-hole'. The three-light belfry windows, which date from the 15th or early 16th centuries (a date of 1515 has been given) have stepped transoms and above the western one is a stone shield. The parapet, of stone, is panelled and not embattled. A distinct change in the texture of the masonry just below the level of the belfry windows indicates that the belfry stage was added at a later date than the lower stages. Towards the summit of the tower the buttresses are slender and polygonal in shape, as in the tower of St. Lawrence. At the time of writing the tower is undergoing restoration and the parapet and pinnacles are being faithfully renewed. The south porch has been greatly restored. A sketch of the church, made by Ogilby in 1674, shows a large and richly decorated porch, with flushwork, battlements and a niche, but when this was reduced to the present structure we do not know. The lateral windows are in the Decorated style and the inner entrance has a fine arch.

Interior

The interior of this church is spacious and well-proportioned. The lofty nave is divided from the aisles by **arcades** of six bays. These have quatrefoil piers, with moulded capitals and fillets in the diagonals. Although the roofs and most of the interior furnishings are not ancient, their design is quite tasteful.

Above the simple tower arch is an excellent set of carved **Royal Arms** of King Charles II, which date from 1661. These are flanked by scrolls bearing texts which appear to be quite early examples of their type. The **door** to the belfry stairs is mediaeval.

The octagonal 15th century **font** stands at the west end of the south aisle (which is extended westwards to the western end of the tower). This is a typical East Anglian font, with the emblems of the four Evangelists, alternating with shields around the bowl and lions, alternating with wodewoses round the base. Wodewoses are wild, hairy men from the world of folklore.

They are depicted on several Suffolk fonts and can often be seen bearing clubs, as is the case on this font. There is a simple font-cover.

The church had a western **gallery**, dating from the 17th century and this has been partially re-erected at the eastern end of the north aisle, where its columns and carved cornice can be seen to their full advantage. There is a **piscina** in the aisle wall, marking the position of a side altar in mediaeval times. The gallery was moved in 1880, when the nave received a new roof. Another restoration took place in 1891 (by Bisshopp) when the benches, stalls, etc., were inserted and the church was refloored.

The **chancel** has great dignity and its **east window** contains some good modern glass, placed there in 1948 by Abbott & Co. of Leicester, to replace glass which was shattered during the second World War. In the **sanctuary** are some fine **Jacobean seats**.

An **organ** by Rayson, much enlarged about 1903 by Bishop & Son, stands on the north side of the choir, and is destined for the parish of Selworthy in Somerset. At present it has two manuals and 17 speaking stops.

Monuments

The church is quite rich in memorials to past worthies. There are two **brasses** in the floor at the east end of the centre aisle. One commemorates John Tye, a merchant and portman who died in 1583, also his two wives, five sons and nine daughters. The other commemorates John Coke, who died in 1607.

Several of the **wall-monuments** have inscriptions which are worth reading. In the south aisle, for instance, is an inscription commemorating Captain Samuel Green, who died in 1723. It warns that "This stone never to be removed, and to disanall the will of ye dead is not good". At the south-west end of the chancel is a wall tablet to John Ward, which bears an inscription in Latin and in Greek. There is another good square tablet above it. Directly opposite is a memorial to a former priest, which has an extremely complimentary inscription and is well worth reading.

The ring of six **bells** was cast in 1680, by John Darbie, the local bell-founder. There is a carillon mechanism in the belfry, which was a gift made at the turn of the century. This is an unusual feature and it enables hymn-tunes to be played on the bells. The tenor weighs 15½ cwt. and is 43 inches in diameter.

This church has been declared redundant and is now under the care of the Ipswich Historic Churches Trust.

St. Helen

This church was largely rebuilt during the last century and the amount of mediaeval work left is small, but not without interest. Much restoration and rebuilding took place during 1835-37 and the transepts were added during this time, but in 1848-49 the church was almost completely rebuilt, except for the tower, porch and south wall of the nave. Of this work the *Ipswich Journal* states that its "architectural faults are not redeemed by a single feature that we can commend". In 1875 the old tower was replaced by the present tower and spire (about 80 ft. high) and the nave was extended westwards and reccived its large west window. The old plaster ceiling was removed and much of the woodwork of the roof was replaced, also the south transept doorway was inserted. The architects were F. Barnes and E. Bisshopp, but Barnes prepared the designs.

The former building had an unbuttressed western tower, which was embattled and had double belfry windows, beneath which on the south side was a blocked Norman window. The south porch is still standing and will be described later. The nave was lit by three-light Perpendicular windows as it is today, but there were only two on the south side, which was lengthened at the restoration to accommodate three. The chancel had, in 1674, a pair of square-headed two-light windows on the south side, but a sketch made in 1841 shows a brick transept in this side, which necessitated the removal of one of the chancel windows.

The church now consists of nave and chancel, under the same roof and with no division, north and south transepts, south porch and a small square south-west tower, with an octagonal belfry stage, surmounted by a spire.

Exterior

The church is built of flint and stone, and most of the windows are in the Perpendicular style. The majority of these windows have three-lights and the two to the east of the porch are restorations of the mediaeval originals and have the same tracery, which is very pleasing.

The Victorian tower and spire are unusual and extremely attractive.

The fine mediaeval porch is the only part of the mediaeval church which remains intact and unaltered. It has two-light lateral windows and a Perpendicular outer entrance, although the stonework in the spandrels has been greatly weathered. There are crowned lion corbels and flowers in the arch. Above it is a canopied niche and at the summit is a restored sundial. The inner entrance has corbel heads and flowers in the moulding. Beside it is the remains of a Holy Water stoup. A frieze of flushwork runs around the base of the porch and the nave wall.

Interior

The church is entered by means of a large mediaeval **door,** which retains its huge closing ring. The interior is spacious and light, but rather barn-like, having no arcades, chancel arch or western tower. All the fittings and furnishings date from the last century or later. Over the main entrance hang the **Royal Arms** of Queen Victoria.

The **font** was made in 1855. It is octagonal and on the bowl are fleurons and foliage within quatrefoils, Davy describes its predecessor as "of brick and plastered over". Standing on the floor on the north side are two **bells.** These were taken from the old tower, hung in the new and then removed here because the tower was unsafe. The larger bell is mediaeval and bears the inscription "Sancta Maria ora pro Nobis". It was made at Bury St. Edmunds. The other bell was cast by Miles Graye in 1621. There are now eight **tubular bells** in the tower.

There are several **monuments** of interest. On the north wall of the nave are plaques to Lt.-General Richard Phillipson (1792), Robert Parish (1774) and Elizabeth Parish (1797). On the south nave wall is a good wall monument to the Rev'd. Richard Canning, Vicar of St. Lawrence, who died in 1775. Another monument commemorates Commander Richard Canning R.N., who died in 1726, together with his wife, daughter and the wife of the Rev'd. Richard Canning. Near the **pulpit** are **ledger slabs**, commemorating Robert Dunkon, Bailiff of Ipswich, who died in 1670, and the Rev'd. Samuel Bantoft (died 1692), which has a Latin inscription.

St. Helen's has a small Bryceson **organ** of 1864, formerly in a local residence. The trumpet originally in this organ is now in use at the English church in Naples. There are two manuals and 13 speaking stops.

At the time of writing, St. Helen's is preparing for a complete re-ordering of interior, with a new sanctuary at the west end and vestries, rooms and a chapel in the present chancel and transepts.

The parish has a Mission Church of St. James in Woodville Road, which was opened in 1919.

St. Lawrence

This is a spacious church, of fine proportions. It was erected during the 15th century and is a superb example of Perpendicular architecture.

It was begun through the generosity of John Buttold, who provided money for the building of the tower and nave. He died in 1431 and is buried somewhere in the church. The wherewithal for building the chancel was provided by John Baldwin, a draper, who died in 1449. Beneath the east window, on the exterior wall, is an inscription asking for prayers for himself, his wife and all Christian souls.

Although this church has been restored and some of the original masonry has decayed through years of weathering, it is a noble building and is certainly one of the finest in the town. The churchyard has, in recent years, been paved and furnished with seats, thus providing a much needed place where the public can rest in comparative peace amidst the bustle of central Ipswich. Unfortunately the church itself is redundant and closed at the time of writing and it is hoped that a useful purpose may soon be found for it.

The building consists of nave, chancel, north vestry and a lofty western tower. There was at one time a south porch, but this has long since disappeared.

Exterior

The church is built of flint, which is strengthened and embellished with stone. The upper parts of the nave and portions of the chancel have been restored with brick. The nave is lit by large and lofty three-light Perpendicular windows, which have transoms and fine tracery. There are four on the north side and three on the south. The fourth window on the south side, at the western end, has been restored with intersecting tracery. This probably happened when the porch was taken down. In the south wall of the chancel are two smaller, but very elegant three-light Perpendicular windows, which have embattled transoms. The five-light east window has been completely renewed, but beneath it is the flushwork inscription requesting prayers for the donor of the chancel.

Flushwork can also be seen around the base of the tower and nave, comprising ogee-headed arches, with stone quatrefoils above. This has been carefully restored in places, but in others it is badly weathered. The buttresses also have flint panelling.

There are fine Perpendicular north and south doorways to the nave. Each of these has a very deep arch with rounded shafts at the centre of the responds. These shafts have capitals which are embellished with tiny fleurons. In the moulding of the jambs and arches are other carved motifs – crowns and foliage can be seen in the south doorway and shields and fleurons in the north doorway, which also has spandrels bearing the weathered remains of foliage.

The small door to the vestry is mediaeval and was obviously moved here from elsewhere when the vestry was built. Perhaps it was an old priest's door. There is carved tracery at the base and the door still has its mediaeval closing handle and iron. There is also a modern doorway in the south of the chancel.

The crowning glory of the church is its magnificent tower. This is 97ft. high and it merits careful examination. It was originally erected in the 15th century and must have looked very fine, but by the 19th century it was but a shade of its former glory, having suffered through injudicious restoration which had taken place probably during the 17th or 18th centuries, when it was given a plain and unembattled parapet with urns at the corners. In 1882, Messrs. F. Barnes and H. Gaye made a splendid effort to restore it to its former glory. This was most successful and this tower is now one of the most beautiful in the town. The upper stages have been rebuilt and a new parapet added. At the base of the tower are processional arches on the north and south sides. That on the south has a mediaeval door which has been turned back to front so that its fine tracery can only be seen from the inside. The large west doors are also traceried and the arch is Perpendicular and flanked by pinnacles. The ringing chamber has two-light Perpendicular windows, but it is in the stage above that the fun starts! From here upwards is a maze of flushwork. There are lozenges, wheels, trefoil-headed panels, roses, two friezes of quatrefoils with shields, one having two angels beneath it on each face, and even the north-east staircase turret, which reaches almost to the top of the three-light belfry windows, has flushwork at its summit. There are four figures above the belfry windows and the tower is crowned with an elegant openwork parapet with eight pinnacles. The weathervane bears the date 1799.

Interior

Entry is gained through the **west door** and on the right can be seen the traceried **mediaeval door** in the south tower arch. The inner doorway and screen are not ancient, but are extremely worthy.

The **nave** is lofty and spacious. Its grand proportions can be seen best by looking westwards from the chancel arch. The **tower arch** is lofty and has three pairs of rounded shafts. The nave roof has arch braces and king-posts and there are huge contemporary stone **corbels**. The stone **pulpit** (reported to be a facsimile of one at Bemerton, Wilts.) is by Wyatt of Bloomsbury. This, together with the seating and the nave roof were inserted in 1863 to the designs of R. M. Phipson; the contractors were Messrs. Luff.

The **seats** are arranged in a most unusual fashion, with a centre block and those on the sides facing inwards. Although reminiscent of the collegiate fashion, this arrangement has been known in some 19th century 'low-church' naves possibly to avoid any idea of reverence towards the altar; this may be so here.

The **rood-loft stairway** is still intact and its upper entrance can be seen on the north side. The original **font** is now in St. Nicholas Church. Its 19th century successor has fleurons and shields on the bowl and trefoil-headed arches round the base. It is said that in mediaeval times this church was noted for its fine glass and one can imagine these huge windows resplendent with mediaeval colour.

The chancel is much lower than the nave and above the chancel arch is a quatrefoil opening. The arch itself has small fleurons in the capitals. The **reredos** (1863) was designed and carved by Williams of Ipswich, with lettering by Henry Day. The **glass** in the **east window** (1855) by Charles Gibbs is good and typical of the period.

Monuments

On the south wall of the chancel is a stone in which is a **brass** shield and two brass inscriptions. These commemorate John Moore (died 1580) and Margery Drury (died 1618). Also in the chancel are wall-monuments to John Pemberton (died 1718) and to Louisa Squire (died 1780).

Among the **wall-monuments** on the south side of the nave are those to John Sparrow, a magistrate (died 1762), which bears a flattering inscription. Henry Jolman (died 1738), and Elizabeth Lyton (died 1605). On the north side are more 17th and 18th century monuments. That to Mrs. Elizabeth

Colman is of particular interest. It is a standing column and coat of arms, beneath which is a skull and a lengthy inscription, which mentions her benefactions of money to the poor for the purchase of 'shirts and shifts'. This monument was erected about 1700.

The five **bells** are a complete pre-Reformation ring. The only other mediaeval ring of five bells in England is at St. Bartholomew's Church, Smithfield, London.

A large two manual **organ** by Holdich, c.1872, with a well stencilled front, stands to the north of the chancel. It has 14 speaking stops.

The Ipswich Historic Churches Trust now has the care of this church.

St. Margaret

This is one of the finest and most interesting churches in the town. The beautiful exterior, with its flushwork, battlements, turrets and handsome windows is seen at its best from the south, where it dominates St. Margaret's Plain.

The core of this building dates from c. 1300. The tower was added about 1400 and the transepts, clerestory and porch about 1450.

The church consists of square west tower, nave with aisles and south porch, north and south transepts and chancel, with vestries on the north and south sides.

Exterior

This contains a great deal of beauty and interest. The lower part of the square tower dates from about 1400, but the belfry stage was rebuilt and heightened in 1871, when the double sets of belfry windows were inserted and the flushwork parapet and battlements were added, also crocketed pinnacles at the corners, which have recently been removed. A staircase ascends to the ringing chamber in the north-east corner. There is a simple west doorway and the window above is a Perpendicular addition. The ringing chamber is lit on the north side by a small cinquefoil-headed window and there is a modern equivalent on the west side. On the south is the fine clock-face, dated 1737.

Sets of four triple windows can be seen in the aisles. Both sets are in the Decorated style but those on the north have intersecting tracery (c. 1300), whilst the southern set have reticulated tracery which is a 19th century embellishment; this aisle is embattled. In the north aisle is a large 14th century doorway with a moulded arch and corbel heads. The south transept is flanked by turrets with carved stone tops and crocketed spirelets. These are absent in the north transept, at the south-west corner of which can be seen the place where people ascended to the former rood-loft. Both transepts have four-light Perpendicular windows. In the western buttress of the north transept is a stone panel with the MR motif (the emblem of Our Lady). The 19th century east window of the church is in the Decorated style and has four-lights. The southern vestry is not mediaeval (it is not shown on Ogilby's sketch of 1674) but the three-light window and the small door are. Perhaps they were moved here from elsewhere in the church, possibly from the south wall of the chancel.

Above the aisles is the magnificent clerestory, with fine sets of ten three-light windows each side. These are in the Perpendicular style and are set amidst richly carved stonework, beneath stepped battlements and pinnacles. This impressive feature is a fine example of the mediaeval stonemasons' art.

The south porch is also noteworthy. This too is embattled and has small pinnacles. Gargoyles can be seen on the east and west sides and there is flushwork on the parapet, buttresses and south wall. Above the entrance arch are three fine niches. The arch itself is a good Perpendicular example, with figures in the spandrels and the remains of crowned lion corbels. There was at one time a sundial on this porch, but it was removed during the last century. The three-light Perpendicular windows on the east and west sides have transoms. The porch roof contains most of its original mediaeval timbers and there are three bosses remaining. The inner doorway is richly moulded. Bequests were made towards the "new porche" in 1453 and 1454.

Interior

Many items of interest may be seen in this bright and cared-for interior. Immediately to the west of the main entrance is a stone **coffin lid** in the wall, which dates from the 12th or 13th centuries and may have come from the Priory of the Holy Trinity which was adjacent to the church. Above the doorway are the **Prince of Wales' Feathers**, dated 1660. The superb set of **Royal Arms** of Charles II, which hang above the tower arch were installed just after this date. The **tower arch** itself is quite simple, but has carved tracery in the stonework beside it. The **glass** in the **west window** of the tower has colourful figures of Faith, Hope and Charity and is by Ward & Hughes.

The aisles are divided from the nave by **arcades** of five bays. These have octagonal piers. The north aisle **windows** have moulded arches and a string course extends along the wall between them and forms hood-moulds around them. The south aisle windows have hood-moulds resting upon animal-head

corbels, and there are three more stone corbel heads high up in this aisle. In the wall of the south aisle is a simple **niche** and at its eastern end is a recess which may once have been an **aumbry**. Nearby is a doorway which once led to the **rood-loft stairs**. A corresponding doorway can be seen in the north aisle and the passage-arch to the former rood-loft is visible high up near the chancel arch. The **chancel arch** itself is supported by **responds** which are decorated with flowers, crowns and shields, and its capitals are embellished with flowers. The roofs of the aisles are largely mediaeval, but the crowning glory of the interior is the magnificent **double hammer-beam nave roof**. This 15th century masterpiece is resplendent with colour which was added during the late 17th century. Carved figures adorn the wall-posts, which rest upon stone corbels. Richly decorated wooden **spandrels** fill the spaces above the clerestory and link the struts with the hammer-beams and collar-beams. The **wall-plates** are decorated with crowns and angels. The glory of all this can best be seen either by viewing from the chancel arch westwards, or better still by laying flat on one's back on one of the benches near the centre of the nave!

The 15th century **font** is octagonal and has an uncommonly thick stem. On the bowl are angels bearing scrolls which have now lost their inscriptions, except one, which reads "Sal et saliva", which refers to the mediaeval custom of using salt and saliva at Baptism. One panel has a cross, which is probably a recent addition.

The *Ipswich Journal* records that the present benches (made by Henry Ringham) replaced the box pews in 1846, when the east window also received new tracery. The writer looked forward to the impending removal of the Classical fittings, particularly because he observed that the Communion Table was fixed to the reredos behind it, thus constituting an altar and not a movable table!

The chancel is much lower than the nave and above the arch are two trefoil headed windows and a circular window. There is a three-light Decorated window in the north wall, behind which is the vestry. The east window has circular shafts with capitals, which are of 14th century date and are much earlier than the present window. The tracery in the north transept window is noteworthy.

Monuments

A huge table tomb once stood in the chancel of this church, commemorating the builder of Christchurch Mansion, Edmund Withipoll. It was removed in 1755, because of the obstruction which it caused and its enormous **top slab** now stands against the wall of the north transept. In the south transept is the canopied tomb of Sir William Roskin, who died in 1512. Some 17th century **wall-tablets** can be seen on the south aisle wall.

The church has several funeral **hatchments**. The four which hang in the nave commemorate members of the Edgar family and a further five, hanging in the chancel, commemorate members of the Fonnereau family.

During very recent years a simple **nave altar** has been installed beneath the chancel arch. This modern liturgical arrangement has been tastefully and successfully executed and is a worthy 20th century addition.

There are eight **bells** in the tower, the original peal of six were cast by Miles Graye in 1630, to which were added two by Mears in 1899. The tenor weighs 15 cwt.

The old **organ** in the west gallery was supplanted by a new one by Hill about 1870, and sent to Dennington Church, where the case may still be seen. The organ was rebuilt by Binns on the south side, the older Hill woodwork remaining as a vestry screen. This organ served from 1908 until 1981, when a three manual tracker organ by Walker was purchased from Holy Trinity, Bedford. It has 26 speaking stops.

St. Mary at the Elms

This church, which was named thus because of the elm trees which stood nearby, is built on or near the site of an earlier building which was dedicated to St. Saviour. The Norman doorway may have come from this church. The brick tower and north aisle were added during the early Tudor period and the church was further enlarged in 1883, when the north aisle was extended two bays eastwards of the transepts and the present chancel was added on to the eastern end of the old chancel (now part of the nave). The architect was E. F. Bisshopp, who replaced the old east window in the new chancel. The north transept is mediaeval and there was at one time a south transept.

St. Mary's now consists of nave, with north aisle and north transept, south porch, chancel, with south organ chamber and north vestry and brick western tower. This church is another example of the way in which the modern development of the town has opened up fine views of its ancient buildings. The view from the west now shows the fine tower to its full advantage.

Exterior

The extent of the original nave, which was very short, can be seen on the south side, because it is capped with brick battlements. The windows, which are in the Perpendicular style, have been mostly renewed. The east window is now blocked. It had three-lights and was in the Decorated style. The north transept and the 1883 extension are built of flint, but the Tudor north aisle is brick built. In the transept can be seen a blocked doorway with a Holy Water stoup beside it and there is another blocked doorway at the west end of the aisle. The sturdy brick western tower, which reaches a height of 54 ft. and dates from the late 15th century, is a very fine example of its period. It is built almost entirely of brick and has polygonal buttresses and stepped battlements. The only stone used can be seen in the restored west window. The double sets of two-light belfry windows, set under wide single arches, can be seen on the west, south and east sides. On the north side are single belfry windows and a large staircase turret in the north-east corner which reaches to the parapet.

The south porch has a Perpendicular doorway, above which are three shallow niches. Its lateral walls, which are about 2½ ft. thick, are pierced by simple 'Y' traceried windows. The solid mediaeval roof of the porch remains intact. Perhaps the greatest treasure of the church is its large Norman doorway, which is quite a plain example, with one order of colonettes and some simple zig-zag moulding round the arch. The door itself is of tremendous age and has some fine ironwork. Many authorities think that it may be contemporary with the doorway and this is certainly possible.

Interior

The interior of this small church is homely and atmospheric. Part of the south wall of the nave leans outwards. Although St. Mary's has been for about half a century a great centre of the Anglo-Catholic movement, the furnishings are quite simple and unprepossessing. There is a Holy Water **stoup** by the south door. The nave has a plaster ceiling and the chancel roof has angels. The aisle and transept **roofs** preserve much of their original mediaeval woodwork. Of the five-bay **arcade** the two western arches separate the original aisle from the nave, the centre one separates the transept and the two eastern arches separate the Victorian extension.

The **font** dates from 1871 and the fine chancel arch, which is emblazoned with painted shields bearing the emblems of the Passion, is by Bisshopp (1883). The base of the tower has been converted into a small chapel during recent years.

The chancel of this church has been cleared of all superfluous pews and is surprisingly light and spacious. There are two small stalls in the chancel, which have beautifully carved ends, although it is very doubtful that they are mediaeval.

In the south nave windows are depicted the Christian Virtues in colourful 19th century **glass** by the firm of Taylor & O'Connor. Sir Ninian Comper designed a window in the north aisle.

An excellent **monument** on the north wall of the chancel commemorates William Acton, who died in 1616. It has kneeling figures with a skeleton above them, and his widow reclining below, with a skull, hour-glass and a vase of flowers. The inscription is in Latin. There are wall-monuments on the south wall of the nave, the best of these being to Elizabeth Hamby (died 1758), the small tablet to Elizabeth Feddeman (died 1653) and the tablet and shield to Robert Hamby (died 1735).

Three **hatchments** hang on the tower wall, above the gallery, also the **Royal Arms** of Charles II, which are a little difficult to see.

The tower contains five **bells**, Nos. 1, 3, and 5 by J. Darbie, 1660. No. 4 is by Miles Graye, 1613. No. 2 is by Richard Hille (of Kent), c.1430. The tenor weighs 10 cwt.

A three manual **organ** by Hunter stands in a chamber south of the chancel; built about 1912, it has pneumatic action, and 23 speaking stops.

St. Mary at the Quay

This church is situated in the heart of dockland, and although it is dwarfed by huge buildings, modern road development has opened out a fine view of it from the north.

Money was provided for the erection of this building in the year 1448 and it has had associations with wealthy merchant adventurers such as Tooley and Pownder. During the last hundred years, however, it has suffered a chequered history. A parishioner, H. M. Eyton, restored it in 1874, when the east window was renewed, a plaster casing was removed from the font, the pulpit was reduced in size (in 1811 it had a large sounding-board) and the box pews were replaced by some benches borrowed from St. Mary-le-Tower. These benches were in turn replaced (under Eyton's supervision) by the beautiful specimens which can now be seen in St. Andrew's Church. On 12th March 1898, the church was pronounced unsafe and closed. This state was largely due to the many times when it had been flooded and it was also reported that water in the vaults beneath it had given rise to an unbearable smell in the church! A great appeal for its restoration was launched and it was re-opened in 1901. It remained a parish church until a bomb dropped near it during World War II, which blasted out the windows and caused other damage. Again the church was closed, but at length it was put in order by the Friends of Friendless Churches and is now in the care of the Redundant Churches Fund.

The nave has been converted for use as a hall, but the altar is still in place and the bells, which have remained intact throughout, are still rung.

The church is an architectural period-piece of the 15th century and consists of nave, with aisles and south porch, north and south transepts, chancel and a square western tower. A large vestry was added to the north in 1882, but this has now been taken down.

Exterior

The dignified proportions of this church, which are enhanced by its elegant Perpendicular windows, are a noteworthy feature. The aisles are lit entirely by three-light windows and each transept has a four-light window, that in the south being blocked. The east window also has four-lights and its lower parts have been bricked up. There is a priest's doorway in the chancel, which contains an ancient door, also a blocked doorway in the north aisle. The fine clerestory comprises eight two-light windows each side, and there is flushwork in the wall between them, although this is now somewhat faded.

The embattled tower (for which money was bequeathed in 1443) is 73 ft. high and was until recently crowned with an attractive 18th century wooden cupola. The weathervane takes the form of a key, some five feet in length. In the base of the tower are carved stone quatrefoils. The Perpendicular west doorway has crowns and fleurons in the arch, shields in the spandrels and crowned lion corbels. Above it is a frieze of flushwork shields. There is flushwork in the buttresses and faint panelling can also be seen on the parapet. The latter is almost certainly restoration, as are the double sets of belfry windows and the west window (the tower is believed to have been restored in 1804). A north-east staircase turret rises to the level of the belfry.

The south porch has a Perpendicular doorway and a blocked window. The inner doorway has fleurons in the arch and there are the remains of a Holy Water stoup beside it. The door itself is mediaeval and it retains its original closing ring and iron.

Interior

The absence of pews emphasises the fine proportions of the interior. There are **arcades** of four bays, with a further bay opening into the transepts. These have quatrefoil piers with moulded capitals.

The **roofs** of the nave and aisles are mediaeval. The aisle roofs have carved spandrels and the nave has a superb double hammer-beam roof, which is magnificently carved and has figures on the wall-posts. This roof and that in St. Margaret's are the two finest in Ipswich. The chancel roof, which is also ancient, is a single hammer-beam. It has modern shields and one remaining corbel head on the north side, near the chancel side. The chancel arch itself has embattled capitals. In the sanctuary is a **piscina** and a window-sill **sedilia** on the south side. The level of these indicates that the floor must have been considerably lower when they were in use.

In the wall of the south transept is a **squint.** This transept contains some monuments, including the large **table tomb** of Henry Tooley, who died in 1551, which bears traces of its original colour, also a pleasant 17th century wall-monument. There were also some fine **brasses** in this church, which can now be seen in Christchurch Mansion. Henry Tooley and his family are commemorated in brass, also Thomas Powndcr, a bailiff of Ipswich, and his family. This is a huge Flemish brass, dating from c.1525, which is an excellent example of its type.

The 15th century octagonal **font** (recently returned here having been used in Brantham Church) is a typical East Anglian font, with angels bearing shields, alternating with the emblems of the four Evangelists, in the panels of the bowl and lions around the stem. The Jacobean **pulpit** from this church has found a new home in Elmsett Church.

Evidence of the Victorians' handiwork survives in the tiles behind the **altar.**

The peal of six **bells,** which date from the 17th and 18th centuries is still rung occasionally. Nos. 2, 3 and 6 are by John Darbie, 1662. No. 4 is by Miles Graye, 1613. No. 1 is by Gardiner of Sudbury, 1732.

The small two manual **organ** by Godball of Ipswich, who had a music shop on the Cornhill at the turn of the century, was put into the church of St. Alban, Lakenham, Norwich after the church was damaged by enemy action. It had 14 speaking stops.

The church possessed an Elizabethan chalice and an alms-dish made in 1721.

St. Mary at Stoke

This church is situated on the south side of the river, in an elevated position on a ridge overlooking the town. Its parish was once a small farming community, but is now large and populous. Because of this growth the building was greatly enlarged during the last century.

Davy's sketch, made in 1839 shows the church to be a small, attractive building, with a western tower, plaster-covered nave and chancel continuous under one roof and a brick two-storied south porch. This porch looked very fine, having polygonal buttresses, ending in crocketed spirelets, three niches and stepped battlements. There was a three-light dormer window at the division of the nave and chancel. The tower was much the same as it is now, but an earlier sketch shows Perpendicular tracery in the belfry windows. In 1824, the ceiling of this small church was painted sky-blue and the back-board of the pulpit was lined with blue velvet, bordered with broad gold lace!

The north transept was added in 1864, when the old church was restored, much of the design being done by P. R. Burrell, although Phipson also appears to have been involved. In 1870-2, a new nave, chancel and south porch were built on to the south side of the church and the original church became the north aisle and Lady Chapel. The architect for the new work was William Butterfield, but this church is a far cry from his great London churches, like All Saints, Margaret Street or St. Matthias, Stoke Newington. He used here the traditional East Anglian flint and the Perpendicular style of architecture, commonly found in mediaeval churches in the locality.

Exterior

Butterfield's nave and chancel have three-light Perpendicular windows and a five-light east window. There are three-light windows in the north aisle. The tower is unbuttressed and has stone quoins. The double belfry windows and the embattled parapet are restorations in white brick, probably executed at the beginning of the 19th century. Butterfield's organ chamber and porch are decorated with chequerwork panelling and the latter is entered by means of a typical Perpendicular doorway, with flushwork above it and flanking it. There are shields in the spandrels.

Interior

The present nave and chancel are bright and spacious and there is an arch-braced roof. The **sanctuary** is pleasant and colourful and a fine **niche** with a crocketed canopy in the north wall provides a fitting home for the reserved Sacrament. An **arcade** of five bays separates the old and new churches.

Behind the **High Altar** is a traceried **reredos**, now hidden by a curtain. The handsome **east window** above is by Clayton & Bell.

The original nave (now the north aisle) is crowned with a good mediaeval **single hammer-beam roof**, which has moulded wall-plates, angels with shields at the ends of the hammer-beams and figures underneath. In the south-east corner is a mediaeval **piscina**. The old tower arch is now blocked.

The present **font** is not ancient. It is octagonal, with a plain base and quatrefoils round the bowl. Its predecessor had leaves and roses on the stem and vine-leaves on the bowl.

One of the two **bells** in the tower was cast by Miles Graye in 1615. There was a third bell, but this was sold during the last century.

A two manual Holdich **organ** was built into a small chamber south of the choir-stalls when the church was restored by Butterfield. In 1966 it was reconstructed by Bishop & Son and the pipework brought forward to better tonal advantage. There are 18 speaking stops.

The church possesses a cup and paten which were made in 1797.

St. Mary-le-Tower

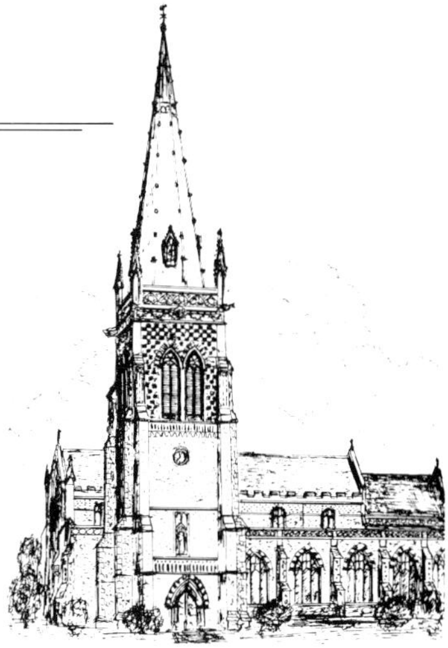

This is the town's Civic Church and it is a fine building, although most of it was rebuilt between 1850 and 1870. The architect for the rebuilding was R. M. Phipson, who built and restored several East Anglian churches. Some work does remain from the mediaeval church, including most of the arcade, the font and other items.

The plan of the previous building was similar to the present church, except that the north aisle was narrower and extended as far east as the chancel arch, and that the tower stood at the west end of the south aisle and attached to it was a large two-storied porch which had polygonal turrets and a sundial. There was a clock at the summit of this porch and there was Early English work in its entrance arch. The church was faced with ashlar and the windows were mainly in the Perpendicular style, except those in the tower and south chancel chapel which had Decorated windows. The tower once had a spire, but this fell during a storm in 1661.

The interior was filled with box pews and had galleries on three sides. Above the west gallery stood the organ, with its fine case, by Thomas and Renatus Harris.

Phipson began his restoration by replacing the chancel roof and redesigning the east window in 1850. The north chancel aisle was also built at this time. During the 1860s the major rebuilding took place, including the chancel arch and the arches of the nave which join it (these are narrower than the others). The clerestory was also heightened. Later in that decade the old tower and porch were replaced by the present tower and spire.

The church now consists of nave, chancel, north and south aisles which extend to the beginning of the sanctuary, a vestry to the north and a south-west tower and spire, the base of which forms a porch.

Exterior

The church stands in a quiet, tree-shaded churchyard near the centre of the town. Although what we can see on the outside is almost entirely work of the 19th century, this exterior is very fine. The aisles are lit by three-light windows, in the Perpendicular style. The west end of the nave has pinnacles, a five-light Perpendicular window and a fine doorway. The chancel windows are in the Decorated style.

Although they may not appear so, the crocketed niches on the east wall and over the south doorway came from the mediaeval church. Phipson thoroughly restored these and most of their old stonework seems to have been replaced. In the same way the present inner south doorway was removed from the former tower, restored and embellished with a carving of the Annunciation. This doorway dates originally from the 13th century.

The tower has angle buttresses, a clock and double sets of two-light Decorated belfry windows. There is chequerwork in the belfry stage and above is an openwork parapet with crocketed pinnacles at the corners. The crocketed spire rises to a height of 176 ft. and has one tier of lucarnes in the cardinal faces.

Interior

The main entrance is through the porch under the tower, which gives access to a somewhat dark interior where there is peace and solemnity. The porch is spacious and vaulted and the 13th century inner entrance arch mentioned earlier is worth pausing to view.

Most of what we see inside the church is Phipson's work, but several ancient features have survived. The aisles are divided from the nave by **arcades** of six bays which retain much 15th century stonework. The two bays which separate the south chancel chapel have 14th century arches. The chancel arch and the first arches west of it are Phipson's work, as are the roofs of the church. The cornices of the north aisle roof, with their Biblical texts, are fine examples of the work of Henry Ringham.

A carved set of **Royal Arms** of Charles II hangs over the west door. The two canopied **churchwardens' seats** at the west end incorporate 15th century benches which have survived from the mediaeval church. Another survivor of the 15th century is the fine octagonal **font,** standing on its original steps which have quatrefoil carving on the top risers. The eight panels of the bowl have lions and set into the borders of these panels are tiny fleurons. Beneath the bowl are human heads at the four corners, with foliage between them. Around the stem are lions, standing on human heads. The font is in an excellent state of preservation, which may be because Dowsing's men could find nothing on it which could be called superstitious.

The handsome **pulpit** and sounding-board also survive from before the restoration and date from c. 1700. This is the Civic Church of Ipswich and the front pews of the nave are the **Corporation pews,** bearing the arms of the Borough and on the piers nearby are the civic **sword** and **mace rests.** Phipson's rood-screen has recently been removed to stand in front of the organ pipes at the east end of the north aisle, and the screen in front of the organ console contains in the two centre divisions, some tracery from the 16th century **parclose-screen** which once divided off the south chapel.

The **sanctuary** contains richly coloured woodwork and ornate **sedilia** and **piscina**, also a fine 17th century oak **chair.** Another chair, dating from about 1630, can be seen in the south chapel. This chapel possesses exact copies of its original windows. In the south aisle, near the chapel entrance, is a restored **piscina.**

This church is rich in 19th century **glass** and some of the most important stained glass manufacturers are represented here. The east and west windows, also others in the south aisle are by Clayton & Bell and two windows in the north aisle are by William Wailes, who produced windows for Pugin, Butterfield and other famous 19th century architects. Other glass in the building shows the work of Michael O'Connor and Lavers, Barraud & Westlake.

Monuments

All the monuments from the old church were taken by Phipson and placed together in two groups. One group can be seen in the choir vestry, behind the organ, and amongst the memorials here is a fine **wall-monument** to John Robinson, a portman, who died in 1694, showing effigies of himself, his wife and four children. The second group of monuments is at the south-west corner of the church. These commemorate many of the important people of Ipswich during the 17th and 18th centuries. There is a curious memorial here to William Smart M.P., who died in 1599. (His ledger slab can be seen in the floor). It is an acrostic verse about him, which is painted on a wooden panel, at the bottom of which are depicted himself, his wife and a contemporary view of the town of Ipswich which he served.

In the chancel floor are four **brasses,** of late 15th and early 16th century date. The brass nearest the west shows an unknown merchant and his two wives (c. 1500). Another brass commemorates Thomas Drayle (also a merchant) and his family. He died in 1518. There is a lawyer with his ink-horn and pen-case. His name is not known, but his brass dates from about 1475.

The fourth brass commemorates Alice Baldry and shows her with her two husbands and nine children. She died in 1506.

The fine three manual **organ**, by 'Father' Henry Willis, of 1860 was rebuilt by Rutt in 1930, and again by Willis in 1964. It contains one old stop probably from the Harris organ of c. 1680. It has 42 speaking stops. This church maintains an extremely high musical tradition.

The fine ring of twelve **bells** has recently been re-tuned and re-hung. No. 11 is by Miles Graye, 1610, (also No. 7, but this was recast in 1946). No. 4 is by Hodson of St. Mary Cray, 1699. Three are by John Darbie, 1671, four by Warner, 1866 and two by Taylor, 1844. The tenor weighs 32 cwt. This church has a fine ringing tradition and many memorable peals have been rung in this tower.

The church also possesses several items of interesting and valuable **plate**, some dating from the 17th and 18th centuries. There was a pre-Reformation chalice here, but this was injudiciously remade in 1867.

St. Matthew

This church now has a superb situation when viewed from the east. This is due, again, to the modern development of the town. Many houses have been taken down in the vicinity and an important main road now runs past the eastern end of the churchyard.

St. Matthew's is a large church which has undergone several changes and extensions during the 19th century, when it was used as the Garrison Church. Old prints of the building show that it had a south porch and a dormer window in the nave roof. The porch disappeared in 1845, when the south aisle was considerably widened. The south chapel and a small porch were added in 1860, when the church was refloored and new benches were made for the nave and aisles. The architect was R. M. Phipson. The widening of the north aisle took place in 1877, under the direction of Sir G. Gilbert Scott. The east wall was rebuilt in 1866 and was again altered in 1890. In the 1884 restoration (by Bisshopp) the upper part of the tower was rebuilt, the present parapet added and also the south aisle was refaced. This list of dates and additions shows that the church has had much alteration during the 19th century, but the work done is very tasteful and conforms to mediaeval tradition.

The church consists of a square west tower, a nave with wide north and south aisles, and a chancel with wide south aisle and narrower north chapel and vestry.

Exterior

Mention has already been made of the imposing situation of this church and it is worth taking time to view it from a distance. The windows are in the Perpendicular style of architecture, the majority having three-lights, except the west window of the north aisle and the east window of the chancel, which have five-lights. Although all the windows have been either renewed or newly inserted during the last century, their style is authentic and a comparison of their structure and tracery shows the great variety of window design used during the Perpendicular period. In the north aisle is a fine Perpendicular doorway, which has lion corbels, shields in the spandrels, fleurons, shields and crowns in the moulding of the arch and more tiny fleurons in the hood-moulds. There are some gargoyles to be seen on the walls of this church and a particularly fine one can be seen to the north of the east window. There is flushwork on the buttresses and parapets of the aisles and tower. The clerestory comprises four double square-headed windows each side.

The tower is unbuttressed and has an embattled parapet. The simple doorway was inserted in 1884 and above it is a two-light window. The ringing chamber, which is accessible by means of a staircase turret at the south-east angle, is lit by single trefoil-headed windows. The two-light belfry windows were carefully replaced in their original places and condition when the upper part of the tower was rebuilt. Above them is an attractive openwork parapet, with battlements, flushwork and a string course in which there are stone carvings.

Interior

This is spacious and colourful, with wide aisles and an impressive sanctuary. The aisles are divided from the nave by **arcades** of four bays. The piers on the south date from the 14th century and are octagonal, with fleurons in the capitals. Those on the north are work of the late 15th century and have concave-sided octagonal piers. As a result of their enlargement in the 19th century, the aisles are as wide as the nave.

The nave **roof** was erected in 1843 and has tie-beams, similar to that in St. Clement's. It replaced a very fine hammer-beam roof and it is sad that this roof was lost. Both aisles have arch-braced tie-beam roofs, also dating from the 19th century and that in the south aisle is a very fine example.

At the west end of the church is the magnificent 15th century **font**, which is one of the finest in Ipswich. It is octagonal and around the base are lions, alternating with carved figures. The bowl, beneath which are angels, depicts the five Joyful Mysteries of the Rosary, which are all incidents in the life of Our Lady. They are the Annunciation, the visit of the Wise Men, the Assumption, the Coronation of Our Lady, and her Glorification with her Son. The remaining three panels have the Baptism of Our Lord, a foliage panel and a rose. The fine state of preservation of this font is remarkable.

At the eastern end of the north aisle are six panels from the mediaeval **rood-screen**. On these panels are painted four saints in episcopal vestments and two groups, one of nine men and the other of seven women. It is thought that these groups may represent the donors of the screen. The **pulpit** was carved by Henry Ringham in 1860.

The **chancel arch** is graceful and has nicely moulded capitals. Beneath it is a modern rood and flanking it are openings to the chancel and south chapel, which were made in 1860, and there is another small opening in the wall to the south. In the north pier of the chancel arch is a curious **squint**, which contains a **piscina drain** and a shelf for Communion vessels. This indicates the existence of an altar nearby in mediaeval times.

The chancel has its original 14th century **single hammer-beam roof**, which has carved wall-plates and angels with shields. In recent years the organ has been moved to the north chapel and the south chapel has been opened up. The south chapel is divided from the chancel by an arcade of two bays, and in its east wall is an ancient **niche**, with fleurons in the arch. This has been removed here from elsewhere in the church and may have been a piscina at one time. The modern oak **Communion rails** in this chapel are carved in 17th century fashion; they flank three central **glass panels**, which are a memorial to the Rev'd. T. A. George, an Indian priest, who was Curate here until his death in 1975. They were made in 1977 and are a worthy example of craftsmanship from our own time which rightly takes its place alongside the work of past ages. The screen (1860) at the entrance to the chapel, originally stood beneath the chancel arch.

The fine **reredos** in the sanctuary was erected as a memorial in 1904. It was designed by J. S. Corder, a local man, and made by Messrs. Bacon of London. In the north chancel wall is an **aumbry**, where the Blessed Sacrament is reserved.

This church has an interesting collection of 19th and early 20th century **glass** by a variety of firms. At the east end of the south aisle is an interesting window of 1853 by George Hedgeland (who designed the great west window of Norwich Cathedral) and the artist, Frank Howard.

There are two fine **wall-monuments** in the north wall of the chancel. The westernmost commemorates Anthony Penning, who died in 1630. It has effigies of him and his wife kneeling, with their children kneeling beneath them. It is interesting to note that two daughters (holding skulls) died before their parents and three died in infancy. To the east of this is a similar monument to Richard Cock, who died in 1629, with effigies of himself, his wife, three sons and five daughters.

There are six **bells** in the tower, including one (No. 2) by Miles Graye, 1605. No. 3 is inscribed "Sancta Katerina ora pro nobis". Nos. 1, 4 and 5 are by Pack & Chapman, 1772. The tenor weighs 11 cwt. and was given in 1933.

Forster & Andrews built a three manual **organ** in 1882, which was later placed against the east wall of the church in 1921. In 1968 it was restored to the north side of the chancel, again by Bishop & Son, with very minor changes. There was formerly a remarkable crank and feeder blowing apparatus. It has 27 speaking stops.

The church possesses an Elizabethan **chalice** amongst its plate.

St. Nicholas

This church stands on the site of the Saxon church of St. Michael and it is possible that parts of it are built of materials taken from the demolished church.

The churchyard to the south is tree-shaded and picturesque and its northern side was nicely opened up when Franciscan Way was made. St. Nicholas Church is now very much dwarfed by the tall modern buildings which have risen around it.

The main body of the church is built of a mixture of stone, flint and septaria rubble, which is unusual in the Ipswich churches. It consists of nave with aisles, chancel, with north vestry, south porch and a western tower of flint.

Exterior

The nave and aisles date from the early 14th century, the north aisle having been extended eastwards to match the south in 1848. The windows of the aisles are built in the early Decorated style, with simple 'Y' tracery, except the easternmost windows on either side, which are Perpendicular. The chancel windows are also in the Perpendicular style. The east window was blocked until the late 1820s.

The north aisle has a good Decorated doorway (now blocked) with corbel heads. The brick south porch was erected in the 18th century. The large sundial above the doorway is noteworthy. The attractive set of two-light dormer windows on each side of the church, near the division between nave and chancel, were probably made to give additional light to the rood. Similar dormer windows could be seen in St. Matthew's and St. Mary Stoke, but these were removed during the 19th century.

The western tower was rebuilt in 1886 by E. F. Bisshopp. It is a fine flint structure, rising to a height of about 57 ft. The rebuilding faithfully restored it to its former mediaeval glory. Photographs taken previous to the restoration show a plain parapet, without pinnacles, and probably of brick. The present parapet is a mass of flushwork, the niches containing statues on each face, with stepped battlements and crocketed pinnacles. The tower has buttresses with flushwork, reaching to the level of the tops of the belfry windows, and a staircase turret in the south-east corner, leading to the ringing chamber. There are double sets of two-light belfry windows in each face and single windows lighting the ringing chamber. The west window is large and has three-lights. Beneath it is the fine west doorway, which is mediaeval and worth noting. It has shields and fleurons in the arch, winged shields in the spandrels and crowned lions for corbels. Above the doorway are three shields, bearing coats of arms.

The main entrance to the church is by means of the porch, which has a 14th century doorway.

Interior

There are many points of interest inside this church. The interior was restored in 1848 and there have been several tasteful additions since then.

The 14th century **arcade**, of five bays, has quatrefoil piers and beautifully moulded capitals, which authorities reckon to be premier examples of their type. The sills of the aisle windows have been lowered to form seats and around the walls of the north aisle, the west end of the nave and part of the south aisle, is 17th or 18th century **panelling**, which came from the box pews which once filled the church.

The octagonal **font** is 15th century and came from St. Lawrence Church, having been purchased for this church in 1862. There is trefoil-headed panelling round the bowl, and the symbols of the four Evangelists. The handsome **pulpit** is Jacobean and has a sounding board. At the eastern end of the north aisle wall is a tall **niche**, and this is flanked by pieces of **lead** which were salvaged from the old lead roof and which bear the names of churchwardens. Notice the imprint of the hand in the easternmost one. At the eastern end of the north aisle can also be seen a good 15th century trefoil-headed **piscina**. Another piscina can be seen in the south aisle.

The chancel contains in its wall some of the oldest **fragments of carved stonework** in the town. They date almost certainly from Saxon times, although some authorities would date them a little later – until 1948, these stones were incorporated into the exterior wall of the south aisle. The westernmost is a carving of St. Michael fighting the Dragon. It bears an inscription in Anglo-Saxon which, translated, reads: "Here St. Michael fights against the Dragon". This stone probably came from the church of St. Michael which stood on this site. The centre stone is semi-circular and it has been suggested that this probably formed the tympanum over the doorway of the lost chapel of All Saints, which stood near Handford Bridge. The carving on it is a boar, and its Latin inscription shows that it was almost certainly the dedication stone of the chapel. The eastern group of stones bear traces of colour. They are fragments of people in Eucharistic vestments, and probably represented apostles.

In the sanctuary is a **piscina**, and some more panelling can be seen under the south window. The **Communion rails**, which have twisted balusters, date from the 18th century and were once three-sided.

The painting on the west wall of the north aisle depicts the meal at Emmaus, and was executed by J. Smart, a local artist in 1807, and hung above the altar. In 1848, the old Royal Arms were taken down and a set of Prince of Wales' Feathers were found nailed to the back.

The floor of the centre aisle contains several stones with the matrices of **brasses**. Those brasses which remain have been removed to the walls of the south aisle. Here they can be studied with the help of well-written notes beside them. On the south wall, the westernmost commemorates William Style and his wife Isabella, who died in 1475 and 1490 respectively. The centre brasses are of an unknown civilian and his wife (c.1600), to the east of which is an inscription and coat of arms to the memory of Susan, wife of Augustine Parker. There is another brass near the division of the nave and chancel (south side) dating from about 1500.

The tower contains a peal of five **bells**, No. 2 is by Miles Graye, 1630. The rest by H. Pleasant of Sudbury, 1706. The tenor weighs 10 cwt. Diameter 39 inches.

A new five-rank unit **organ** by Rutt was installed in 1935. It is placed in the north aisle at first-floor level and has no facade. There are two manuals and 26 speaking stops.

Amongst the church **plate** is an Elizabethan chalice and a paten, flagon and alms-dish made in the 18th century.

It is thought that Cardinal Thomas Wolsey lived in this parish as a boy. His father and mother were buried here and his father bequeathed money to the church in his will.

St. Peter

St. Peter's Church is situated near the dockland and next to the gateway of Cardinal Wolsey's College. The views of this fine building have been greatly improved by the demolition of some of the buildings around it and the building of a new road on its north side.

This is an edifice of considerable size and beauty. The nave is known to date from the early 14th century and nine bequests towards the erection of the present fine tower were made between 1452 and 1473. The belfry stage and parapet were rebuilt in 1882.

Considerable restoration took place during Victorian times, to the plans of Sir G. Gilbert Scott. In 1878 the aisles were lengthened, the organ chamber was built and the church was given a new chancel arch and east window. Before this there was no east window, the inside of the east end being filled with a large altar-piece. The south clerestory received new windows and the chancel was re-roofed.

The church consists of nave and chancel, north and south aisles, south porch (rebuilt 1874) and square western tower.

This church has seen great prosperity in its time, but now its parish has a tiny population and during recent years the building has been declared redundant and closed. Vandals have broken in and caused damage and it has been necessary for the windows to be boarded up. It is to be hoped that a useful and worthy purpose may soon be found for this lovely church.

Exterior

St. Peter's has a noble exterior, although many of the windows were renewed during the last century. Those in the aisles are in the Decorated style, and have two-lights, except the ornate Victorian windows in the north chapel which have three-lights. Scott's five-light east window is also in the Decorated style. The clerestory has two-light windows on the south side and circular windows on the north side. The porch is lit by two-light Perpendicular windows. Its outer entrance arch is also Perpendicular, with fleurons in the spandrels and crowned lion corbels. The inner entrance has a good moulded arch and crowned corbel heads and the roof of the porch contains some mediaeval timbers. There is a doorway with a moulded arch in the north aisle.

High on the northern buttress which supports the east wall is a piece of weathered carving. This is the remains of a set of the Royal Arms of Henry VII carved in stone.

The tower is both sturdy and lofty. It rises to a height of 93ft. and dominates the exterior. It dates from the late 15th century and has a large four-light west window, the arch of which is almost flat. The three-light belfry windows have intersecting tracery (which is post-mediaeval) and there are tiny stone shields beneath them. Above is a flushwork parapet with stepped battlements. Remains of the stone shields which were carved round the base of the tower can be seen on the north side. Also on this side is the staircase turret, which reaches to the level of the belfry and is pierced by its original tiny openings.

At the base of the parapet are gargoyles which drain the rainwater from the tower roof.

The enormous west doorway merits close inspection. Its tremendous proportions and its carved stonework are unrivalled in Ipswich and greatly reward examination. The doorway is flanked by large canopied niches, which have small pinnacles. The doorway itself has three minor shafts in its moulding and between them can be seen shields, Tudor roses, thistles, angels, fleurons, male and female heads and crowns.

Interior

The condition of the interior of this church at the time of writing is rather pitiful. Many of the furnishings have been cleared away, the organ has been reconstructed at Clare Church, some of the windows are broken or boarded up and the hoof-mark of the vandal can be seen everywhere. The absence of pews does, however, emphasise the fine proportions of the building and also its excellent acoustics.

The **arcades**, of four bays, date from the 14th century and have good quatrefoil piers. The **tower arch** is lofty and handsome and has minor shafts. The southern entrance is flanked by corbel heads.

The fine open **roof** is mostly mediaeval and the aisle roofs also have ancient timbers and wall-plates, although Davy was told in 1811 by the Clerk that the roof was restored some years before that date, using timbers from the demolished Brightwell Hall in the restoration of the cornices. In the north aisle is the blocked entrance to the former **rood-loft stairs,** with an ancient arched recess beside it (maybe for a piscina). These were discovered in 1880, when the chancel was also refurnished. In the south aisle opposite is a trefoil-headed **piscina.**

The great treasure of the church is the massive **font.** The square bowl is made of black Tournai marble and dates from the latter half of the 12th century. It is one of only seven examples in the country. It measures 3 ft. 6 inches across each side and the carvings around it represent lions. The stone base is later, having been made for the bowl in the 15th century. Around the base are four standing figures.

The **stained glass** in the church was placed there during Scott's restoration and is by Heaton, Butler & Bayne.

In the north chancel chapel is a **memorial** to Manuel Sorrell, a portman and bailiff of the town, who died in 1669. Another slab commemorates Thomas Blith, who died in 1652.

The church also possesses a **brass** to the Knapp family, which shows Sir John Knapp (who died in 1604), his wife, their four sons and eight daughters. This brass has now been taken to Christchurch Mansion.

There are six **bells** in the tower, Nos. 1 and 5 are by Thomas Gardiner of Sudbury, 1733. No. 4 is by Darbie, 1683. No. 6 (the tenor) is by Miles Graye, 1630, and weighs 9 cwt.

The **organ** by Gray, which stood in the gallery as early as 1832 was enlarged by Rayson and squeezed into a small space built out from the south wall during Scott's restoration. It had a finely carved case by Scott, much impaired in appearance when it was brought out of the chamber in 1907 and left without sides. The organ and case went to St. Rhedwy's Church, Llanllyfni, Caern., in 1952 when the Bishop organ from Herne Hill Congregational Church was installed. This was removed to Clare in 1976. When at St. Peter's this two manual organ had 23 speaking stops.

This church is now in the care of the Ipswich Historic Churches Trust.

St. Stephen

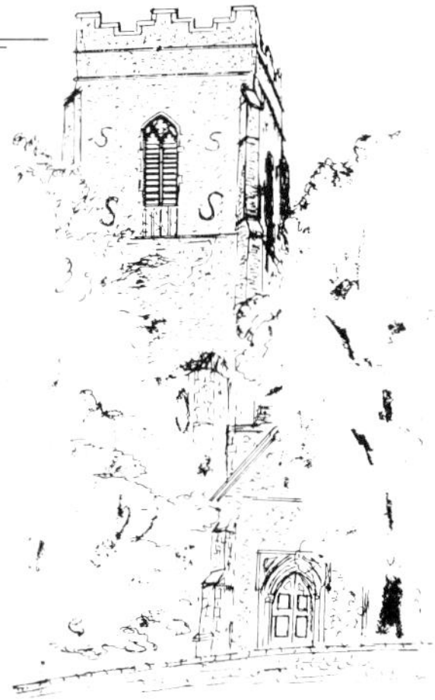

This church was founded before the Domesday Book was compiled in 1086. It is a humble building, situated in a quiet lane, amongst trees. The churchyard has been made into a place where people can sit in peace and quiet.

Several building materials have been used in the fabric of this church, including flint, stone and brick in the exterior and Purbeck marble in the arcade. The building shows signs of the wear of centuries, which has mellowed it and given it great character.

It has been restored several times. The walls have been patched with brick in several places and Davy's sketch shows that the tower was entirely faced with brick or plaster. In 1881, the battlements of the tower were rebuilt, the organ chamber was erected and the church was generally restored. The vestry was built in 1885.

The church consists of nave, chancel, south aisle (of which the eastern part was built as a chapel), south porch and square western tower.

Exterior

The nave and south aisle are lit by the characteristic three-light Perpendicular windows, which were greatly renewed during the general restoration in 1881. There is a blocked square-headed four-light window at the east end of the aisle and the east window of the chancel is a large four-light Perpendicular window, renewed in 1866. Traces of an entrance (in use in 1810) to the south chapel through a buttress can be seen. Davy recorded the date 1535 on this buttress in the aisle, which received its parapet in 1881. In the north wall of the nave there is a blocked doorway which has fleurons in its arch.

The western tower is 59 ft. high and has been patched and restored with red brick. The stepped battlements were renewed in 1881, and during a very recent restoration the parapet has lost its flushwork of vertical panels and quatrefoils. Flushwork can still be seen however beneath the belfry windows and on the base at the west end. The belfry windows have two-lights and the chamber below is lit by a small single window. A staircase turret on the south side leads to the ringing chamber. Beneath the restored west window is a weathered west doorway, which must have looked quite splendid in its heyday. Beside it, in the battered flushwork, is a Holy Water stoup. In the buttresses flanking the west doorway are two lofty niches. Careful examination reveals that these are vaulted and in their canopies can be seen tiny carved heads.

The south porch is at the western end of the aisle. It has two-light windows and a Perpendicular entrance arch, with fleurons. The inner entrance arch has fleurons, also a deep hood-mould which rests upon corbel heads. There was formerly a gallery, and the stairs which led up to it were approached by means of a door in the north-east corner of the porch.

The interior was re-ordered in 1866, when new seating, pulpit, etc., designed by Barnes and made by Godbolt of Harleston, were inserted.

Interior

Above the main entrance hangs the **Prince of Wales' Feathers**, which are dated 1661. A similar set can be seen in St. Margaret's Church and there is no clear explanation as to why the fleur-de-lis were set up in churches at this time. In 1660 the rule of the Cromwellians finished and England again had a king. The return of the monarchy meant also the return of the Church of England and its Prayer Book and no doubt there was a move by loyal churchmen to celebrate this in our churches with symbols of the monarchy. This is also apparent by the fact that most of the sets of Royal Arms in the Ipswich churches are those of King Charles II. A set of these **Royal Arms** also hangs in this church, beneath which are **lead fragments** from the old roof, bearing the names of the churchwardens at the time when it was erected.

The south aisle is divided from the nave by an **arcade** of three bays and from the chancel by a further two bays. An unusual feature of this arcade is that the piers are built of Purbeck marble. The **tower arch** rests upon angels, bearing shields. Two funeral **hatchments** hang on the tower wall.

In the north wall of the nave, near the blocked doorway, is an extremely beautiful **niche**, which probably once contained a statue. It retains the pedestal on which the statue stood and its canopy has miniature fan-vaulting.

The south aisle **roof** is original, and there are several 15th century beams in the nave roof, which has tie-beams and queen-posts. The arched openings either side of the chancel arch are probably 19th century insertions. The chancel roof is of single hammer-beam construction. It has been greatly restored, but it still preserves its mediaeval wall-plates.

The ends of the two **priests' stalls** in the chancel are fine and probably date from the 15th century.

The west window showing the Stoning of Stephen is by James Powell & Son.

In the sanctuary can be seen two **brass inscriptions.** The southern inscription commemorates William Sherman, who died in 1585 and that on the north is to John Wingfield, who died in 1594.

The church has other **monuments** which are of interest, the finest being in the north wall of the chancel, and commemorating Robert Leman and his wife. He was at one time Lord Mayor of London. The inscription reads:

Beneath this monument entombed lie
A rare remark of a conjugal tye.
Robert and Mary, who to show how neere
They did comply, How to each other deere.
One loath behind the other long to stay
(As married) Died together in one day.
3rd Sept. 1637

Beneath the kneeling couple are their one son and four daughters.

On the south aisle wall, near the entrance to the chapel, is a monument to John Reynolds, his wife and daughter.

In the tower are three **bells.** Nos. 1 and 2 are pre-Reformation. No. 3 (the tenor) weighs 6 cwt. and was cast by Miles Graye in 1630.

A two manual **organ** by Hunter, built in the late 19th century, stands in a chamber north of the chancel. It has 14 speaking stops.

The church possesses a set of 18th century **Communion plate.**

The Ipswich Historic Churches Trust now look after St. Stephen's.

St. Andrew's - Rushmere

We see in St. Andrew's a village church in a peaceful and picturesque village setting, sedately away from the modern housing developments where the majority of its many parishioners reside. It stands in a large and attractive churchyard and in its fabric can be seen a mixture of contrasting building styles.

The western tower rose during the late 15th and early 16th centuries and money was left for it in 1496 and 1521. It was restored in 1861 and 1863, when a new west window (with its figure of St. Andrew) was inserted and the pinnacles and emblems of the four Evangelists were added to its flushwork parapet; the gargoyles at the base of the parapet on three sides are, however, largely original.

The nave and chancel were rebuilt, and the north aisle added in 1861, to the designs of Edward Hakewill (who lived at nearby Playford), but the fine Norman south doorway – preserved by centuries of shelter from a former porch – was carefully replaced and forms the main entrance. Hakewill used the Early English style of architecture for his new windows, replacing larger Perpendicular windows which had weakened the former structure.

In 1967-68 the church was enlarged by an eastern extension and porch, also a vestry complex to the north-west of the nave. The old nave and chancel (with the exception of the east wall) remain, the new part being a continuation of the chancel. The modern work is in brick and the architecture is distinctive and contemporary in style. Reactions to a major work of extension such as this differ but, although the proportions of the exterior now look rather strange, there is a certain grandeur and quality in the design. The architect was George Pace of York, who supervised the rebuilding of Llandaff Cathedral and designed several modern churches. One of his most remarkable works was the rebuilding of the mediaeval church of St. Mary, Bishopshill Senior in York as Holy Redeemer, Acomb, a suburb of the city.

Interior

What was internally a small, largely Victorian village church has been transformed into a light and spacious building, ideally suited to modern liturgical requirements. The **central altar**, standing in the old chancel, is the focal point of the church, uniting the Victorian Gothic nave to the west, with its carved benches and stained glass, and the light and airy extension to the east, with its brick walls, large windows and contemporary fittings.

The **nave roof** retains some of its mediaeval timber framework and the 1861 **chancel roof** has been painted, forming a canopy for the altar. The **oak benches**, with their poppyhead ends and array of fine armrests, were beautifully carved in 1861 in mediaeval fashion by William Polley of Coggeshall. The armrests near the centre aisle depict angels, bearing scrolls and musical instruments, except the two rear benches, where they carry the tower and chancel of the mediaeval church. Those in the north aisle show the emblems of the four Evangelists and other symbolic creatures. The **font** at the west end is large, square and typically Victorian.

Amongst the colourful 19th century **glass** (by Lavers, Barraud & Westlake) in the windows, the three lancets in the south chancel wall (which are lowered to form sedilia) contain glass given in memory of E. C. Hakewill, the architect, who died in 1872. Other memorials of note are three attractive **wall-plaques** opposite the main entrance, commemorating members of the Edge family.

The **organ** was rebuilt in its fine case (originally made by Barnes of Ipswich) at the west end by Hill, Norman & Beard in 1948. Its detached console has two manuals, pedals, 15 speaking stops and eight couplers. The instrument was originally built (1882) by J. D. Dixon of Cambridge and much of Dixon's work has been preserved in the rebuilding.

The **tower** contains six bells. Three are pre-Reformation and bear the marks of William Chamberlain, who worked between 1426 and 1456; two are by John Darbie of Ipswich and are dated 1695 and the tenor (8¾ cwt.) was cast by Mears and Stainbank in 1885.

St. Mary Magdalen-Westerfield

Westerfield is a small and picturesque village, about two miles north of the town centre, now included in the Borough of Ipswich. Its church is small and unprepossessing, yet of considerable interest, showing craftsmanship from the 11th century onwards.

The nave and chancel have no structural division and, unusually, were not altered externally during the Perpendicular period. The simple rendered walls form a pleasing contrast to the flint tower. A single 13th century lancet window can be seen on the north side and the remaining windows were inserted about 1300 and show the characteristic 'Y' tracery. The south-west window was inserted in 1867 to replace the former Norman south doorway and south porch. The large 'Gothick' brick vestry on the north side was built as a schoolroom in 1840.

The core of the tower probably dates from c. 1300, but it was given a major face-lift in the early 15th century, when it received its flushwork parapet, elegant Perpendicular west window and handsome west doorway, which has an arch studded with fleurons, and roses in the spandrels; it retains its mediaeval door. The belfry windows have unfortunately lost their mullions and tracery (the western one has been entirely reframed with brick); these were once two-light windows.

Interior

This is colourful and cared-for. The earliest workmanship is seen in the **carved Norman stonework** from the former south doorway which now surrounds the south-west window of the **nave.** Nearby is the **niche** for a Holy Water **stoup** for the former entrance (there is another outside).

The **font** is of traditional East Anglian design, and is a fine piece of 15th century stonecarving. In the panels of the bowl are the emblems of the four Evangelists, alternating with the Cross of St. George and the emblems of the Holy Trinity and the Blessed Sacrament.

The original **rood-beam** straddles the church at the division of nave and chancel and nearby in the south wall are the remains of the rood-loft stairs.

The crowning glory of this building is the magnificent **single hammer-beam roof.** It was fashioned in the 15th century and is one of the finest in the county. What is particularly fortunate here is that it is low enough to be examined and enjoyed at unusually close quarters!

The **piscina** and window-sill **sedilia** remain in the **sanctuary**.

Above the **tower arch** hang the framed **Royal Arms** of King George III. These, together with the Lord's Prayer, Creed and Commandments which now hang beneath the tower, were all fixed to the east wall of the chancel before the 1867 restoration.

Most of the furnishings date from 1867 onwards and some good craftsmanship of our own century is represented here, including the **altar** and **reredos** (1930), the **pulpit crucifix** from Oberammergau, the list of Rectors (1966), the locally-made **kneelers** (1960s) and the beautiful **pictorial map** of the parish (1977).

Several **memorials** can be seen on the walls and in the floors and windows. A mediaeval slab near the font once contained a brass and some ledger slabs commemorate the Collett family of Westerfield Hall. Of particular interest to 'church-crawlers' is the memorial to Henry Munro Cautley (1875-1959), who wrote major text-books on Suffolk and Norfolk churches and on Royal Arms in churches. As Diocesan Architect and Surveyor he designed three new churches in Ipswich and work of his design can be seen in the reredos, lectern and war memorial in this church, where he worshipped for 65 years.

The **organ**, by Bishop & Son, has two manuals, pedals and nine speaking stops.

Two of the three **bells** in the tower date from c. 1400 and were probably cast in John Langhorne's London foundry. The other, originally made at Bury in 1535, was recast by Mears in 1852.

St. Mary's - Whitton

Situated at the north-west corner of Ipswich, overlooking open countryside at the end of Whitton Church Lane, this unprepossessing building is probably one of the most difficult of the Ipswich churches to find; its spire is usually dwarfed by the surrounding trees.

A church has existed on this spot for many centuries and the humble mediaeval building was small and towerless. In 1852, this was rebuilt to the designs of Frederick Barnes; the chancel was remodelled and a new nave and north aisle (with a bell-cote at the west end of the former) were built. In 1862, much of the stonework which remained of the little ruined church of Thurleston (closed in the early 16th century and united with Whitton parish) was brought up to St. Mary's and was used to build the south aisle and tower.

The church we see today is therefore predominantly a Victorian building, which stands aloof in a far corner of its densely populated parish. It is a fascinating structure because, although it is by no means a tiny church, its features are on what can only be described as a miniature scale, giving it a certain quaintness. Barnes mainly used the architecture of the Early English and early Decorated periods in his rebuilding, with a pleasant diversity of window tracery, thus giving the 'feel' of a typical small Suffolk village church. The small tower, which is crowned by a stone broach spire, capped with a carved finial, also serves as the south porch. Its doorway is thought to be original, of 13th century date, re-used from the mediaeval church.

Interior

Inside, the church is bright and homely; it is a very humble building and is a far cry from the airs and graces of the High Victorian heights of the Gothic Revival. Once again there is the feeling of smallness, particularly in the

arcades. The building is also remarkably low (structurally rather than liturgically) and this is particularly apparent in the **chancel**, which retains its original 14th century roof and simple **piscina** in the south wall of the **sanctuary**. The position of the piscina suggests that the floor-level of the chancel has been raised considerably. Also in the sanctuary is a small and plain **chest** of considerable age.

The 19th century **pews** in the nave have individual doors, but the **chancel stalls** have poppyhead ends (note the little faces in the ends of the rear stall on the south side). The **reading desks** have misericords and traceried fronts; these incorporate mediaeval woodwork and were brought here during recent years from a Sudbury church. The **reredos** which stood behind the **altar** is now at the west end of the nave and nearby is the 19th century **font**, which has a circular arcaded bowl.

There is some attractive **stained glass** including three windows by Hardman of Birmingham, of which the west window is particularly noteworthy. The Madonna and Child, in the north aisle is by the firm of William Morris.

The **organ** is a recent acquisition from the House of Bethany in Bournemouth. It was built by Walker and has two manuals, pedals and 14 speaking stops.

The **bell** in the tower is of interest because it is the earliest dated bell in the county. It was cast in 1441, probably by a Flemish bell-founder.

The parish has a daughter church, dedicated to the Ascension of Our Lord, which is a spacious dual-purpose building, situated at the junction of Larchcroft and Congreve Roads. It was built in 1964.

19th & 20th century Churches

As the population of Ipswich grew and the town extended outwards during the last 150 years, it became necessary for new churches to be built, mostly away from the centre of the town. As a result ten comparatively new churches have been erected for the parishes which have been formed. Also three dual-purpose hall-churches have been built within existing parishes.

These modern buildings do not have the antiquity of the mediaeval churches, but each is a piece of original design and, viewed for its own sake, is of some interest. Also deserving of record in connection with these churches are several generous and hard-working priests and lay people, by whose untiring efforts the new parishes were born and the life of the churches grew, and by whose generosity land was given for the sites and money donated for their erection and beautification.

All Hallows

All Hallows serves the Gainsborough Estate area on the east side of the town. It stands in Landseer Road and was erected in 1939 to the designs of H. Munro Cautley, providing an interesting contrast to his conventional Gothic church of St. Augustine, whose parish adjoins this one.

The church is built of brick and although not particularly large or ornate, it is certainly conspicuous and manages to dominate its surroundings, particularly when viewed from the east across the playing field. It is lit by rectangular windows at the sides and has a circular west window. The hipped roof and the oblong tower on the north side are distinctive features. There are chapels on the north and south sides and a baptistery at the west end.

Interior

All Hallows has a dignified and devotional interior which is lofty, spacious and bright. The red brick is exposed inside and beneath the windows are blank semi-circular headed arches. The architect has successfully created dignity out of simplicity. The panelled roofs of the nave and chancel are pleasantly painted and the nave floor has an unobtrusive but effective downward slope towards the east.

The **benches** were originally in Ely Cathedral and a 17th century **chair** in the north chapel, also a 17th century **Communion table** in the south chapel have been brought here from elsewhere. The south chapel (which is being re-ordered at the time of writing) has much evidence of the church's connection with the Boys' Brigade, including a framed carving of its founder, Sir William Smith. The Lady Chapel was tastefully refurnished as a memorial in 1951.

A fine feature of the interior is the excellent **woodwork**, in walnut veneer, which can be seen in the **twin pulpits**, **reading desks** and **stalls**, also in the **altar** and its **rails**. The octagonal **font** is crowned with a beautiful wooden cover which was given as a memorial by members of the Mothers' Union.

A two manual **organ**, dating from 1939 by Binns, Fitton & Haley is placed in a shallow recess north of the choir-stalls. There are 16 speaking stops.

The **bell**, cast by John Draper in 1609 was the tenor of three bells at the disused church at Knettishall, near the Norfolk border.

All Saints

This large red brick church stands in Chevallier Street, on the western side of Ipswich. Its distinctive tower is a familiar landmark to travellers along the by-pass.

The parish was formed out of St. Matthew's parish and the incomplete church was consecrated in 1887. Architects had been invited to submit designs to compete for a prize of £50 which was to be given to the winning design. The eminent architect, Ewan Christian, judged the entries and the winning architect was S. Wright, from Morecambe. The bricks used in the building of this church were all manufactured in the parish, but its design has the flavour of many Victorian Lancashire and Cheshire churches and would have looked splendid had it been built in pink Runcorn stone!

All Saints was the dedication of a lost mediaeval church which stood near Handford Bridge, the original dedication stone is preserved in St. Nicholas Church. The carving on this stone has been reproduced in the foundation stone of the present All Saints Church.

The building was completed in 1893. It consists of nave with aisles, chancel, north porch and a lofty tower at the west end of the south aisle, the base of which forms a south porch. The style of architecture is Perpendicular. The aisles are lit by triple windows, there is a five-light east window and a set of three lofty two-light windows in the west end of the nave. The unusual **tower** is octagonal and is capped by a short spirelet. A gabled turret ascends one side to the level of the large single belfry windows. There is one **bell** (cast by Warner of London) which is the treble of what was to be a peal of five.

Interior

The red brick is exposed in the interior walls and in the six-bay **arcade**, which has slender quatrefoil pillars. The **screen** and **reredos** were designed by the architect and the **pulpit** is a fine piece of carved woodwork. The Lady Chapel in the south aisle has an oak screen which has been made during recent years.

The glass in the **east window** was inserted about 1947 by Campbell of London.

The Binns **organ** was enlarged to three manuals by Fitton & Haley in 1935; it stands at the east end of the south aisle, and has 26 speaking stops.

Holy Trinity

This was the first church to be built in Ipswich during the 19th century. It was begun in 1835 and was designed by Harvey, a local architect. In 1895 the existing building was extended and the present chancel, vestries and organ chamber were added. The designs were by the versatile and adaptable E. F. Bisshopp. At this time the font and pulpit arrived.

Holy Trinity occupies a fine and commanding position on the hillside, overlooking the town at its eastern end, and it is rather a pity that the exterior is so plain and uninspiring. It is built of 'white' Suffolk bricks, which have considerably darkened over the years. The walls are pierced by large semi-circular headed windows and there is a plain oblong tower at the west end.

Interior

The interior of Holy Trinity is, by contrast, surprisingly colourful and attractive. A great deal of thought and effort has obviously been given to make it as beautiful and atmospheric as possible. The chancel, which has panelled **arcades** in the style of the 17th and 18th centuries, was greatly beautified in 1960. This was done to commemorate the 125th anniversary of the church. During this restoration the organ was moved to the south side, and the existing **high altar** was placed in the north chapel. A new **free-standing altar** was made for the sanctuary and the chancel was painted sky-blue and white. This careful use of colour is most effective. The church has a fine **pulpit** which is fittingly made in the Jacobean style.

The glass in the **east window** (c. 1920) is by L. A. Pownall of Falmouth, who was related to the vicar of the time.

The Bishop **organ** of 1908 was moved to the south side of the chancel in 1960, greatly enhancing the appearance of the church by allowing a Lady

Chapel to be formed. Until this time the organ was blown by a water engine, which gave rise to frequent flooding. It has two manuals and 18 speaking stops.

The **bell** in the tower was cast by Thomas Gardiner in 1751. This is obviously second hand but its former home is not known.

A dual-purpose church of St. Luke was opened in 1954 in Cliff Lane. This has a western bell-cote, with one bell by Gillett & Johnston, and a small three-light east window containing stained glass by F. Stephens.

St. Andrew

An appeal was launched at the beginning of the 1930s by the Bishop of the diocese to provide three new churches for Ipswich. As a result the churches of St. Thomas, All Hallows and St. Andrew were all built. The majority of the money was spent on St. Thomas and All Hallows because it was felt that these areas had the greatest need for churches. St. Andrew's was erected in 1936 from what little money remained, to serve a Conventional District which was formed out of St. John's parish. This was not granted parochial status until 1974.

St. Andrew's is a small and unassuming building, which is situated just off Britannia Road. It is built of red brick and was designed by H. Munro Cautley. The church, which comprised nave and chancel only, was recently enlarged by the addition of an entrance and baptistery at the west end.

Interior

Although St. Andrew's is a simple and unpretentious church, the interior is homely and feels 'lived-in'. The nave is furnished with fine 19th century **benches** with poppyheads, which came from the disused church of St. Mary at the Quay. These are a handsome addition and they blend well with their surroundings. The painted chancel **roof** and **reredos** add a pleasing splash of colour to the interior.

The **organ** is an electronic instrument.

The small **bell** was cast by Bowell of Ipswich.

St. Augustine

This cement-coloured cruciform church stands beside a roundabout at the eastern edge of the town, on the road to Felixstowe. Its tower is a landmark along the by-pass and at night the bright illuminated cross above the tower can be seen for some distance.

This building is the generous gift of one man, who saved and sacrificed for years to provide it. His name was Charles Bantoft and the church was a thank-offering for his mother, to whom he owed his Christian faith. Hence the church is dedicated to St. Augustine of Hippo, who also owed much to his Christian mother, St. Monica. The only record he left of his benefaction in the church he had built was a tablet in the Lady Chapel which reads: "This church has been given by an Ipswich tradesman as a thank-offering to Almighty God for the blessing of a pious and affectionate mother. 1927." Lady de Saumarez gave the land on which the church was built and the foundation-stone was laid by her. The builders and stonemasons were Ipswich firms and the architect was H. Munro Cautley, who gave his services in the designing of this church.

The exterior walls of St. Augustine's are faced with rough-cast. The nave has low, narrow, passage-like aisles on the north and south sides and a small baptistery at the west end. The south transept contains the Lady Chapel and has a small eastern projection. The rectangular central tower rises 80 ft. from the ground and at the summit of its 35 ft. flagpole is the unusual illuminated cross which shines out at night. The lofty two-light nave windows and the belfry windows are in the Decorated style, but the larger windows (at the cardinal points) are in the Perpendicular style. The splendour of the exterior is enhanced by the use of buttresses, although the flying buttresses which support the south transept were erected during comparatively recent years, when the transept was in danger of collapse. The total length of the church is 126 ft. and the apex of the nave roof is 50 ft. from the ground.

Interior

The interior is equally handsome. The nave roof has arch-braces and large tie-beams and the vaulted roof of the crossing is enriched by carved bosses. There is stone panelling above the low arcades of the nave.

Mr. Bantoft died in 1935 and in his will he left money for the purchase of the two manual Walker organ, the stained glass in the **east window** (which depicts Our Lord's Ascension), the **east window** of the Lady Chapel (depicting St. Monica and St. Augustine) and the **oak benches**, which were to replace the existing chairs. These were all in place by 1937. The **reredos** was given in memory of Mr. Bantoft by his nephews and nieces in 1938.

The church does contain one mediaeval treasure, which was fashioned 500 years before St. Augustine's was thought of! This is the octagonal 14th century **font**, which was a gift from the church-people of Linstead Magna, near Halesworth, and came from their long disused church. It is a typical East Anglian font and is in a very good state of preservation. Around the bowl are angels bearing shields, alternating with lions (notice also the tiny fleurons in some of the panels). Beneath the bowl are angels with wings outstretched, also a frieze of fleurons. Supporting the stem are four lions.

This church serves a parish of some 20,000 people and has a live and active congregation, who have recently added new vestries, etc., to the north side of the church.

J. W. Walker & Sons provided a part-extension **organ** in a transeptal gallery north of the tower, with the console on the opposite side, c. 1936. In 1978 additional pipework was put in, lessening the proportion of extension ranks. There are 20 speaking stops.

St. Augustine's was given the pre-Reformation **bell** (made in Norwich c. 1450) from Linstead Magna Church, but this is cracked and disused. The other bell was made by Bowell in 1927.

St. Bartholomew

This church has always been a great centre of the Catholic Movement within the Church of England and it was built to cater for this form of worship. It stands in Newton Road, on the eastern side of the town, not far from Derby Road Station and its parish was formed out of Holy Trinity parish. This fine building was erected through the generosity of Anna Frances Spooner, (daughter of John Cobbold of Holywells and wife of Dean Spooner of Hadleigh), who had been brought up at St. Mary-le-Tower, which was the first Ipswich church to come under the influence of the Catholic Revival. The church was consecrated in 1895, although its western end was not completed until 1907, when the sacristy was also built and the present font added. The architect was Charles Spooner and this church is considered to be one of the finest examples of his work.

The first Vicar was Fr. George Cobbold, who was instituted in 1894 and served St. Bartholomew's for 21 years. He was a nephew of Mrs. Spooner and was a fine preacher and teacher. In 1899 Fr. Charles Curtis joined him as assistant priest. His zeal for visiting and for youth work complemented the scholarship of the Vicar and this excellent team built up a sound tradition and a live congregation. All this was achieved in spite of considerable persecution in a predominantly Protestant town and a few people can still remember seeing Fr. Cobbold being pelted with rotten tomatoes. Fr. Cobbold died in 1915 and in that year his curate moved to Southend. The next Vicar, Fr. Powell, continued to build up the Catholic tradition, which has been maintained by successive incumbents of the church.

The building, which is superbly proportioned and beautifully furnished, consists of nave with aisles, chancel, with a chapel to the south and the sacristy to the north, and a western porch. There is no clerestory and the nave and aisles are contained beneath one vast roof. The exterior walls are built of brick.

Interior

The interior of the church is spacious and light. The tremendous amount of space available has made it possible for several altars, statues and shrines to be inserted without in any way giving the church the appearance of being 'cluttered'. Fr. Cobbold's memorial is the **Blessed Sacrament Chapel**, which was designed by H. Munro Cautley and was dedicated in 1925. The stone **arcades** of the nave have three wide bays and a smaller bay at the west. Most of the beautiful **furnishings** and **adornments** were given as **memorials** and their inscriptions tell of many people who have been associated with St. Bartholomew's, yet one feels here that these gifts glorify God rather than the givers!

The **sanctuary**, which has great dignity, is surprisingly simple and is most effective. The oak servers' bench was made in 1949. Above the curtain-canopy to the **high altar** is the circular **east window**, which has elegant tracery and attractive coloured glass.

The fine three manual Norman & Beard **organ** stands high above the chancel with the console below, and has 24 speaking stops.

The small **bell** is appropriately inscribed "St. Bartholomew, our Patron, pray for us".

St. Francis

Here we have a mid-20th century church situated in the nucleus of a large and populous mid-20th century estate and providing a worthy centre of Anglican worship for the Chantry conurbation.

St. Francis' was erected in 1959 in a contemporary style of architecture. The exterior is faced with brick and pebble-dash, with large windows, a shallow copper roof and a tall, thin and distinctive tower at the west end which, with its illuminated cross provides an effective landmark.

Interior

Inside, the church is light and spacious; colour has been used judiciously and there is an atmosphere of devotion. The **sanctuary** is narrower but has the same height as the **nave**; there is no east window and light is provided by windows at the sides. The **furnishings** are tasteful and strangely conventional. A small and attractive **portable font** was given in the late '70s as a memorial.

The Chapel of the Holy Cross, on the left-hand side, provides a small, colourful, carpeted, homely setting for small services and for the reserved Sacrament.

The **organ** is an electronic instrument.

The architect of St. Francis' was Basil Hatcher, who also designed the church at Chelmondiston, rebuilt after the war.

St. John the Baptist

The original St. John's, which was built in the year 1857, still stands to the south of the churchyard. It is a small flint building in the Perpendicular style, consisting of nave and small apsidal sanctuary. It was designed by Woolnough and was never consecrated.

Looming above it is its vast red-brick successor, which was erected in 1899 and was designed by Sir Arthur Blomfield, a famous and prolific architect who designed churches all over England. St. John's, Felixstowe is another of his churches. The architecture of this church is an adaptation of the Early English style and the windows are mostly groups of lancets. The west front, although not easily visible from close quarters, is most effective with its lofty windows and bell-turret containing two **bells.** The church was to have a large tower at the eastern end of the south aisle, with its base serving as a porch. This tower was to be square, with corner pinnacles and three-light belfry windows. Had it been built, it would have been visible from a considerable distance.

Interior

The interior of this church emphasises its huge proportions and great length. The walls have exposed red brick and the furnishings are pleasant. The **reredos** dates from 1913 and the **east window** above it was filled with stained glass during the previous year. The fine **pulpit** and **tester** were given in 1926, in memory of a former vicar. In 1945 the eastern end of the south aisle was furnished for use as a chapel.

A considerable amount has been done during very recent years to add to the beauty and comfort of this church. The wooden **screens** for the organ and chapel were made in 1969 and the modern clusters of lights are most effective.

A re-ordering of the eastern end of the nave has recently been completed, with a new **Communion table** in front of the chancel arch.

The **organ** was built by Binns, Fitton & Haley in 1938 and occupies a loft south of the chancel, with the console opposite. There are three manuals and 40 speaking stops.

St. Michael

This is the only church of 19th century foundation which stands in the central part of the town. Its foundation-stone was laid in 1880 and it is interesting to note that buried in the wall with it is a bottle, containing a copy of *The Times,* a description of the church, some coins and a list of the Building Committee. The architect was E. F. Bisshopp. The nave was consecrated in 1881, the transepts followed in 1884 and the chancel and organ chamber were added in 1890.

St. Michael's is a large and lofty brick church. Its total length is 96 ft. and the height to the summit of the bell-turret is 64 ft. The architecture was influenced by the Early English and Decorated styles and the building consists of nave with aisles, transepts, chancel with north organ chamber, west porch and gabled bell-turret containing two **bells**, by Warner of London.

Interior

The interior is vast and has several distinctive features. The seven-bay **arcade** rests upon heavy stone pillars with intricately carved capitals. The chancel arch is enriched with dog-tooth ornament and the vestry door has a trefoil-headed arch. The great feature of the church is the enormous **east window**, which is made up of three sets of lofty triple Decorated windows. The stained glass in this window was inserted in 1929 and one panel commemorates the Rev'd. W. J. Garrould, the first incumbent. The **pulpit**, which has some fine woodcarving, was made by a churchwarden of St. Michael's.

The **organ** is a Norman & Beard of about 1880, with a choir organ added by Rayson, there are three manuals and 18 speaking stops.

This building was threatened with demolition in 1956 and again in 1960. It still stands however, and its small but faithful congregation are using it and keeping it alive.

St. Thomas

This church is situated between Norwich Road and Bramford Road and serves a parish which was formed out of All Saints parish. The present building replaces a corrugated iron church and was erected on land given by Alderman E. Coleby Ransome. It was built in 1937.

The architect was N. F. Cachemaille Day, who has also designed several 20th century churches in London. He made a careful study of Suffolk churches and from it he created an original and distinctive building using a development of the Perpendicular style which is found in our Suffolk churches, also flint-work facing on the exterior walls.

The exterior is built of flint and brick and at the east end of the south aisle rises a fine, sturdy tower, 60 ft. high, which terminates in an openwork brick parapet. There are three-light windows in the aisles, above which is a low clerestory.

Interior

The interior is bright, homely and tastefully furnished. The east end in particular is most effective with its exposed brickwork, tiny single windows and judicious use of colour. The unusually long **high altar** is particularly effective.

A rebuilt two manual **organ** was provided by Hill, Norman & Beard in 1939, standing under the tower on the south side of the sanctuary. It has 13 speaking stops.

The **bell**, made by John Draper in 1628, is from the disused church at Knettishall, near the Norfolk border.

Glossary

Although some words listed below have more and wider definitions, this glossary is confined only to the context in which they are used here.

Arcade	A set of arches, usually dividing the aisles from the nave.
Aumbry	A rectangular aperture in a wall, usually near the altar, and used in Mediaeval times for storing Communion Vessels.
Ashlar	Large blocks of masonry which give a wall an even facing.
Baluster	Small (usually circular) supporting columns or posts – as seen in 17th century Communion rails.
Baptistery	A part of the church set aside to accommodate the font.
Buttress	Projections from an exterior wall made to strengthen it, particularly at the corners.
Capital	The top of a pier, upon which the arch rests.
Clerestory	The part of the nave above the roof of a side aisle.
Corbel	A piece of carved stone which supports a hood-mould or part of a roof, etc.
Crockets	Carved decoration on the sloping sides of spires, arches, etc.
Cupola	A small domed turret on a roof or top of a tower.
Finial	Carving at the apex of an arch, pinnacle or spire.
Fleuron	A carved flower.
Flushwork	Patterns made in the masonry using flint and stone.

Foils	Lobes used to embellish the head of an arch or a circular opening. Trefoil – three lobes, Quatrefoil – four lobes, Cinquefoil – five lobes.
Gargoyle	A piece of carved stone used as a spout to drain rain-water from a roof.
Hammer-beam	Beam jutting out horizontally at right angles at the top of the wall. This supports other beams and arch braces.
Hood-mould	Projected moulding immediately above an arch or doorway.
Lancet windows	Single windows with sharply pointed arches of the Early English period (1190-1280).
Lucarnes	Small arches or openings in spires which let in light.
Misericord	A hinged seat, which often has a carving underneath, which is revealed when the seat is lifted up.
Niche	A recess (usually arched) made in a wall to contain a statue.
Ogee-headed arch	Moulding; showing in section a double continuous curve, concave below passing into convex above; (onion-shaped!).
Pinnacles	Ornamental spire-like projections which decorate the corners of towers or sides of doorways, niches, etc.
Piscina	A basin for washing Communion Vessels, usually found to the south of an altar.
Queen-post	Two vertical pieces of wood, set side by side on a tie-beam and supporting the upper timbers of the roof. (When it is a single vertical piece of wood it is called a **King-post**).
Reredos	Panelling or decorative structure behind an altar.
Responds	Half-piers found in the jambs (vertical sides) of arches.
Reticulated	Early 14th century tracery which creates a satisfying net-like appearance.
Sedilia	These were seats for officiating clergy to occupy during parts of the mediaeval Mass. (Usually in the south wall of the sanctuary.
Spandrel	The space (roughly triangular in shape) between an arch and its square hood-mould.

Splay	The internal aperture of a window.
Squint	Hole through a wall, usually cut to give a better view of the altar.
Stoup	Receptacle for Holy Water, usually near an entrance. The water was used to make the sign of the Cross as an act of purification on entering and leaving the sacred building.
Tester	A suspended canopy over a pulpit (also called a sounding-board) or altar.
Tie-beam	Large horizontal beam stretching from wall to wall at the base of a roof.
Tracery	The decorative stonework in the upper part of a window.
Tympanum	The stonework filling the space between the horizontal lintel of a doorway and the arch above it.

Dates of earliest Registers in the Ipswich churches

Parish registers for the recording of Baptisms, Marriages and Burials were first ordered in 1538, although compulsory entry in a book was not ordered until 1598. The earliest registers of Ipswich parishes date from the following years:

St. Clement	1563	St. Mary Stoke	1565
St. Helen	1677	St. Mary-le-Tower	1538
St. Lawrence	1539	St. Matthew	1559
St. Margaret	1538	St. Nicholas	1539
St. Mary at the Elms	1557	St. Peter	1662
St. Mary at the Quay	1559	St. Stephen	1585

Approx. Architectural Dates:

Saxon	– Before 1066
Norman	– 1066-1190
Early English	– 1190-1280
Decorated	– 1280-1377
Perpendicular	– 1377-1547
Tudor	– 1450-1600

By kind permission of Ipswich Borough Council. Department of Recreation and Amenities

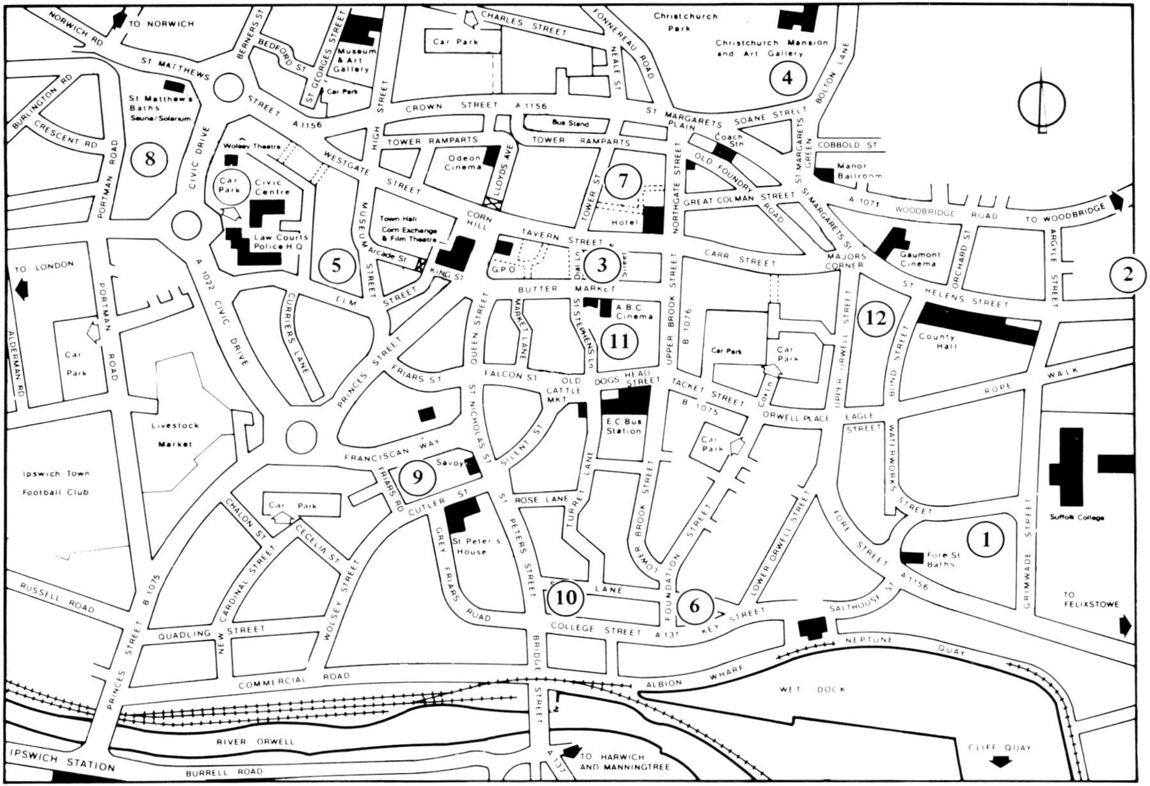

1. St. Clement
2. St. Helen
3. St. Lawrence
4. St. Margaret
5. St. Mary at the Elms
6. St. Mary at the Quay
7. St. Mary-le-Tower
8. St. Matthew
9. St. Nicholas
10. St. Peter
11. St. Stephen
12. St. Michael

By kind permission of Ipswich Borough Council, Department of Recreation and Amenities

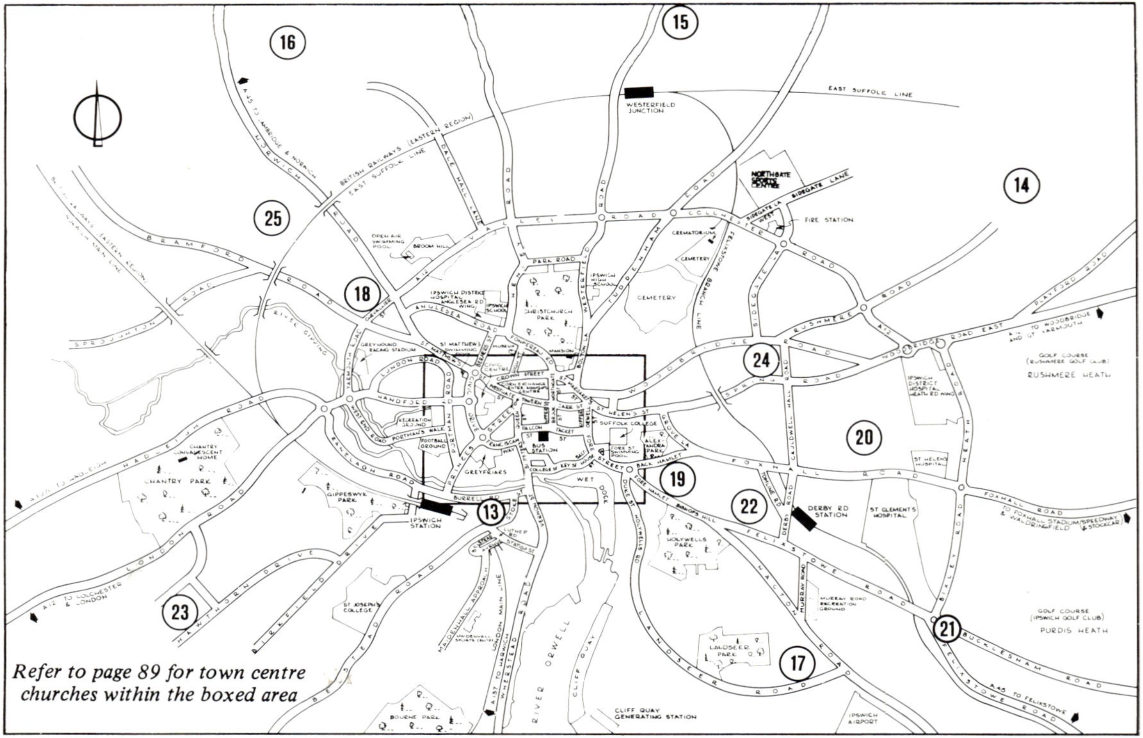

Refer to page 89 for town centre churches within the boxed area

13. St. Mary at Stoke, Stoke Street
14. St. Andrew, Rushmere St. Andrew
15. St. Mary Magdalen, Westerfield
16. St. Mary, Whitton
17. All Hallows, Landseer Road
18. All Saints, Chevallier Street
19. Holy Trinity, Back Hamlet
20. St. Andrew, Britannia Road
21. St. Augustine, Felixstowe Road
22. St. Bartholomew, Newton Road
23. St. Francis, Hawthorn Drive
24. St. John the Baptist, Cauldwell Hall Road
25. St. Thomas, Bramford Lane

THE

THAXTED BRANCH

THE
THAXTED BRANCH

Peter Paye

Oxford Publishing Co.

ISBN 0-86093-184-6

Typesetting by:
Aquarius Typesetting Services, New Milton.

Printed in Great Britain by:
S&S Press, Abingdon, Oxon.

Published by:
Oxford Publishing Co.
Link House
West Street
POOLE, Dorset

Key to Diagrams

lc	level crossing
ld	loading dock
gs	goods shed
cp	cattle pens
sc	signal box
wr	waiting-room
sb	station buildings
cb	coach body
es	engine shed
wt	water tank
wc	water crane
lg	loading gauge
gf	ground frame

CONTENTS

ACKNOWLEDGEMENTS

The publication of this history would not have been possible without the help of many people who have been kind enough to assist. In particular I should like to thank:

The late Mr A. R. Cox
The late Mr W. Fenton
Mr J. Mott
Mr R. Debenham
Mr H. C. Casserley
Mr R. C. Riley
Mr B. D. J. Walsh
Mr J. Watling
Mr G. Parslew
Mr M Barnes
Dr I. C. Allen
Mr D. Taylor
The late Mr J. Haylock
Mr F. Dever
Mr S. C. Nash
Mr S. Moss
Mr P. Webber
Mr M Brooks

and the many other active and retired railway staff some of whom worked on the line, also members of the Great Eastern Railway Society.

Thanks are also due to:

The Public Record Office
British Rail, Eastern Region
The Editor & Staff, *Herts & Essex Observer*, Bishop's Stortford
The House of Lords Record Office
The British Museum Newspaper Library
Essex County Record Office, Chelmsford
County of Cambridgeshire Library

Special thanks go to my mother who typed the manuscript and to my wife, Madge, for helping in checking the text.

Class J67/2 0-6-0T, No. 68609, stands at Sibley's (for Chickney & Broxted) Station, with the 11.50 a.m. Thaxted to Elsenham train, on 16th April 1949. The coaching stock is open third, No. 61471 and brake third No. 62450. A coal wagon stands in the goods siding.

W. A. Camwell

BIBLIOGRAPHY

General Works

Allen, C. J. — *The Great Eastern Railway* Ian Allan
Gordon, D. I. — *Regional History of Railways of Great Britain Volume 5 – Eastern Counties* David & Charles
Gordon, W. J. — *Our Home Railways Volume 1*
Joby, R. S. — *Forgotten Railways of East Anglia* David & Charles
R.C.T.S. — *Locomotives of the LNER (Various Volumes)*
Aldrich, C. L. — *GER Locomotives*

Periodicals

Bradshaws Railway Guide
British Railways (Eastern Region) Magazine
Buses
Essex Countryside
Essex Review
Great Eastern Railway Magazine
Locomotive Carriage & Wagon Review
Locomotive Magazine
LNER Magazine
Railway Magazine
Railway Times
Railway World
Railway Year Book
Trains Illustrated

Newspapers

Herts & Essex Observer
Saffron Walden Weekly News

Also

Minute books of:
Great Eastern Railway
London & North Eastern Railway

Working and Public Timetables: GER, LNER and BR (ER)
Appendices to Working Timetables: GER, LNER and BR (ER)

INTRODUCTION

The Elsenham & Thaxted Light Railway was truly a farmers' line, promoted by local gentry and financed partly by the Treasury and partly by the GER to serve an area with a traffic potential of less than 3,000 passengers. It relied heavily on agriculture for freight, and finally failed to withstand the competition of motor transport to become a victim of the pre-Beeching era of railway closures.

Unfortunately, with Thaxted lying on the edge of a broad declivity, the avoidance of the construction of major earthworks for economy reasons forced the railway to terminate nearly three quarters of a mile away on the opposite side of the Chelmer Valley. This factor weighed heavily against potential traffic from the town which the railway was supposed to serve. Likewise, the intermediate halts were also a considerable walking distance from the villages they served, and it was no surprise that financial difficulties were met at an early stage.

Nevertheless, the branch served the locality with quiet efficiency for 40 years, but in spite of all efforts to keep running and maintenance costs down to a minimum, efficiency deteriorated, and by 1950 the line was described as an 'antiquated branch railway from Elsenham'.

Inefficient though it was at the last, 'The Thaxted Flier', the 'Club Room on Wheels', or the 'Gin & Toffee' – so named because of the line's association with the Gilbey family and Lees, the confectioners – served its purpose by lifting the depression from the agricultural area of north-west Essex in the early years. Surprisingly, many who had advocated its coming were alive to witness its passing. That so few objected to the closure was surely a sign of the rapid increase in ownership of, and dependence on, the private car, for many had forgotten their branch line existed. The replacement bus service, although taking twice as long on the journey, provided a more convenient service for those who relied on public transport, especially in wet weather, but even this service has now dwindled to one bus a week.

This area of north-west Essex is now part of the London commuter belt, with a regular clientele travelling daily to the City, and motoring to the railhead at Elsenham. The former junction is now served by morning and evening peak hour trains to and from Liverpool Street, and off-peak by the semi-fast diesel connecting Cambridge to London. In the near future the scene will be transformed again, for it is proposed to electrify the route from Bishop's Stortford to Cambridge.

I have attempted to trace the history of the branch, and details have been checked with available documents, but apologies are offered for errors which may have occurred.

P. Paye
August 1983

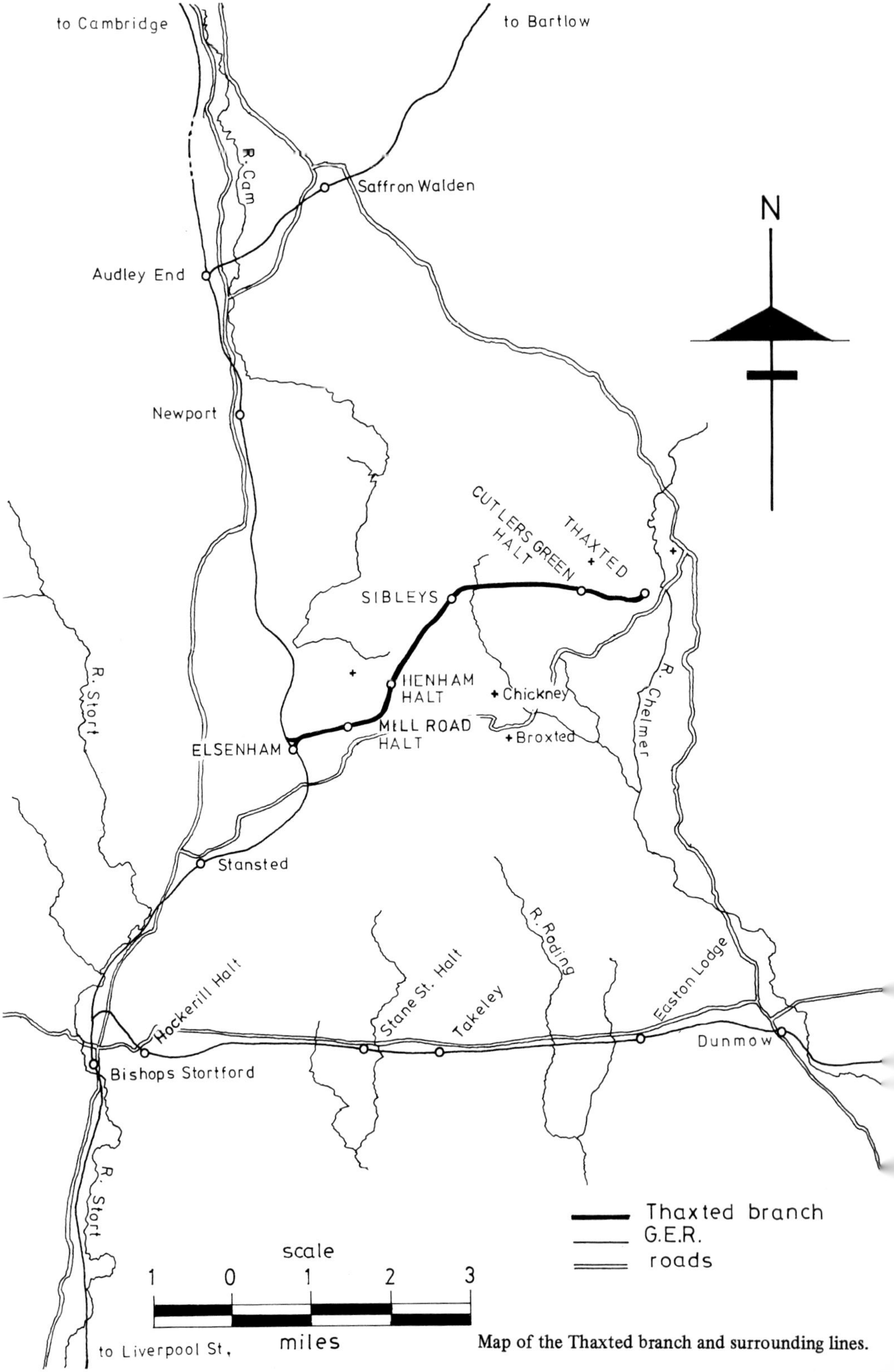

Map of the Thaxted branch and surrounding lines.

Thaxted is a small picturesque town in the north-west corner of Essex, close to the East Anglian Heights and near the source of the River Chelmer. In medieval times it was one of the foremost cutlery manufacturing centres and later one of the East Anglian wool towns. The cutlery trade declined because of the great difficulty in obtaining coal, but for this the area might have developed into another Sheffield. During these halcyon days the town became a borough, and was granted a charter by Philip and Mary with additions by Elizabeth I and James I. Evidence of the former wealth is found in Thaxted's church of cathedral like proportions, with a spire that can be seen for miles, and the famous Moot Hall, both popular today with tourists.

Despite the presence of such traders as blacksmiths, grinders, carvers, hafters and sheathers, the area suffered the agricultural depression of the mid-nineteenth century, and the population of the town decreased from 2,556 in 1851 to 1,659 at the beginning of the twentieth century. Maltings, granaries and other businesses fell into decay and except for the establishment of Lee's confectionery business employing 170 people, few jobs were available.

Although the town was served by an undulating cross-country road linking Cambridge and Chelmsford, the decline was partially attributable to the absence of any railway connection. As early as 1835 some excitement was caused when Joseph Gibbs surveyed the route of a railway from London through Dunmow, passing close to Thaxted, thence to Saffron Walden and Cambridge and on to York. Presented to Parliament as the Great Northern Railway, the bill was defeated at the second reading in 1836 and the scheme fell into oblivion. When the Great Northern Railway was again mooted ten years later it followed a course to the west through Hitchin and Huntingdon. Gibbs' survey was not the only one to be carried out, for James Walker surveyed a route for the proposed Northern & Eastern Railway from London to Cambridge. Walker's route followed the gradual rise of the Lea and Stort valleys to Bishop's Stortford and thence over the watershed at Elsenham to Newport and Great Chesterford, by-passing Thaxted six miles to the west. The line was duly opened to traffic from Stratford to Broxbourne, on 15th September 1840, to Harlow on 9th August 1841, Spelbrook on 22nd November 1841 and Bishop's Stortford on 16th May 1842. From 1st January 1844 the activities of the Northern & Eastern Railway were taken over by the Eastern Counties Railway. The Northern & Eastern Railway had obtained powers in 1843 to extend the line to Newport, and the Eastern Counties Railway subsequently obtained the Royal Assent on 4th June 1844, to build a line from Newport to Brandon, via Cambridge and Ely, effecting an end on junction with the Norfolk Railway. The section from Bishop's Stortford to Brandon was opened throughout on 30th July 1845. The lack of industry in the district never attracted railway promoters, and subsequently branch lines opening between Audley End and Saffron Walden on 23rd November 1865, and between Bishop's Stortford and Braintree on 22nd February 1869 bypassed Thaxted seven miles to the north and south respectively.

Acknowledged to be one of the most inaccessible towns in Essex, Thaxted, almost entirely dependent on agriculture, was thus in a badly depressed state at the end of the nineteenth century. Landowners and inhabitants became increasingly alarmed by the unemployment position and about losing business because of their isolation from the main railway system. Then in 1896 Parliament gave agreement to a statute that was to help overcome the problem.

The Light Railways Act of 1896 was promoted to alleviate the distress of the agricultural depression by allowing inexpensive railways to be constructed in rural areas, with the proviso that those so constructed would be freed from the obligation to build to the high standards laid down by the Board of Trade for main lines. Section 5 of the Act stated that where the Board of Agriculture certified that the provision of a light railway would benefit agriculture, the Treasury might agree to aid the building of the line out of public money. Another significant feature was that application to the Light Railway Commissioners for an order could be made by the county, borough or district through which the railway would pass, or by any company or individual. The latter was particularly relevant to the Thaxted proposal, for Sir Walter Gilbey of Elsenham Hall, a prominent landowner of the district, had been advocating a light railway in this area for some years prior to the passing of the Act.

Anticipating the outcome, Gilbey called a meeting at his home on 4th July 1896 to engender support for a railway, at which he discussed plans with other landowners in the area, including the Earl of Warwick of Easton Lodge, Charles Gold, MP for Saffron Walden, William Fuller Maitland, F. Smoothy of Braintree, F. Payne of Wixoe and George Lee the confectionery manufacturer. Others attending the semi-private meeting included T. W. Raven, J. H. Raven, T. Franklin and Walter Davis, the secretary of the Light Railway Association of Great Britain.

As engineer to the scheme, Gilbey had engaged Walter Hopkins, of 30 Parliament Street, Westminster, and after the formal introductions, Hopkins was asked to explain his proposals. It was the intention to construct a line from the GER main line at Elsenham to Thaxted and on to Finchingfield, originally to follow close to the roads, but this idea was abandoned because of the severe gradients. The alternative route, which followed the ideals of the Light Railway Order, was for the line to follow the surface of the land as far as possible to obviate cuttings and embankments. The proposed route was to run south of Henham past Chaureth Green and Cutler's Green to Thaxted. Passing south of the town the route crossed the Thaxted to Little Bardfield road on the level, continuing via Hawkspur Green and terminating midway between Great Bardfield and Finchingfield. Hopkins concluded by telling the meeting that it was the intention to ultimately join up with the Colne Valley Railway at Castle Hedingham.

Questioned as to the cost of such proposals, the engineer quoted estimates for standard and narrow gauge lines. The standard gauge railway was to cost £3,000 per mile for the 10¾ mile line if all roads were crossed on the level. The alternative, favoured by Sir Walter Gilbey and some of the others, was for a 2ft. 6in. gauge line costing £25,000, or £2,500 per

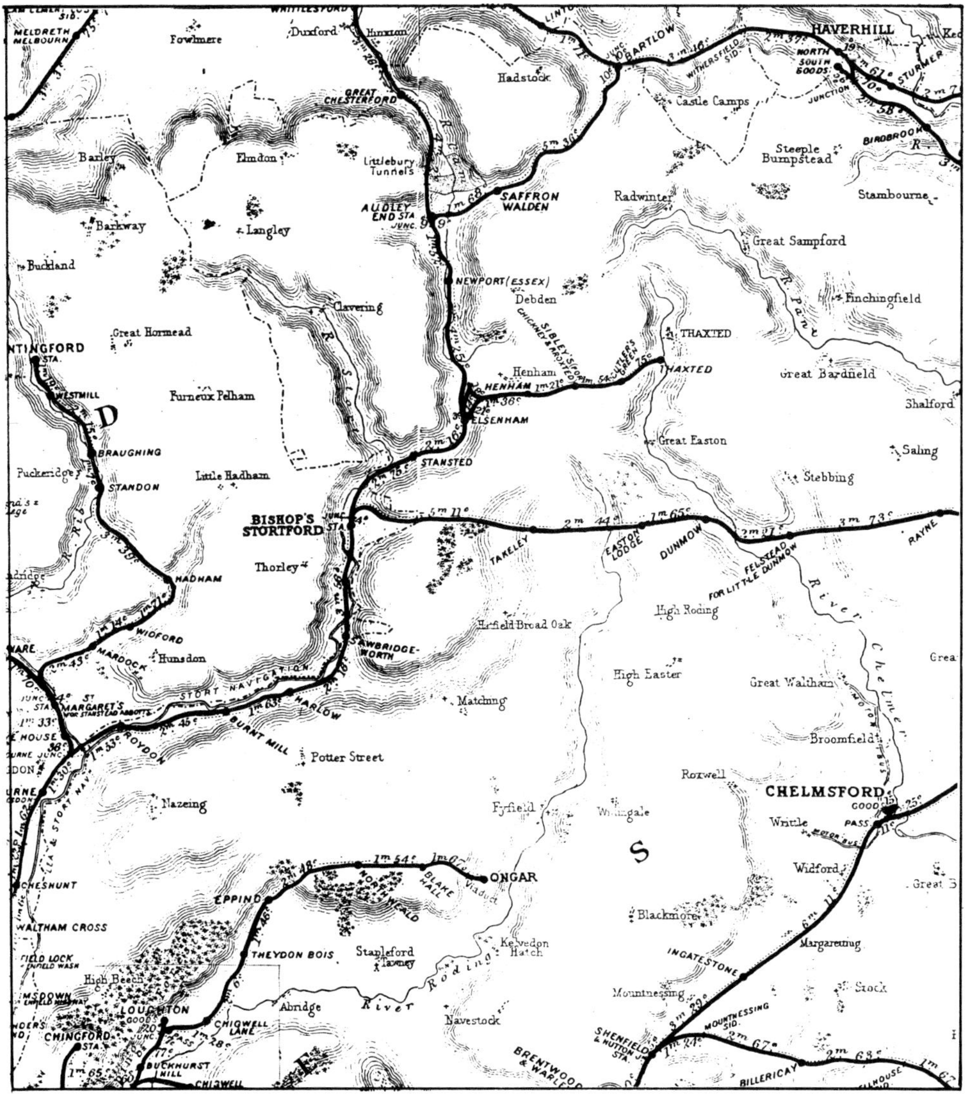

Railway Clearing House Map of the Thaxted branch and surrounding lines in 1928.

mile, a figure which excluded rolling stock and bridges. Hopkins added that both schemes envisaged the provision of stations with low platforms, each equipped with single sidings and small goods sheds. The engineer reiterated that if narrow gauge was adopted, special rolling stock would have to be provided, whereas if standard gauge was adopted, Great Eastern Railway rolling stock could be utilized.

The private meeting was generally in favour of the proposed line, Sir Walter Gilbey restricting the route from Elsenham to Thaxted only, whilst the Earl of Warwick was adamant that as much land as possible should benefit from the railway and favoured the line to Bardfield.

After the initial meeting in July, Hopkins visited the Hunslet workshops at Leeds to inspect narrow gauge rolling stock destined for service in India. During the visit he was shown a transporter car which ran on the narrow gauge track and was capable of conveying standard gauge wagons. The engineer was obviously impressed by the sales talk at Hunslet, for he expounded the simplicity of the system and proposed it for the change-over of vehicles between the GER and the new railway that he envisaged at Elsenham. When questioned, later, as to the cost of the narrow gauge rolling stock, Hopkins thought £7,000 would suffice.

Flushed with success Sir Walter and other promoters held a public meeting at Thaxted on 9th September 1896. Sir Walter had promised to purchase shares to the value of £1,000 to launch the scheme, and it was suggested that in addition to other landowners purchasing shares, local working-class villagers from Bardfield and Finchingfield might be offered £1 shares which would realize a further £290 to £300. The gathering was also told that the scheme to join up with the Colne Valley Railway at Castle Hedingham was considered too ambitious and had been abandoned. At the conclusion of the meeting Hopkins was requested to prepare a submission for the narrow gauge light railway for presentation to the Light Railway Commissioners by November.

The Great Eastern Railway directors were duly notified of the proposals by Mr Franklin of Thaxted. The board noted the proposals with interest, but decided to await further developments before taking any action.

A preliminary meeting of the promoters was held in the Great Eastern Hotel, Liverpool Street, on Monday, 26th October 1896, the costs being borne by Sir Walter Gilbey. After introduction by Sir Walter, Hopkins gave details of his submission for the light railway with the following estimated costs:

	£
Earthworks	5,130
Bridges over public roads	550
Accommodation bridges and works	1,500
Culverts and drains	350
Metalling roads and level crossings	420
2 gatekeepers' houses at crossings	250
Permanent way 10 miles 5 furlongs at £1,300 per mile	13,812
Permanent way for sidings, etc.	736
Stations	1,000
Contingencies at 10 per cent	2,344
Land and buildings, 45 acres at £15 per acre	675
	26,767

Hopkins was duly awarded £50 expenses for his services. At the conclusion of the proceedings the initial committee was elected, and comprised Sir Walter Gilbey, The Earl of Warwick and Messrs Brise, Parker, West, Bradridge and Lee.

J68 Class 0-6-0T, No. 8645, eases round the curve away from Elsenham with the Thaxted branch train in the summer of 1947.

Dr I. C. Allen

Such was the success of the idea that the application for the Elsenham, Thaxted & Bardfield Light Railway was submitted on 18th November 1896, with copies to the Essex County Council and local parish councils. The application provided for a Light Railway No. 1, 10 miles 6 chains, or thereabouts, in length, commencing at a point at the southernmost end of Elsenham Station of the GER in field No. 50 on the Ordnance Survey map of the Parish of Henham, and terminating in the Parish of Great Bardfield at a point at, or near, the western side of the High Road linking Great Bardfield and Finchingfield, about 12 chains from the entrance to Pake's Farm. The light railway would run through the parishes of Henham, Chickney, Debden, Broxted, Thaxted, Little Bardfield and Great Bardfield. Light Railway No. 2, 1 furlong 8 chains long, and wholly in the parish of Henham, was to commence at a point on the east side of the easternmost siding at Elsenham Station, a quarter of a chain south of the footbridge across the GER main line north of the station. After passing over the high road from Henham village to Elsenham Station, the line was to terminate in field No. 25 by a junction with line No. 1, 19 chains east of the commencing point.

The proposed line, taking 80 acres of land and laid to a gauge of 2ft. 6in., was to cost £30,565. The GER, which over the years had built up a network of branch lines chiefly dependent on the rich farming areas of East Anglia, at first showed little interest in the scheme, but after a deputation from the promoters met the GER Board on Monday, 20th December 1896 it was keen to assist. After protracted negotiations it was agreed that the light railway would be built by an independent company but financed and worked by the GER.

Later, on 30th July 1897, the GER directors, attempting to offset some of the cost, stated that the company was willing to work and construct the line on condition that the Treasury made a free grant of money to cover half the cost of construction, and that the condition in Section 5 of the Light Railway order was complied with.

On 17th June 1898, another deputation, representing the Thaxted promoters, met the GER Board. At the meeting the directors advised that the main line company was not sufficiently rich to finance the whole of the railway. However, if half was subscribed by the local promoters, the GER would find the remainder. The directors also advised that they would construct the line similar to their Wisbech & Upwell, and proposed Kelvedon to Tollesbury lines, with no large stations, and cattle guards alongside open level crossings, at an estimated cost of £36,000. Hopkins and members of the Thaxted committee were urged to inspect the Wisbech & Upwell line, after which Hopkins and the GER Engineer, Wilson, would confer to draw up amended plans.

Negotiations with the Treasury were lengthy and protracted. By 1902 estimates were agreed, but inflation was causing problems. On 4th November 1903, the GER General Manager reported that it was necessary to increase the price of labour and materials and revise the estimates for the cost of construction of the line. To this total was to be added the cost of exchange sidings and connection at Elsenham, which had not previously been accounted for. The revised estimate of £50,700 had been agreed by the Treasury, who would now subscribe the balance to half the cost of the works, free of expenses, leaving the GER to find £25,300.

A Class J68 0-6-0T stands at Thaxted Shed. Note the distance of the station from the town, almost a mile away on the opposite side of the valley, denoted in this photograph by the spire of the church and the adjacent windmill.

C. Bayes

The insistence on a narrow gauge line for economy, and the arguments which later developed in support of a standard gauge railway, delayed implementation. The need to bridge the valley of the River Chelmer near Thaxted, and the reluctance of the GER to work anything except the standard gauge, led to difficulties in raising the necessary capital. After ten years of argument and counter-argument the original scheme was finally abandoned, in 1906, in favour of the more modest plan for a standard gauge line connecting Elsenham and Thaxted, following the same route.

The promoters backing the new scheme were Sir Walter Gilbey, Lancelot and Hugh Cranmer Byng of Folly Mill, Thaxted, George Lee, the confectionery manufacturer, and four farmers of the district; John Tredgett, John Jeffery, Benjamin Tyler and James John Prior. Neogtiations proceeded apace and the deposited plans for the new light railway from Elsenham GER Station to Hill Farm, Thaxted, were submitted to the Light Railway Commissioners, on 29th May 1907, with copies deposited with the Essex County Council at Chelmsford and the parish councils through which the line passed. The estimated cost of single track standard gauge railway No. 1, 5 miles 47 chains in length, commencing at the southernmost end of the platform at Elsenham GER Station, and terminating at Hill Farm, Thaxted, was:

	£	s
Earthworks	2,737	10
Accommodation (bridges and works)	538	10
Culverts and drains	778	0
Metalling of roads and level crossings	1,600	0
Permanent way, including fencing, at £2,500 per mile	13,968	15
Permanent way for sidings and cost of junction	1,920	0
Stations	5,565	5
Contingencies	3,388	10
Land and buildings, 43 acres	770	0
	31,266	10

Line No. 2 connecting the branch to Elsenham goods yard, 18 chains in length, was costed at:

	£	s
Earthworks	7	10
Accommodation (bridges and works)	42	10
Culverts and drains	22	0
Metalling of roads and level crossings	200	0
Permanent way	540	0
Sidings and cost of junction	80	0
Contingencies	111	10
Land, 2 acres	30	0
	1,033	10

The combined cost totalling £32,300.

On the 45 acres of land required for the railway the removal of 36,600 cubic yards of soil for earthworks would be necessary. Most of this was subsequently replaced, as 34,370 cubic yards of soil required for the embankments. Halts were to be erected at Henham and Sibley's (named after a local farm).

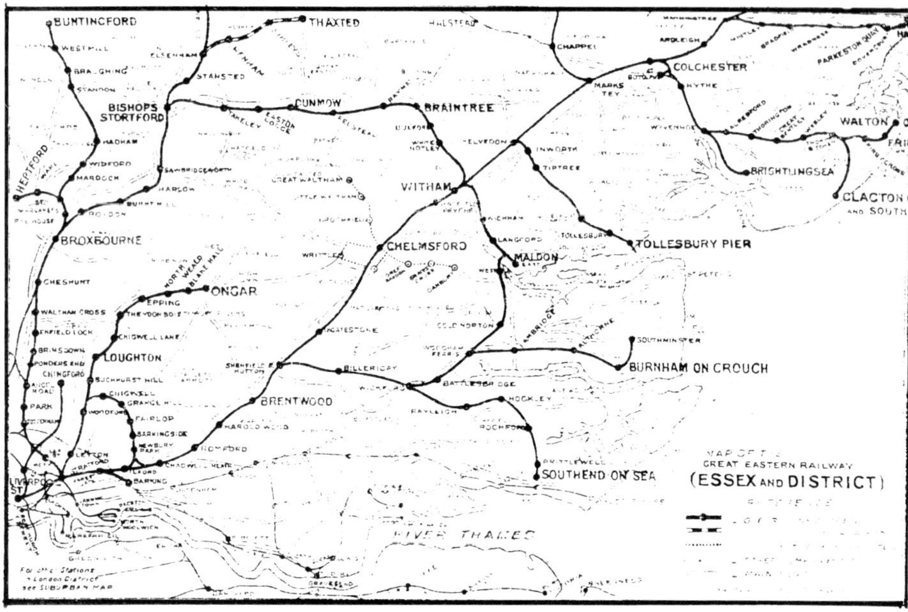

Map from GER Passenger Timetable for 1910 showing the Thaxted line as authorized for construction.

The plans, as published, were readily accepted by all but one of the eleven landowners who had freely donated the land for the railway. Alfred Paget Humphrey of Horham Hall, however, was only at variance regarding the location of some occupational crossings linking his fields, and the siting of an additional halt near Plonk's (later Cutler's Green Halt). The Land Commission of the Treasury, after much badgering by J. A. Pease, MP, and members of the GER Board, agreed to provide a free grant of £15,000, but stipulated that the main line company should work the line. The GER directors, at a meeting on 31st July 1908, agreed to this and also authorized the provision of £15,750 of the remaining capital to build the light railway. The application attracted little opposition and was passed to the Board of Trade, who, after an enquiry, approved the issue of a Light Railway Order.

LIGHT RAILWAYS ACT, 1896.

ELSENHAM AND THAXTED LIGHT RAILWAY ORDER, 1911.

ORDER

MADE BY THE

LIGHT RAILWAY COMMISSIONERS,

AND MODIFIED AND CONFIRMED BY THE

BOARD OF TRADE,

AUTHORISING THE CONSTRUCTION OF A

LIGHT RAILWAY IN THE COUNTY OF ESSEX, BETWEEN ELSENHAM STATION AND THAXTED.

Presented to both Houses of Parliament by Command of His Majesty.

LONDON:
PUBLISHED BY HIS MAJESTY'S STATIONERY OFFICE.
To be purchased, either directly or through any Bookseller, from
WYMAN AND SONS, LIMITED, FETTER LANE, E.C., and 32, ABINGDON STREET, S.W.; or
OLIVER AND BOYD, TWEEDDALE COURT, EDINBURGH; or
E. PONSONBY, LTD., 116, GRAFTON STREET, DUBLIN.

PRINTED BY
DARLING AND SON, LIMITED, BACON STREET, E.
1911.

[Cd. 5694.] *Price 2d.*

LIGHT RAILWAYS ACT, 1896.

ELSENHAM AND THAXTED LIGHT RAILWAY ORDER, 1911.

ORDER authorising the construction of a Light Railway in the County of Essex, between Elsenham Station and Thaxted.

PREAMBLE.

WHEREAS an application was in May 1907 duly made to the Light Railway Commissioners by the Promoters therein named in pursuance of the Light Railways Act 1896 for an Order to authorise the construction of the light railway hereinafter described AND WHEREAS it has been arranged with the approval of the said Commissioners that the Order should be granted to the Great Eastern Railway Company in the place of the said Promoters and the proprietors of the Great Eastern Railway Company at a meeting called for the purpose and held on the 31st day of July, 1908, have approved that arrangement AND WHEREAS the Treasury have agreed subject to the fulfilment of certain conditions to grant the sum of fifteen thousand five hundred pounds for the purpose of the light railway NOW we the Light Railway Commissioners being satisfied after local inquiry of the expediency of granting the said application do in pursuance of the Light Railways Act 1896 and by virtue and in exercise of the powers thereby vested in and of every other power enabling us in this behalf ORDER as follows—

PRELIMINARY.

Short title.

1. This Order may be cited as "The Elsenham and Thaxted Light Railway Order 1911" and shall come into force on the date on which it is confirmed by the Board of Trade.

Interpretation.

2. Words and expressions to which by the Light Railways Act 1896 or by any enactment incorporated with this Order meanings are assigned have in this Order (unless the context otherwise require) the same respective meanings and in this Order—

"The Company" means the Great Eastern Railway Company;

"The principal Act" means the Light Railways Act 1896;

"The railway" means the light railways and works by this Order authorised or (as the case may be) any part thereof;

"The undertaking" means the undertaking by this Order authorised;

"The Plan" "the Section" and "the Book of Reference" mean respectively the plans sections and book of reference deposited in respect of the application for this Order with the Board of Trade and signed by an assistant-secretary of the Board of Trade;

"Road authority" means the council of any county urban district or rural district commissioners trustees or other body or persons who are charged with the duty of maintaining or repairing any public road;

The Interpretation Act 1889 applies for the purposes of this Order as if this Order were an Act of Parliament.

Incorporation of Acts.

3.—(1) Subject to the provisions of this Order the Lands Clauses Acts as varied by the principal Act the Railways Clauses Consolidation Act 1845 (except the Sections thereof numbered respectively 11 to 15 25 to 29 46 to 48 59 60 63 and 64) and Sections 7 and 8 of the Railways Clauses Act 1863 are hereby incorporated with this Order and Section 19 of the Regulation of Railways Act 1868 and the Regulation of Railways Act 1889 (except paragraphs (a) and (b) of Section 1 and Section 4) are hereby made applicable to this Order;

The Elsenham & Thaxted Light Railway Order 1911, granted on 19th April 1911, authorized the building of:

A Railway (No. 1) 5 miles 4 furlongs 7 chains or thereabouts in length wholly situate in the County of Essex commencing in the parish of Henham in the field numbered 84 on the 1/2500 Ordnance Map of the said parish (1897 edition) at a point at the southern-most end of the eastern side of the up platform at the Company's Elsenham Station proceeding thence in a north-easterly direction on the south side of the village of Henham and into the parish of Chickney passing between Lovecott Farm and Sibleys thence in an easterly direction into the parish of Broxted and terminating in the parish of Thaxted in the field numbered 290 on the 1/2500 Ordnance Map of the said parish (1897 edition) near the road from Elsenham and Dunmow to Thaxted about 10 chains north of the Hill Farm and opposite Dairy Green Farm.

A Railway (No. 2) 1 furlong 8 chains or thereabouts in length wholly situate in the said parish of Henham commencing by a junction with the eastern-most siding north of Elsenham Station aforesaid 2 chains or thereabouts south of the foot-bridge north of the said station over the Company's main line and sidings crossing the high road from Henham village to Elsenham Station and terminating by a junction with the Railway (No. 1) at a point 2 furlongs or thereabouts from the commencement of that Railway.

Three years were allowed for the compulsory purchase of land and five years for the completion of the works.

The GE Company was bound by the Light Railway Order to erect and maintain gates at the level crossing where the railway crossed the road or the connecting spur with the goods yard. Clause 16 covered the arrangements at the other level crossings on the line, where no gates were to be erected:

Level crossings without gates

16. With respect to every level crossing of a public carriage road other than a level crossing where gates are erected and maintained in accordance with the foregoing provisions of this Order the following provisions shall apply; (that is to say) –

a) Cattle-guards or other suitable contrivances shall be constructed at each side of the road and so maintained and kept as to prevent cattle or horses passing on the road from entering upon the railway;
b) At each of two points one two hundred yards along the railway in one direction from the level crossing and the other two hundred yards along the railway in the other direction from the level crossing there shall be erected and maintained a white post standing five feet about ground and bearing upon it and so as to be plainly legible by the driver of an engine approaching the level crossing a figure indicating the number of miles an hour which is fixed under the provisions of this Order as the maximum rate of speed of a train or engine approaching and within a distance of two hundred yards from the level crossing;
c) At each of two points one fifty yards or thereabouts along the road in one direction from the point of crossing and the other fifty yards or thereabouts along the road in the other direction from the point of crossing there shall be erected and maintained by the Company a notice board cautioning the public to be aware of the trains.

With negotiations duly completed, the GER solicitor notified the board on 17th May 1911 that the company had possession of the required land, but it was necessary for it to be fenced off as a matter of urgency to enable farmers to arrange their crops. A contract was placed with George Wood & Sons of Brandon, and by 15th June 1911 standard paling and fencing had been provided on site at a cost of 1s 8d per yard. Wood, however, sought guidance regarding the 53 (later reduced to 21) occupational and level crossings on the line, asking whether they were to have fixed warning notices on oak posts at a cost of £5 17s 6d at each crossing.

The ceremony of the cutting of the first sod was held on Tuesday, 25th July 1911, on the site of Thaxted Station. Sir Walter Gilbey, who had advocated a light railway in the district for over 20 years before his ideas came to fruition, prepares to perform the deed, watched by a gathering of GER officers and local people.

Sir Walter Gilbey sinks the blade of the silver spade into the turf of Hill Farm, Thaxted, on 25th July 1911. The inscription engraved on the blade reads 'Presented by the Directors of the Great Eastern Railway Company on the occasion of the cutting of the first sod of the Elsenham & Thaxted Light Railway, July 25th 1911'.

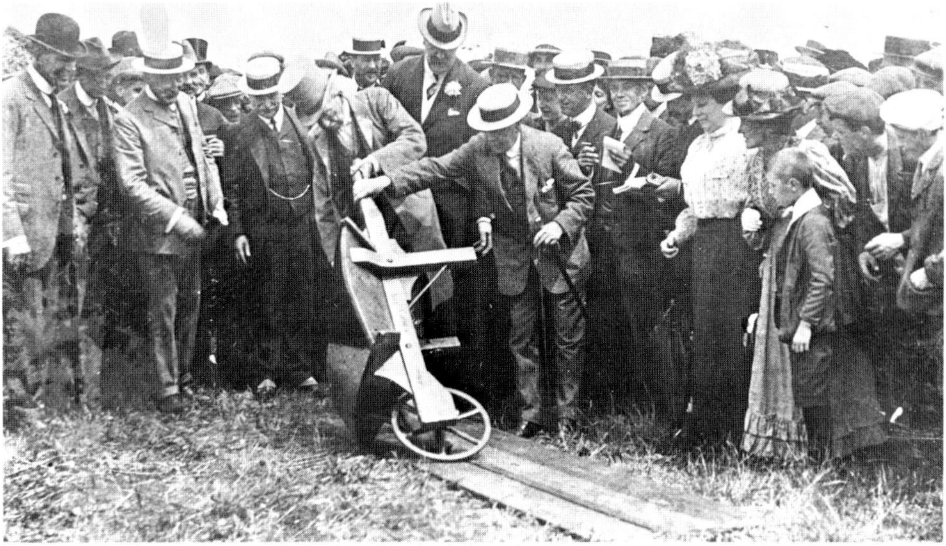

The first sod of earth is tipped out of the wheelbarrow. After some of the GER directors had also dug spits of earth with the spade, W. J. Galloway pushed Sir Walter, seated in the barrow, for a short distance along the route of the intended light railway.

The ceremony of cutting the first sod was held on Tuesday, 25th July 1911, on the proposed site of Thaxted Station. In addition to the two local Members of Parliament, J. A. Pease and Cecil Beck, the occasion was treated with some importance by the GER, who were represented by their General Manager, W. H. Hyde, Chief Civil Engineer, H. Jones and F. G. Randall, the Superintendent of the line. With other local landowners present, Sir Walter Gilbey performed the actual deed using a silver spade presented to him by the directors of the GER. The inscription engraved on the blade read, 'Presented by the Directors of the Great Eastern Railway Company on the occasion of the cutting of the first sod of the Elsenham & Thaxted Light Railway, July 25th 1911'. The ceremony was accompanied by a certain amount of light-hearted banter, and at one stage Sir Walter Gilbey was seated in a navvy's barrow to allow W. J. Galloway, a director of the GER, to push him for a short distance along the line of the intended railway. The GER officials, confident in the success of their latest and, indeed, last promotion at building a complete new branch line, then entertained guests in a marquee erected nearby. The day was rounded off with speeches advocating the extension of industry at Thaxted and the surrounding area, as a result of the advent of the railway.

No time was lost in making a start on the construction, and by the second week in August the land released by the benevolent landowners was fenced off. On Monday, 6th September 1911, the GE commenced preliminary work on the formation of the permanent way from Elsenham, under the supervision of Mr J. Tyler, Inspector of Permanent Way for the Cambridge District.

In September 1911, tenders were invited for the construction of the Light Railway and on 19th October 1911 three replies were considered:

H. V. Smith tendered at £4,167 0s 10d
Wm. Griffiths & Co. tendered at £4,244 2s 11d
Charles Wall tendered at £5,347 5s 0d

The offer of H. V. Smith of 20 Victoria Street, London S.W., was accepted with the proviso that work was to be completed by 19th April 1913. The contractor subsequently employed many local men on the construction work, paying above agricultural rates to attract suitable men from the land.

In April 1912, tenders for the construction of stations and buildings were invited, and on 20th June the following were considered:

William Bell & Son	£1,537 0s 0d
H. V. Smith & Co. Ltd.,	£1,887 17s 2d
A. Parnell & Son	£1,904 0s 0d
Kirk & Randall	£2,305 8s 0d
A. J. Bateman	£2,428 10s 0d

The offer of William Bell & Son of Cambridge was duly accepted, with work to be completely concurrent with the permanent way formation.

The GER Board, having authorized, on 2nd June 1911, the outlay of £15,750 towards the £31,750 total cost of the construction, found the amount made no provision for a new goods shed at Elsenham to deal with the interchange of traffic between the light railway and the main line. It was thought that the old wooden shed could be repaired for £200, but when the goods manager declared the building unsuitable for traffic requirements, tenders were invited, on 18th July 1912, for the construction of a new brick shed estimated to cost £500. On 7th November 1912, the offer received from J. Glasscock & Son, Successors of Bishop's Stortford, who tendered at £365, was accepted, and the building was completed the following year.

Construction of the light railway proceeded without incident until Monday, 1st July 1912, when a labourer was killed in an accident near the site of Mill Road Halt. On the fateful Monday morning a ballast train departed Elsenham at 9.15 a.m. and proceeded to a site near Mill Lane crossing, where the 20 loaded wagons were detached from the locomotive 300 yards beyond the crossing. The train was left on level track with brakes pinned down and in the charge of the guard, whilst the Y14 class tender locomotive, in the charge of Driver William Braybrooke and Fireman Herbert Bannister, proceeded to Lovecoates Farm crossing to bring 20 men back to the site to work on ballasting. As no other vehicle was provided, the 20 men rode, 5 in the cab of the locomotive, and 15 sitting on the tender, some sitting on the water tank with their legs dangling over the side of the vehicle. On the return journey with the locomotive running tender first, Driver Braybrooke's sighting was partially impaired by the workmen sitting on the tender. After passing Carter's Lane crossing he saw the guard signalling, and realized, too late, that he was approaching the stationary ballast wagons at a speed of 4 to 5 m.p.h.

Driver Braybrooke reacted quickly by shutting off steam and applying the brakes, but despite the preventative measures the locomotive hit the wagons at a speed of 2m.p.h., with the result that Charles Clayden of Quendon, aged 43, was pinned between the tender and leading ballast wagon, which, being half loaded, rose up on impact. Clayden suffered a crushed thigh and as a guard iron entered his back, he died almost instantly. One of his colleagues, Walter Denison of New Hall, suffered a fractured leg and was conveyed to Cambridge Hospital by express train, which stopped especially at Elsenham. Others injured in the accident included William Neville and Arthur Weaver of Henham, who suffered bruises to their legs, and Horace Digby of Debden and William Butcher of Cherry Green who suffered shock. These four were treated on site by Doctor Cayling of Stansted.

The inquest was held the following day, when the Braintree Coroner, Doctor Harrison, conducted the hearing at the Congregational Schoolroom, Henham. The GER was represented by J. S. Fitzjohn, District Superintendent, Cambridge, J. Sherlock, District Engineer, Cambridge, and H. F. Hilton, the District Locomotive Superintendent, Cambridge. Other people included W. Wilson, the assistant permanent way engineer who was in charge of the work on the light railway, and a solicitor, G. A. Wootton, who represented the Amalgamated Society of Railway Servants, of which the driver was a member. Fitzjohn had only been appointed Superintendent and taken up his appointment on the day of the accident. The jury, after hearing the reports of Driver Braybrooke, Fireman Bannister and some of the navvies, also questioned Smith Winters, the ganger in charge of 31 men employed on ballasting the new light railway.

Thaxted Station nearing completion. Contractors' spoil wagons stand in the loading dock siding on the right. Note the sacking covers over the axleboxes to stop dust falling into the boxes. The station building and engine shed are complete, but the water tank house is being constructed, with scaffold poles in position, behind the wagons on the left hand siding. On the main single line stands a Class Y14 0-6-0 tender locomotive with a train of spoil wagons, whilst on the passenger loop line is a small mobile crane. The exposed position of the site can be judged by the distant spire of Thaxted Church and windmill in the left background.

Elsenham 'up' main line platform and Thaxted bay platform in March 1913, just before the light railway was officially opened. A line of wagons stand on the main branch line, whilst 4 of the 5 six wheel vehicles, converted by the GER, from main line stock specially for use on the branch, stand on the run-round loop. The six wheelers are, from left to right, third class to Diagram 613, Nos. 97, 439 and 43, and brake third to Diagram 612, No. 253. Station Master H. Butters stands on the platform, whilst the line of the new railway can be seen curving away out of the picture.

Cutler's Green Halt, before the opening of the line, with the painters adding the finishing touches.

Recording a verdict of accidental death, the jury was critical of the number of men allowed to ride on the engine and tender, a factor which distracted the driver's attention and unsighted him on the approach to the wagons. It was thought that a brake van ought to have been provided to convey them to and from the site.

Despite the shock of the accident, work continued towards the completion of the railway, although hampered slightly by wet weather during the autumn. Early in the new year construction was completed ahead of schedule, and at the end of January 1913, application was made to the Board of Trade for official inspection to enable the line to be opened. The official Board of Trade inspection was carried out by Lieutenant-Colonel P. G. von Donop on 28th February 1913. The Inspector found that the light railway had been constructed almost exactly as described in the authorizing order, with no cuttings or embankments 'calling for mention'. The six public road crossings and twenty one occupational crossings complied with all safety aspects required by the Board of Trade. The girders of the one underbridge at Horham Lane were found to have sufficient theoretical strength and gave satisfactory deflections under test. Von Donop was satisfied with the method of locking the points to the sidings at Elsenham, Sibley's and Thaxted, but requested the provision of a checkrail on the 8¾ chain radius curve at Elsenham, and for fencing to be provided on the wing walls adjacent to the underbridge. The Lieutenant-Colonel, concluding 'the line appears to be in all respects substantially constructed and to be standing well', duly recommended that the Board of Trade sanction the opening of the line for passenger traffic.

On 15th March 1913, the GER announced that the new line would open for passenger and goods traffic on and from Tuesday, 1st April 1913, with a weekday service of 5 trains from Elsenham to Thaxted, and 4 in the reverse direction. Trains would call at Henham and Cutler's Green to pick up and set down passengers only when required.

For the official opening, on Monday, 31st March 1913, Sir Walter Gilbey, now 82 years of age, travelled by car from Brighton to perform the ceremony, accompanied by his daughter Mrs Hine. A train carrying officials of the GER, and press representatives, departed from Liverpool Street at 12noon for Elsenham. After reversing the train into the goods yard, two 'Jubilee' Class R24 0-6-0 tank locomotives, Nos. 168 and 196, backed on to haul the first trip to Thaxted. The locomotives were coupled bunker to bunker, 168 facing Elsenham and 196 facing Thaxted. Prior to departure at 1.25p.m. Sir Ailwyn Fellowes, Deputy Chairman of the GER, welcomed Sir Walter and his daughter aboard. The occasion was viewed with considerable importance in the locality, and many farmers and other employers gave their employees a half day holiday. Thus the train attracted attention from most of the population of the locality, who gathered by the crossings and lineside to cheer and wave it past, and greet the arrival at the terminus.

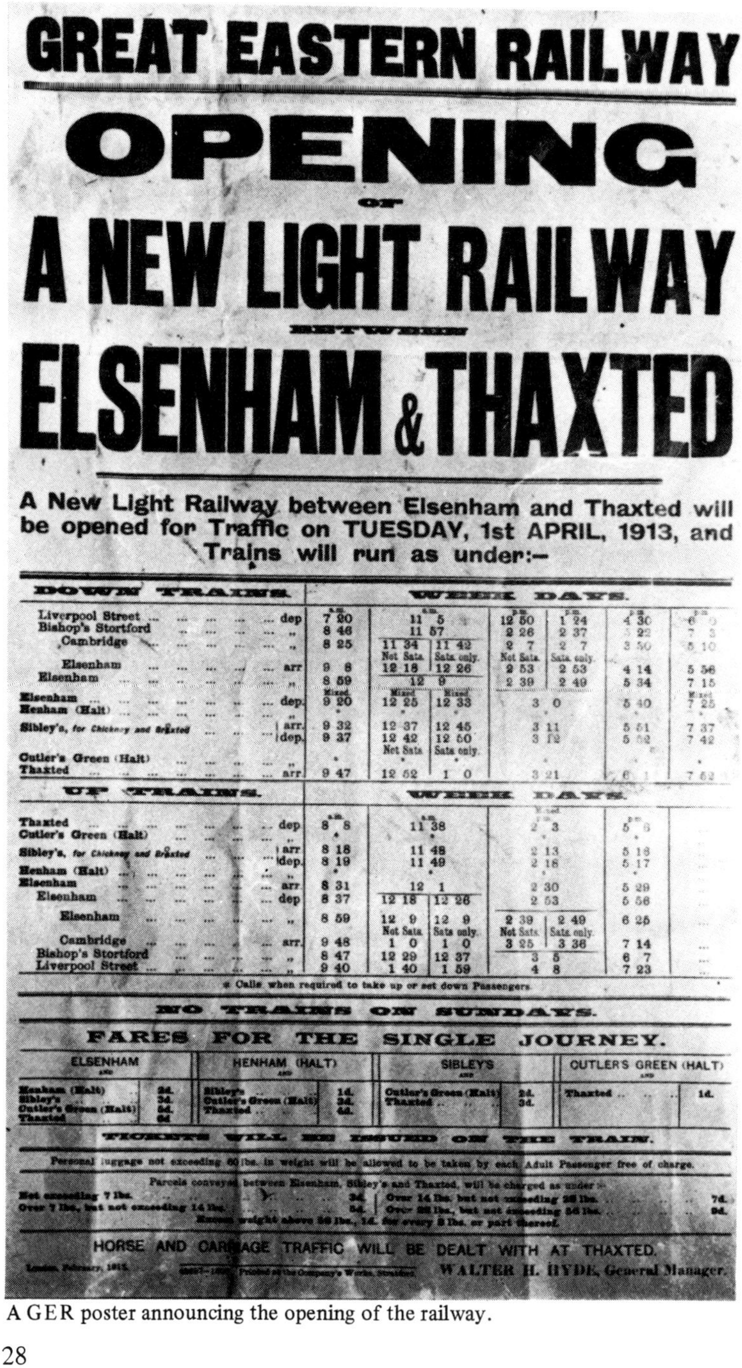
GREAT EASTERN RAILWAY

OPENING

OF

A NEW LIGHT RAILWAY

BETWEEN

ELSENHAM & THAXTED

A New Light Railway between Elsenham and Thaxted will be opened for Traffic on TUESDAY, 1st APRIL, 1913, and Trains will run as under:–

DOWN TRAINS.		WEEK DAYS.						
		a.m.	a.m.		p.m.	p.m.	p.m.	p.m.
Liverpool Street	dep	7 20	11 5		12 50	1 24	4 30	6 0
Bishop's Stortford	"	8 46	11 57		2 26	2 37	3 22	7 3
Cambridge	"	8 25	11 34	11 42	2 7	2 7	3 50	5 10
			Not Sats.	Sats. only.	Not Sats.	Sats. only.		
Elsenham	arr	9 8	12 18	12 26	2 53	2 53	4 14	5 56
Elsenham	"	8 59	12 9		2 39	2 49	5 34	7 15
		Mixed.	Mixed.	Mixed.				Mixed.
Elsenham	dep	9 20	12 25	12 33	3 0		5 40	7 25
Henham (Halt)	"	*	*	*	*		*	*
Sibley's, for Chickney and Broxted	arr	9 32	12 37	12 45	3 11		5 51	7 37
	dep	9 37	12 42	12 50	3 12		5 52	7 42
			Not Sats.	Sats. only.				
Cutler's Green (Halt)	"	*	*	*	*		*	*
Thaxted	arr	9 47	12 52	1 0	3 21		6 1	7 52

UP TRAINS.		WEEK DAYS.						
		a.m.	a.m.		Mixed p.m.		p.m.	
Thaxted	dep	8 8	11 38		2 3		5 8	
Cutler's Green (Halt)	"	*	*		*		*	
Sibley's, for Chickney and Broxted	arr	8 18	11 48		2 13		5 16	
	dep	8 19	11 49		2 16		5 17	
Henham (Halt)	"	*	*		*		*	
Elsenham	arr	8 31	12 1		2 30		5 29	
Elsenham	dep	8 37	12 18	12 26	2 53		5 56	
Elsenham	"	8 59	12 9	12 9	2 39	2 49	6 25	
			Not Sats.	Sats. only.	Not Sats.	Sats. only.		
Cambridge	arr	9 48	1 0	1 0	3 25	3 36	7 14	...
Bishop's Stortford	"	8 47	12 29	12 37	3 5		6 7	...
Liverpool Street	"	9 40	1 40	1 59	4 8		7 23	...

* Calls when required to take up or set down Passengers.

NO TRAINS ON SUNDAYS.

FARES FOR THE SINGLE JOURNEY.

ELSENHAM AND		HENHAM (HALT) AND		SIBLEY'S AND		CUTLER'S GREEN (HALT) AND	
Henham (Halt)	2d.	Sibley's	1d.	Cutler's Green (Halt)	2d.	Thaxted	1d.
Sibley's	3d.	Cutler's Green (Halt)	3d.	Thaxted	3d.		
Cutler's Green (Halt)	5d.	Thaxted	4d.				
Thaxted	6d.						

TICKETS WILL BE ISSUED ON THE TRAIN.

Personal luggage not exceeding 60 lbs. in weight will be allowed to be taken by each Adult Passenger free of charge.

Parcels conveyed between Elsenham, Sibley's and Thaxted, will be charged as under:–

Not exceeding 7 lbs.	3d.	Over 14 lbs. but not exceeding 28 lbs.	7d.
Over 7 lbs., but not exceeding 14 lbs.	5d.	Over 28 lbs., but not exceeding 56 lbs.	9d.

Excess weight above 56 lbs., 1d. for every 8 lbs. or part thereof.

HORSE AND CARRIAGE TRAFFIC WILL BE DEALT WITH AT THAXTED.

London, February, 1913. [illegible] Printed at the Company's Works, Stratford. WALTER H. HYDE, General Manager.

A GER poster announcing the opening of the railway.

On arrival at Thaxted, and in the presence of W. H. Hyde, the General Manager of the GER, F. G. Randall, Superintendent of the line and A. J. Hill, the newly appointed Locomotive Superintendent, H. Jones, Civil Engineer, G. J. Hyde, Chief Assistant to the General Manager, J. S. Fitzjohn, Cambridge District Superintendent, and many others, Sir Walter declared the line open to traffic.

In the absence of Claud Hamilton, the Chairman of the GER, Sir Ailwyn Fellowes reviewed the efforts made by Sir Walter and his fellow promoters over the previous 20 years to obtain the benefit of a railway for agriculture and trade in the district, and finally thanked the engineers, contractors and others concerned with the building of the light railway. Henry Gilbey replied on behalf of his father, who felt unable to make a speech. Walter Hyde then issued the first ticket, a sixpenny one to Elsenham, to Sir Walter. Later, luncheon was served to invited guests in the dining car on the train.

The special train, carrying officials of the GER and press representatives from Liverpool Street for the official opening of the light railway, stands at Thaxted Station on Monday, 31st March 1913. It is hauled by two 0-6-0T Class R24 locomotives, No. 196 facing Thaxted and No. 168 facing Elsenham, working bunker to bunker. Note the burnished buffers and well turned out appearance of the locomotives which hauled the train from Elsenham goods yard to Thaxted and back.

Sir Walter Gilbey, aged 82, accompanied by his daughter, Mrs Hine, declares the Thaxted Light Railway open to traffic on 31st March 1913. In attendance on the loading dock, at Thaxted, are W. H. Hyde, General Manager of the GER and Sir Ailwyn Fellowes. Lunch was late, and was served to invited guests in the dining car of the special train.

Part of the crowd watching the opening ceremony of the light railway, at Thaxted Station, on 31st March 1913. In the crowd are Percy Reeve, the Thaxted guard who was in charge of the train on the branch and, in bowler hat, George Archer, a noted Thaxted cattle dealer, who provided much traffic to the railway.

Two views of Thaxted Station and the crowd watching the opening ceremony on 31st March 1913. The coaching stock utilized on the special train from Liverpool Street was in immaculate condition, the wheels having white painted tyres. Unlike the stock specially allocated to the branch, these main line vehicles were devoid of steps to allow passengers to alight on to the low platform. Portable steps were provided for VIPs.

At 3.30 p.m. the special departed, and after reversal and change of locomotives at Elsenham, arrived at Liverpool Street at 4.57 p.m. With the public opening of the line scheduled for the following morning, Class R24 0-6-0T No. 196 returned to Thaxted Shed, whilst No. 168 ran light to Bishop's Stortford. The horse-drawn omnibus, owned by George Rogers, which had connected Thaxted with Elsenham Station, ran for the last time during the evening, after 27 years service.

The following morning, over fifty passengers travelled on the first train, hauled by Class R24 No. 196, and in the evening no less than 200 availed themselves of a journey on the last train of the day, including over 150 inhabitants of Thaxted who walked to Cutler's Green in order to ride into the terminus. Although railways had been in operation for over 70 years, rural folk were still wary of the 'iron horse' and two amusing incidents involving local people gave evidence of such trepidation.

On 31st March 1913, the horse-drawn omnibus, which had connected Thaxted with Elsenham Station for 27 years, ran for the last time. The last bus, ready to depart, stands outside the Crown Inn at Elsenham, with George Rogers, the owner, on the far side, and Sim Harvey, the driver, in the nearside driving seat. Thaxted guard, Percy Reeve, is second from the left and H. W. Butters, Elsenham Station Master, fourth from the left. Thaxted-based driver and fireman stand in front of the bus.

The first train for public use departed from Thaxted at 8.08a.m. on Tuesday, 1st April 1913. All five of the six wheel coaches were used, although this train was far from full with about 50 passengers travelling on a train with a capacity for 192. Class R24, No. 196, with a full head of steam, awaits departure.

Railway staff, police and passengers, pose, on 1st April 1913, in front of the first train to depart from Thaxted. Even W. H. Smith provided a news stand and the newsboy stands in the foreground. The station and rolling stock are spotlessly clean. The brake third at the end of the train is No. 94.

The first day of public passenger service on the Elsenham & Thaxted Light Railway, 1st April 1913. As passengers hurry for the train, heads look out of carriage windows, and Conductor Guard, Percy Reeve, far left, takes fares. The steps attached to the sides of the vehicles, for passengers to board or alight at the low platforms, are prominent. On these converted six wheelers, only the end doors opened. The intermediate doors were sealed and the handles were removed.

A labourer who had never seen a train in his life was dressed in his Sunday best for the event, but when a young man offered to buy him a ticket for the round trip to Elsenham and back he declined the offer. The other involved an old lady standing on Thaxted Station, who kept repeating to her friends that she could not understand how the wheels kept on the rails. Despite the refusal of these two people to join the train, 575 tickets were issued for travel on the light railway on the first day.

From the outset the line fulfilled the hopes of the promoters and became an essential part of the life of the local community. No longer had they to rely on the poor narrow byways, thick with mud in winter, for their communications. Local farmers, reliant in the past on slow ponderous horse-drawn farm carts to get their produce to the local markets at Bishop's Stortford, Braintree and Saffron Walden, readily turned to the railway for help. Traffic increased to reasonable proportions, with sometimes over 500 passengers travelling on Thursdays to Bishop's Stortford market. Farm produce was sent further afield, with regular wagon consignments to Spitalfields and Cambridge as well as intermediate stations.

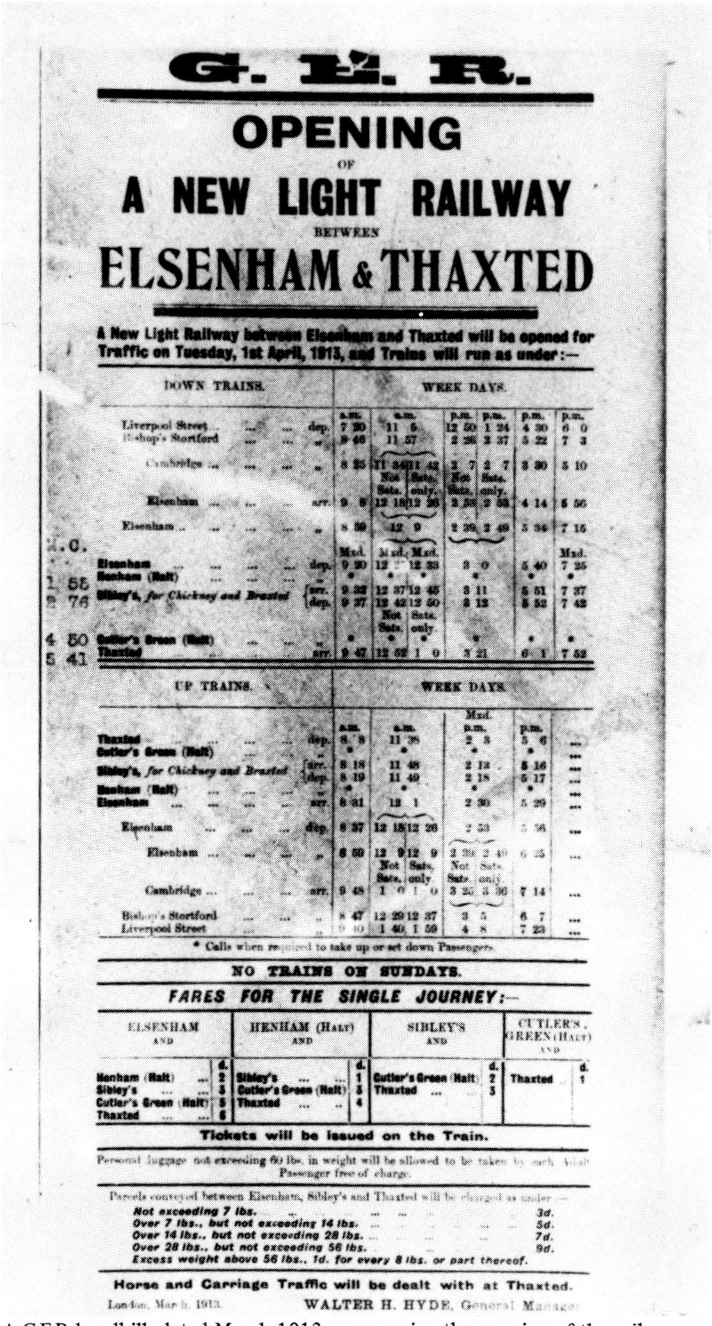

G. E. R.

OPENING

OF

A NEW LIGHT RAILWAY

BETWEEN

ELSENHAM & THAXTED

A New Light Railway between Elsenham and Thaxted will be opened for Traffic on Tuesday, 1st April, 1913, and Trains will run as under:—

M.C.	DOWN TRAINS.		WEEK DAYS.						
			a.m.	a.m.		p.m.	p.m.	p.m.	p.m.
	Liverpool Street ...	dep.	7 20	11 5		12 50	1 24	4 30	6 0
	Bishop's Stortford ...	,,	8 46	11 57		2 26	2 37	5 22	7 3
	Cambridge ...	,,	8 25	11 34	11 42	2 7	2 7	3 30	5 10
				Not Sats.	Sats. only.	Not Sats.	Sats. only.		
	Elsenham ...	arr.	9 8	12 18	12 26	2 58	2 53	4 14	5 56
	Elsenham ...	,,	8 50	12 9		2 39	2 49	5 34	7 15
			Mxd.	Mxd.	Mxd.				Mxd.
	Elsenham ...	dep.	9 20	12 [illegible]	12 33	3 0		5 40	7 25
1 55	**Henham (Halt)** ...	,,	*	*	*	*		*	*
3 76	**Sibley's,** *for Chickney and Broxted*	arr.	9 32	12 37	12 45	3 11		5 51	7 37
		dep.	9 37	12 42	12 50	3 12		5 52	7 42
				Not Sats.	Sats. only.				
4 50	**Cutler's Green (Halt)** ...	,,	*	*	*	*		*	*
5 41	**Thaxted**	arr.	9 47	12 52	1 0	3 21		6 1	7 52

UP TRAINS.		WEEK DAYS.						
					Mxd.			
		a.m.	a.m.		p.m.		p.m.	
Thaxted ...	dep.	8 8	11 38		2 3		5 6	...
Cutler's Green (Halt)	,,	*	*		*		*	...
Sibley's, *for Chickney and Broxted*	arr.	8 18	11 48		2 13		5 16	...
	dep.	8 19	11 49		2 18		5 17	...
Henham (Halt) ...	,,	*	*		*		*	...
Elsenham ...	arr.	8 31	12 1		2 30		5 29	...
Elsenham ...	dep.	8 37	12 18	12 26	2 53		5 56	...
Elsenham ...	,,	8 50	12 9	12 9	2 39	2 49	6 35	...
			Not Sats.	Sats. only.	Not Sats.	Sats. only.		
Cambridge ...	arr.	9 48	1 0	1 0	3 25	3 36	7 14	...
Bishop's Stortford ...	,,	8 47	12 29	12 37	3 5		6 7	...
Liverpool Street ...	,,	9 40	1 40	1 59	4 8		7 23	...

* Calls when required to take up or set down Passengers.

NO TRAINS ON SUNDAYS.

FARES FOR THE SINGLE JOURNEY:—

ELSENHAM AND	d.	HENHAM (HALT) AND	d.	SIBLEY'S AND	d.	CUTLER'S GREEN (HALT) AND	d.
Henham (Halt) ...	2	Sibley's ...	1	Cutler's Green (Halt)	2	Thaxted ...	1
Sibley's ...	3	Cutler's Green (Halt)	3	Thaxted ...	3		
Cutler's Green (Halt)	5	Thaxted ...	4				
Thaxted ...	6						

Tickets will be issued on the Train.

Personal luggage not exceeding 60 lbs. in weight will be allowed to be taken by each Adult Passenger free of charge.

Parcels conveyed between Elsenham, Sibley's and Thaxted will be charged as under:—

Not exceeding 7 lbs.	*3d.*
Over 7 lbs., but not exceeding 14 lbs.	*5d.*
Over 14 lbs., but not exceeding 28 lbs.	*7d.*
Over 28 lbs., but not exceeding 56 lbs.	*9d.*

Excess weight above 56 lbs., 1d. for every 8 lbs. or part thereof.

Horse and Carriage Traffic will be dealt with at Thaxted.

London, March, 1913. WALTER H. HYDE, General Manager

A GER handbill, dated March 1913, announcing the opening of the railway.

The impressive and spotlessly clean station and engine shed, at Thaxted, on 1st April 1913. A line of oil lamps provides illumination on the approach road, whilst the platform is well supplied with 3 wall lamps and 1 post lamp. Two ornate platform seats are provided for passengers and a Pooley weighing machine for parcels. Note the doors on the engine shed which were later removed.

A view facing Thaxted of Sibley's for Chickney & Broxted Station and goods yard on the opening day. The goods loop, complete with loading gauge and access road, is on the right. The station was named after a local farm and generated very little passenger traffic. The GER, however, handled quite considerable goods traffic at the station in the early years, and B. Jakes, who lived in the house beyond the station, acted as goods agent for the railway company. Note the roller, used for levelling the ash and clinker platform, on the left of the photograph.

Receipts from April to June 1913, on the new railway, totalled £531 whilst working expenses totalled £544. The GER was not disappointed with the £13 deficit, as it was considered that the contributory earnings eliminating the estimated value of traffic diverted from Elsenham to the light railway were £763, with 60 per cent for working expenses less £13 for local working, showing a profit of £294 to the Company.

Earnings for the subsequent six monthly periods were:

		Receipts	*Working Expenses*
6 months ending	December 1913	£1,105	£950
6 months ending	June 1914	£1,070	£918
6 months ending	December 1914	£1,063	£994
6 months ending	June 1915	£977	£1,067

Henham Halt from the approach road, with 3 six wheel coaches and a van forming an 'up' train. Note the absence of the coach body as a waiting shelter.

The outbreak of World War I, on 4th August 1914, found the GER, with other British railway companies, under Government control. Train services continued to pre-war schedules on the branch, and goods traffic flourished as increased produce was despatched from the north-west Essex farmlands to towns and cities to make up for the loss of imported food.

ELSENHAM AND THAXTED LIGHT RAILWAY.

66

See page		morn	morn	morn	SO even	NS even	even	even	
57, 58	LON- (Liverpool St. dep.	7 20	9 57	...	1 21	1 41	[illegible] 13	7 2	...
	DON (St Pancras — „	—	10 30	—	—	—	—	—	—
	Bishop's Stortford........ „	8 46	11 23	...	2 39	2 49	5 59	7 50	...
	Elsenham — — — —arr.	9 0	11 36	—	2 45	3 2	6 12	8 3	—
60, 61	Cambridge ....dep.	7 56	9 21	11 36	2 30		5 28	...	...
	Elsenham — — — —arr.	8 43	10 7	12 22	3 16		6 15	—	—
		Mxd		Mxd				Mxd	
	ELSENHAM ....dep.	9 5	11 42	12 48	3 20		6 20	8 7	...
	Henham (Halt) — — — „	C	C	C	C		C	C	—
	Sibley's, *for Chickney and* arr.	9 17	11 53	1 0	3 31		6 31	8 19	...
	Broxted — — — — dep.	9 22	11 54	1 5	3 32		6 32	8 24	—
	Cutler's Green (Halt) ...... „	C	C	C	C		C	C	...
	THAXTED — — — —arr.	9 32	12 3	1 17	3 41		6 41	8 34	—

See page		morn	morn	even	Mxd SO even	Mxd NS even	even		
	THAXTED ....dep.	8 13	11 2	12 9	2 11	2 28	5 4[illegible]	...	...
	Cutler's Green (Halt) — „	C	C	C	C	C	C	—	—
	Sibley's, *for Chickney and* arr.	8 23	11 12	12 19	2 21	2 38	5 5[illegible]	...	...
	Broxted — — — — dep.	8 24	11 13	12 20	2 26	2 43	5 5[illegible]	—	—
	Henham (Halt) .... „	C	C	C	C	C	C	...	...
	ELSENHAM — — —arr.	8 36	11 25	12 32	2 38	2 55	6 [illegible]	—	—
57, 58	Elsenham ....dep.	9 0	11 36	...	2 45	3 2	6 12	...	...
	Cambridge — — — —arr.	9 45	12 18	—	3 27	3 45	6 56	—	—
60, 61	Elsenham ....dep.	8 43	12 A22	...	3 16	3 16	6 15	...	...
	Bishop's Stortford— —arr.	8 53	12 A32	—	3 26	3 26	6 25	—	—
	LON- (St. Pancras ... „	....	1 35	...	....	....	7 22	...	...
	DON (Liverpool St. „	9 46	2 7	—	5 2	5 2	7 54	—	—

A On Thursdays leaves Elsenham 11.30 and arrives Bishop's Stortford 11.40 a.m. **C** Calls when required to take up or set down passengers. **NS** Not Saturdays. **SO** Saturdays only.

Only one class of accommodation is provided between Elsenham and Thaxted and single journey tickets only are issued. Tickets are issued on the train.

SINGLE FARES.

ELSENHAM AND		HENHAM (HALT) AND	
Henham (Halt)	2d.	Sibley's	1d.
Sibley's	3d.	Cutlers' Green (Halt) ...	3d.
Cutlers' Green (Halt) ...	5d.	Thaxted	4d.
Thaxted	6d.		
SIBLEY'S AND		CUTLERS' GREEN (HALT) AND	
Cutlers' Green (Halt) ...	2d.	Thaxted	1d.
Thaxted	3d.		

Personal luggage not exceeding 60 lbs. in weight is allowed to be taken by each adult passenger free of charge.

Parcels conveyed between Elsenham, Sibley's and Thaxted are charged as under:—

Not exceeding 7 lbs.	3d.
Over 7 lbs., but not exceeding 14 lbs.	5d.
Over 14 lbs., but not exceeding 28 lbs.	7d.
Over 28 lbs., but not exceeding 56 lbs.	9d.

GER Passenger Timetable : 1915

ELSENHAM AND THAXTED LIGHT RAILWAY.

62

Single Line.

Worked by Train Staff, without tickets. For regulations for working this Light Railway see Special Instruction No. 1045.

DOWN WEEK DAYS.

Miles from Elsenham.				1	2	3	4	5	6	7
				Mxd.	Pass.	Mxd.	Pass.	Pass.	Mxd.	
M. C.				a.m.	a.m.	p.m.	p.m.	p.m.	p.m.	
	Elsenham	S	dep.	9 5	11 42	12 48	3 20	6 20	8 7	
1 55	Henham Halt		„	*	*	*	*	*	*	
2 76	Sibleys		arr.	9 17	11 53	1 0	3 31	6 31	8 19	
			dep.	9 22	11 54	1 5	3 32	6 32	8 24	
4 50	Cutlers' Green Halt		„	*	*	*	*	*	*	
5 41	Thaxted	S	arr.	9 32	12 3	1 17	3 41	6 41	8 34	

UP WEEK DAYS.

			1	2	3	4	5	6	7	8
			Pass.	Pass.	Pass.	Mxd.	Mxd.	Pass.	Gds	
						SO	NS			
			a.m.	a.m.	p.m.	p.m.	p.m.	p.m.	p.m.	
Thaxted	S	dep.	8 13	11 2	12 9	2 11	2 28	5 40	[illegible]	
Cutlers' Green Halt		„	*	*	*	*	*	*		
Sibleys		arr.	8 23	11 12	12 19	2 21	2 38	5 50	[illegible]	
		dep.	8 24	11 13	12 20	2 26	2 43	5 51	[illegible]	
Henham Halt		„	*	*	*	*	*	*		
Elsenham	S	arr.	8 36	11 25	12 32	2 38	2 55	6 3	[illegible]	

=1 May work one truck of cattle to Elsenham on Tuesdays and Thursdays if the truck is fitted with Westinghouse brake pipes.

GER Working Timetable : 1916

The suggestion to extend the railway beyond Thaxted was again raised in 1919, when the Essex County Council Special Committee reported to the Ministry of Reconstruction on the proposals for the construction of nine light railways in the county. One of these proposals envisaged a light railway linking existing GER stations, from Ongar to Haverhill, with a branch from Thaxted to the Hedinghams. As with the other eight schemes, no attempt was made to produce statistics showing expense and likely traffic, and the proposals were soon forgotten. In the same year, from 26th September to 5th October, a general railway strike brought a suspension of train services on the Thaxted line.

Mill Road Halt with short 25ft. long platforms, opened by the GER on 18th December 1922, after pressure from local inhabitants of the west end of Henham village. Note the cattle guards in the track, and fencing to prevent animals from straying on to the line.

Photomatic

The complacent attitude of the GER authorities was rudely shattered when their monopoly on branch passenger services was questioned at a meeting held in Thaxted on 29th January 1920. The gathering met to discuss and support the proposal for the introduction of a motor coach service linking Cambridge and London via Saffron Walden, Thaxted and Dunmow. The National Bus Company (later Eastern National), and other smaller companies were spreading their infant wings through north and west Essex in the succeeding years, troubling the GER Board. In an endeavour to arrest the flow of passenger traffic from the light railway, and in answer to pressure from local inhabitants, a new halt was opened at Mill Road, Henham, on Monday, 18th December 1922, to serve the west end of the village. The provision of the halt was a parting gesture from the GER, for at the end of the month the company was amalgamated with the Great Northern, Great Central and other minor railways to form the London & North Eastern Railway.

From 1st January 1923 the Thaxted line changed ownership to the London & North Eastern Railway. Few alterations were made but industrial strife soon changed matters.

A seven day railway strike, from 20th January 1924, brought a decline in branch receipts, whilst services were again curtailed during the General Strike of 1926. These industrial disputes began the decline in railway freight. Farmers and growers realized for the first time that with improving roads, goods could be sent by lorry, using, in some cases, second-hand Army vehicles, thus making short-haul journeys cheaper than rates charged by the LNER. The door-to-door service was more convenient than the double handling caused by loading and unloading railway wagons. The primitive commercial road vehicles of the day were not, however, capable of continuous long hauls, and the middle and long distance freight traffic remained safely in the hands of the railway company.

Receipts from parcels and season-ticket traffic at stations in the years after grouping were:

	Parcels despatched	*Receipts £*	*Season-tickets issued*	*Receipts £*	*Total £*
Sibley's 1923	720	64	1	5	69
Sibley's 1924	783	66	1	4	70
Sibley's 1925	802	66	1	15	81
Sibley's 1926	366	32	2	31	63
Sibley's 1927	462	38	–	–	38
Sibley's 1928	1,340	72	2	41	113
Thaxted 1923	3,026	429	16	189	618
Thaxted 1924	1,753	378	18	237	615
Thaxted 1925	2,971	355	17	222	577
Thaxted 1926	3,896	332	18	236	568
Thaxted 1927	3,887	306	21	287	593
Thaxted 1928	3,850	288	20	234	522

Passenger totals were not available, as they were included with figures for Elsenham Station.

Snow blocked the light railway in December 1927, falling on the evening of Christmas Day. Swirling snow beating in the wind across the ridges and high land of north-west Essex quickly filled some of the shallow cuttings. As the main lines and neighbouring Saffron Walden and Dunmow branches were all blocked, efforts were made to clear these before the engine and snowplough from Cambridge attempted to clear the Thaxted line. Despite the assistance of permanent way staff, it was 27th December before the branch train was again able to run through to Elsenham.

Fortunately the troubles besetting local freight were not as acute with the branch passenger traffic. In the late 1920s and early 1930s few local people owned cars, and in the absence of a directly competitive bus service the local populus were reliant on the light railway for local and long distance journeys. Thus despite the cut-backs made by the LNER, and the withdrawal of passenger services from Somersham to Ramsey East, and Downham to Stoke Ferry on 22nd September 1930, and Ely to St. Ives, and Mellis to Eye on 2nd February 1931, the Thaxted line continued its useful existence.

Passenger traffic receipts showed some improvement in the mid-1930s when holidays and rambles in the country became popular. The branch trains on Saturdays and bank holidays carried more than an average number of passengers eager to take advantage of their free time in the countryside.

A Thaxted branch train of the 1930s. J69/1 Class 0-6-0T, No. 7193, on 15th August 1936, approaches Henham Halt with a Thaxted to Elsenham train formed of a six wheel third and a six wheel brake third.

T. Middlemas

The remote Thaxted Station, in August 1935, looking towards Elsenham. This view shows two of the six wheel coaching vehicles standing at the platform. Note the large stocks of coal in the yard.

L&GRP

The 4.25p.m. waits to depart from Elsenham for Thaxted, on 22nd April 1935, with a train of original six wheel coaches hauled by Class J69/1 locomotive, No. 7193 (later 68600).

LCGB/Ken Nunn Collection

No. 7193 leaves Elsenham for Thaxted with six wheeled stock in 1938.

J. E. Kite

With the outbreak of World War II the LNER merged with other major railway companies under the Railway Executive Committee, from 1st September 1939. Some evacuees were conveyed on the branch, but numbers were small when compared with other lines in the area.

To safeguard against air raids, especially at night, the oil lamps in the halts and stations remained dimmed, and staff utilized shielded hand lamps to attend to train and shunting duties. As a further precaution, station nameboards were also removed and stored in lamp rooms or Thaxted Engine Shed.

Table 47.

ELSENHAM AND THAXTED.

(LIGHT RAILWAY.)

For Local Service see Table			WEEKDAYS									
					SX	SO	SO	SX				
			a.m.	a.m.	a.m.	noon	p.m.	p.m.	p.m.	p.m.	p.m.	
9	LONDON (Liverpool Street)	dep.	7 18	10 5	....	....	1 19	12 49	2 48	4 45	6 30	....
9	Bishop's Stortford	"	8 45	11 4	..	..	2 8	2 9	4 3	5 37	7 17	..
9	Elsenham	arr.	8 58	11 17	....	....	2 20	2 19	4 18	5 47	7 28	....
9	Cambridge	dep.	B8 29	9 32	11 57	12 0	1 10	..	2 30	4 5	5 38	..
9	Elsenham	arr.	9 17	10 14	12 42	12 46	1 55	....	3 9	4 48	6 24	....
	ELSENHAM	dep.	9 19	11 22	12 50	12 55	2 24	2 26	4 23	5 53	7 34	..
	Mill Road (Halt)	"	9 23	11 26	12 54	12 59	2 28	2 30	4 27	5 57	7 38	....
	Henham (Halt)	"	9 27	11 30	12 58	1 3	2 32	2 34	4 31	6 1	7 42	....
	Sibley's for Chickney and Broxted	arr.	9 32	11 34	1 3	1 8	2 36	2 39	4 35	6 5	7 46	....
		dep.	9 37	11 35	1 8	1 13	2 37	2 40	4 36	6 6	7 47	..
	Cutler's Green (Halt)	"	9 43	11 40	1 14	1 19	2 42	2 46	4 41	6 11	7 52	....
	THAXTED	arr.	9 47	11 44	1 18	1 23	2 46	2 50	4 45	6 15	7 56	..

For Local Service see Table			WEEKDAYS									
					SX	SO				SO	SX	
			a.m.	a.m.	p.m.	p.m.	p.m.	p.m.	p.m.	p.m.	p.m.	
	THAXTED	dep.	8 15	10 42	12 13	12 17	1 45	3 25	5 19	6 23	6 34	....
	Cutler's Green (Halt)	"	8 19	10 46	12 17	12 21	1 49	3 29	5 23	6 27	6 38	..
	Sibley's for Chickney and Broxted	arr.	8 25	10 52	12 23	12 27	1 55	3 35	5 29	6 33	6 44	....
		dep.	8 26	10 57	12 24	12 28	2 0	3 36	5 30	6 34	6 49	..
	Henham (Halt)	"	8 31	11 2	12 29	12 33	2 5	3 41	5 35	6 39	6 54	....
	Mill Road (Halt)	"	8 35	11 6	12 33	12 37	2 9	3 45	5 39	6 43	6 58	..
	ELSENHAM	arr.	8 39	11 10	12 37	12 41	2 13	3 49	5 43	6 49	7 4	....
9	Elsenham	dep.	8 58	11 17	..	1 32	2 19	4 18	5 47	6 53	7 28	..
9	Cambridge	arr.	9 40	11 55	....	2 12	2 55	4 58	6 47	7 28	8 4	....
9	Elsenham	dep.	8 43	..	12 42	12 46	3 9	3B55	6 24	7 16	7 16	..
9	Bishop's Stortford	arr.	8 53	....	12 52	12 56	3 19	4B 5	6 34	7 26	7 26	....
9	LONDON (Liverpool Street)	"	9 47	..	1 57	2 9	5 10	5 19	7A55	8 20	8 20	..

A On Saturdays arrives Liverpool Street 7.47 p.m.
B On Saturdays runs 5 minutes later.
SO Saturdays only.
SX Saturdays excepted.

Only one class of accommodation is provided between Elsenham and Thaxted and single journey tickets only are issued. Tickets are issued on the train.

LNER Passenger Timetable : 1934

Table 47.

ELSENHAM AND THAXTED.

(LIGHT RAILWAY.)

Local Service Table			WEEKDAYS								
					SX	SO	SO	SX			
			a.m.	a.m.	a.m.	noon	p.m.	p.m.	p.m	p.m.	p.m.
9	LONDON (Liverpool St.)	dep.	7 18	10 5	...	...	1 19	12 49	2 48	4 45	6 30
9	Bishop's Stortford	"	8 46	11 6	—	—	2 10	2 14	4 6	5 36	7 20
9	Elsenham	arr.	8 59	11 19	...	...	2 23	2 27	4 19	5 49	7 32
9	Cambridge	dep.	8 31	9 28	11 50	12 0	1 10	—	2 26	4 6	5 38
9	Elsenham	arr.	9 16	10 13	12 37	12 47	1 55	...	3 12	4 52	6 25
	ELSENHAM	dep.	9 19	11 24	12 45	12 55	2 27	2 31	4 25	5 55	7 38
	Mill Road (Halt)	"	9 23	11 28	12 49	12 59	2 31	2 35	4 29	5 59	7 42
	Henham (Halt)	"	9 27	11 32	12 53	1 3	2 35	2 39	4 33	6 3	7 46
	Sibley's for Chickney and Broxted	arr.	9 32	11 36	12 58	1 8	2 39	2 44	4 37	6 7	7 50
		dep.	9 37	11 37	1 3	1 13	2 40	2 45	4 38	6 8	7 51
	Cutlers' Green (Halt)	"	9 45	11 42	1 9	1 19	2 45	2 51	4 43	6 13	7 56
	THAXTED	arr.	9 47	11 46	1 13	1 23	2 49	2 55	4 47	6 17	8 0

Local Service Table			WEEKDAYS									
						SO	SX	SO	SX		SO	SX
			a.m	a.m	p.m.	p.m	p.m	p.m	p.m	p.m	p.m.	p.m.
	THAXTED	dep.	8 10	10 40	12A 7	1 45	1 50	3 25	3 47	5 20	6 27	6 27
	Cutlers' Green (Halt)	"	8 14	10 44	12A11	1 49	1 54	3 29	3 51	5 24	6 31	6 31
	Sibley's for Chickney and Broxted	arr.	8 20	10 50	12A17	1 55	2 0	3 35	3 57	5 30	6 37	6 37
		dep.	8 21	10 57	12A18	2 0	2 5	3 36	3 58	5 31	6 38	6 49
	Henham (Halt)	"	8 26	11 2	12A23	2 5	2 10	3 41	4 3	5 36	6 43	6 54
	Mill Road (Halt)	"	8 30	11 6	12A27	2 9	2 14	3 45	4 7	5 40	6 47	6 58
	ELSENHAM	arr.	8 34	11 10	12A31	2 13	2 18	3 49	4 11	5 44	6 53	7 4
9	Elsenham	dep.	8 59	11 19	1 36	2 23	2 27	4 19	4 19	6 57	6 57	7 32
9	Cambridge	arr.	9 44	12 0	2 17	3 4	3 7	5 0	5 0	7 35	7 35	8 7
9	Elsenham	dep.	8 42	—	12A37	3 12	3 12	3 55	4 52	6 25	7 18	7 18
9	Bishop's Stortford	arr.	8 53	...	12A47	3 22	3 22	4 5	5 2	6 35	7 28	7 28
9	LONDON (Liverpool St.)	"	9 47	—	1A57	5 9	5 9	5 19	6 10	7B55	8 26	8 26

A On Saturdays runs 10 minutes later.
B On Saturdays arrives Liverpool Street 7.48 p.m.
SO Saturdays only
SX Saturdays excepted.

Only one class of accommodation is provided between Elsenham and Thaxted and single journey tickets only are issued. Tickets are issued on the train.

LNER Passenger Timetable : 1939

The agricultural nature of the freight handled by the Thaxted branch was of the utmost importance, as the vital provisions of home grown food, vegetables, grain and fruit were despatched to the markets. In addition to the outward flow of produce, the war years brought an influx of tinned food by rail to Thaxted for distribution to the Ministry of Food storage depots in the area.

During the early years of the war, services were drastically reduced to two trains each way, nevertheless the line carried its fair share of traffic, as petrol rationing forced passengers to use the railway, and by 1943 an additional train, in each direction, was introduced.

The route of the light railway crossed a proposed defence line just beyond Sibley's Station, and in the early days of hostilities a train of eight condemned wagons was hauled to the required site and rolled down the bank to form a tank trap. The wagons, wired together, remained in situ for some time after the war as a reminder of those dangerous days.

The close proximity of airfields at Debden, Hadstock, Wethersfield, Stansted and Easton Lodge was no insurance against air attack by the Luftwaffe, and the branch train was attacked on two occasions in 1941 and again the following year. Fortunately, the most serious damage received was splintered woodwork in the rear coach of the train, which was sustained during the last attack. The five airfields received considerable quantities of supplies via Saffron Walden, Bartlow, Easton Lodge and Takeley stations during hostilities. Thaxted was also used occasionally when the other stations were at full stretch, and on two occasions armaments, bombs and explosives were routed via the light railway, off loaded and conveyed to Stansted and Easton Lodge airfields, at night.

Class J68 0-6-0T, No. 8645, stands at Thaxted with the branch train.

A close up of the remote Cutler's Green Halt, with the five compartment four wheel coach body used as passenger accommodation. Note also the ornate cast-iron and wooden seats which were allocated to the halts and stations on the branch.

A two coach train, the 9.55a.m. from Thaxted, hauled by No. 68530, approaches the junction points near Elsenham, on 14th July 1951.

LCGB/Ken Nunn Collection

The railway resumed peacetime services with run-down rolling stock and equipment and stations in need of repair. Questions were raised in Parliament regarding the poor condition of rolling stock, and the deteriorating services offered by the railways. The Thaxted branch was no exception, for despite an increase in the number of trains, engine failures during 1945 and 1946 were frequent.

Early in 1947 heavy snowfalls brought delays to services, and in February the line was blocked for two days, necessitating the use of the Cambridge snowplough to clear the line after the branch locomotive, booked to run all night between Thaxted and Elsenham, failed to keep the line clear. The nationalization of the railways from 1st January 1948 brought little change to the branch which retained its Great Eastern atmosphere, although new posters, paperwork and uniforms gradually appeared. Unfortunately, the new regime failed to stem the flow of passengers away to road transport. Despite the introduction of two extra trains, passenger traffic declined in favour of road transport, and except for Thursday, Bishop's Stortford market day, barely 50 passenger journeys were made daily. On one occasion when Class J69/1 No. 68530 failed on the branch in the summer of 1950, a taxi conveyed all the passengers on to Elsenham. With such a reduction in receipts it was inevitable that pruning would take place.

Class J68 0-6-0T, No. 8645, departing from Thaxted with the two coach branch train in 1948.

T. Middlemas

Class J67/2 0-6-0T, No. 68609, waits hopefully for passengers before departing from Thaxted on 16th April 1949. The working is the 11.50 a.m. from Thaxted to Elsenham, and in true GE branch line fashion, the wrong headcode is displayed on the locomotive. *W. A. Camwell*

Class B2, 4-6-0, No. 61617 *Ford Castle* pulls into the 'up' main line platform at Elsenham with the 11.00 a.m. Ely to Liverpool Street train, on 16th April 1949. In the bay platform Class J67, No. 68609, stands with the 11.50 a.m. from Thaxted. *W. A. Camwell*

Class J69/1, No. 68530, pulls away from Elsenham round the 8¾ chain radius right-hand curve, on 14th July 1951, with a two coach train, the 8.55 a.m. for Thaxted. The run-round loop is in the foreground. The wooden waiting shelter, on the 'up' main line platform, is behind the last coach, whilst the brick building to the right of the picture is the booking office.

LCGB/Ken Nunn Collection

The 11.50 a.m. Thaxted to Elsenham, negotiating the 8¾ chain curve on the approach to Elsenham Station, on 28th April 1951, headed by Class J68 0-6-0T, No. 8645.

LCGB/Ken Nunn Collection

Class J68 0-6-0T, No. 8645, waits hopefully in the branch platform at Elsenham, with the 1.43p.m. to Thaxted, on 28th April 1951. The open countryside, traversed by the branch, is exemplified by the exposed ridge behind the railway.

LCGB/Ken Nunn Collection

The first intimation of closure came on 16th March 1951, two months before passenger services were withdrawn from another Essex light railway linking Kelvedon and Tollesbury. The Railway Executive notified Dunmow Rural District Council, by letter, that the Elsenham & Thaxted line was wholly unremunerative, and it was proposed to withdraw passenger services at the earliest opportunity. The plan was subject to the Eastern National Bus Company providing an alternative service.

Table 30 **ELSENHAM and THAXTED (Light Railway)**

Miles		Week Days only a.m	p.m S	p.m E	p.m	p.m E	p.m
	4 London (Liverpool St. dep	6 56	1230	1255	3F35	5 24	6 36
—	Elsenham .... dep	8 35	1 55	2 28	5 0	6 42	7 55
1	Mill Road Halt	8 39	1 59	2 32	5 4	6 46	7 59
1¾	Henham Halt	8 43	2 3	2 36	5 8	6 50	8 3
3	Sibley's for Chickney arr	8 48	2 8	2 41	5 13	6 55	8 8
	and Broxted dep	8 49	2 9	2 42	5 14	6 56	8 9
4¼	Cutler's Green Halt	8 55	2 15	2 48	5 20	7 2	8 15
5½	Thaxted .... arr	8 58	2 18	2 51	5 23	7 5	8 18

Miles		Week Days only a.m	a.m	a.m		p.m	p.m	p.m E
—	Thaxted .... dep	7 36	10 0	1150	..	4 0	5 50	7 23
1	Cutler's Green Halt	7 40	10 4	1154	..	4 4	5 54	7 27
2¼	Sibley's for Chickney arr	7 46	1010	12 0	..	4 10	6 0	7 33
	and Broxted dep	7 47	1011	12 5	..	4 11	6 5	7 34
3¾	Henham Halt	7 52	1016	1210	..	4 16	6 10	7 39
4½	Mill Road Halt	7 56	1020	1214	..	4 20	6 14	7 43
5½	Elsenham .... arr	8 0	1024	1218	..	4 24	6 19	7 48
41	4 London (Liverpool St.) arr	9 14	1153	1 56	..	6B0	8T12	1119

B Third class only between Elsenham and Bishop's Stortford. **E** Except Saturdays. F Dep. 3 42 p.m on Sats.
S Saturdays only. T Arr. 8 4 p.m on Sats.
One class only between Elsenham and Thaxted. Tickets (single only) issued on the train.

The final LNER Passenger Timetable : October 1947

Table 40 **ELSENHAM and THAXTED (Light Railway)**

Miles		Week Days only a.m	p.m S	p.m E	p.m	p.m E	p.m
	4 London (Liverpool St.) dep	6 56	1227	1255	3P36	5 18	6 36
—	Elsenham .... dep	8 55	1 43	2 28	5 0	6 24	7 55
1	Mill Road Halt	8 59	1 47	2 32	5 4	6 28	7 59
1¾	Henham Halt	9 3	1 51	2 36	5 8	6 32	8 3
8	Sibley's for Chickney arr	9 8	1 56	2 41	5 13	6 37	8 8
	and Broxted dep	9 14	1 57	2 42	5 14	6 38	8 9
4¼	Cutler's Green Halt	9 20	2 3	2 48	5 20	6 44	8 15
5½	Thaxted .... arr	9 23	2 6	2 51	5 23	6 47	8 18

Miles		Week Days only a.m	a.m.	a.m	p.m	p.m E	p.m S	p.m E
—	Thaxted .... dep	7 36	9 55	1150	4 0	5 45	6 0	7 23
1	Cutler's Green Halt	7 40	9 59	1154	4 4	5 49	6 4	7 27
2½	Sibley's for Chickney arr	7 46	10 5	12 0	4 10	5 55	6 10	7 33
	and Broxted dep	7 47	10 6	12 5	4 11	6 0	6 15	7 34
8¾	Henham Halt	7 52	10 11	1210	4 16	6 5	6 20	7 39
4½	Mill Road Halt	7 56	10 15	1214	4 20	6 9	6 24	7 43
5½	Elsenham .... arr	8 0	10 19	1218	4 24	6 14	6 29	7 48
41	4 London (Liverpool St.) arr	9 16	11 30	1B58	5Y58	8 3	8 3	1117

E Except Saturdays P Dep. 3 42 p.m. on Saturdays B Arr. 1 55 p.m. on Saturdays
Y Arr. 6 2 p.m. on Saturdays **S** or S Saturdays only
One class only between Elsenham and Thaxted. Tickets (single only) issued on train

BR (ER) Passenger Timetable : June 1951

Dunmow Rural District Council questioned the decision of the Railway Executive, who replied that the scheme was part of a general review of unremunerative branch lines, which included the neighbouring line linking Bishop's Stortford, Dunmow and Braintree. The council's finance committee, discussing the proposal, was tentatively agreeable to a bus replacement service, but then circularized the Railway Executive's statement to local parish councils and the National Farmers' Union for their views. Somewhat surprisingly both Elsenham and Henham Parish Councils raised no objections to the proposed closure, somewhat to the dismay of their neighbours at Thaxted.

Class J68, 0-6-0T, No. 68645, pulls into Cutler's Green Halt on a bright sunny summer day in 1951. Although the 'buckjumper' was considered a small tank locomotive when compared with other classes, it completely over-shadows the small station.

D. Trevor Rowe

J68 Class 0-6-0T, No. 8645, on 28th April 1951, climbs the 1 in 50 away from Elsenham with the 1.43 p.m. to Thaxted.

Ken Nunn

Class J69/1 0-6-0T, No. 68530, simmers in the sunshine at Thaxted, on 30th June 1951, with her two coach train. No. 68530 was built in March 1892 as GER No. 353, and was finally withdrawn from traffic in February 1961.

H. C. Casserley

Class J69/1 0-6-0T, No. 68530, trundles down the 1 in 50 from Mill Road towards Elsenham on 14th July 1951. The mixed train comprises two bogie ex-GER corridor coaches and a van.

LCGB/Ken Nunn Collection

Class J68 0-6-0T, No. 8645, approaches Mill Road Halt with a 'down' train in 1951.

Despite vehement protests by many Thaxted people, including a petition sent to the Railway Executive requesting retention of the railway, the disturbing aspect which emerged was that few travelled regularly by train. Most of the parish councils had no strong objections to the withdrawal of passenger services if adequate replacement buses were to be provided. Early in the new year the Eastern National Omnibus Company made application to the Traffic Commissioners for consent to extend and divert their infrequent Bishop's Stortford to Debden service to Cutler's Green and Thaxted, to run on weekdays. Opposition to this railway-backed application was made by C. E. Moore Ltd., of Saffron Walden, and Premier Travel Ltd., of Cambridge, both of whom objected to the possibility of further inroads by the nationalized company in their operating area. Because of these objections the licence to operate the new service was refused, much to the dismay of the Eastern National Omnibus Company and the Railway Executive.

A shock to many people fighting for the retention of the Thaxted branch was the withdrawal of passenger services between Bishop's Stortford and Braintree on 3rd March 1952, after a considerable struggle by local interested parties, including a hearing by the newly-formed Transport Users' Consultative Committee for East Anglia.

As might be expected, an appeal was made against the objection to divert the Eastern National bus route to Thaxted, and on Wednesday, 2nd April 1952, a hearing, chaired by the Ministry of Transport Inspector, E. C. P. Lascelles, was held at Cambridge. After digesting evidence from both parties, Lascelles advised in favour of the granting of a licence to the Eastern National Bus Company, a decision upheld by the Ministry of Transport and the Traffic Commissioners.

A poster advertising the withdrawal of passenger train services in September 1952.
D. Trevor Rowe

The licence was duly granted the following month, when Eastern National formally advised British Railways that they were agreeable to operating a service of four buses each way between Bishop's Stortford and Thaxted, serving the villages on the branch. In addition to running their services at similar times to the trains, the Eastern National Bus Company offered to maintain the necessary connections with main line trains at Elsenham. Subsequently on Tuesday, 12th August 1952, British Railways announced that passenger services would be withdrawn from the Thaxted branch from Monday, 15th September 1952, but as no Sunday services ran on the line the last train would run on the previous Saturday.

Last minute attempts were made by Thaxted townsfolk to save the line, and even an approach to R. A. Butler, MP for Saffron Walden brought no firm support, thus the inevitable happened.

Class J69/1, No. 68579, waits in the bay platform at Elsenham on the last day of passenger working, 13th September 1952, with a train formed of the three ex-GER bogie coaches.

T. Middlemas

With a full train and all three coaching vehicles in service, Class J69/1, No. 68579, waits to depart from Thaxted, with the 4.10 p.m. to Elsenham, on the last day of passenger operation, 13th September 1952. The coaching vehicles are third No. 61471, and brake third No. 62450, both 53 ft. long, and brake third No. 62461, 57 ft. long.

J. Watling Collection

The last day of passenger working, 13th September 1952, and Class J69/1 0-6-0T, No. 68579, pulls round the curve into Thaxted with the 5 p.m. from Elsenham with all three ex-GER corridor coaches. At this point, the railway was on an embankment above the surrounding land.

D. Trevor Rowe

The last 'up' train departs from Thaxted on the evening of Saturday, 13th September 1952. The train is packed with local people and enthusiasts taking a last ride on the 'Gin & Toffee'. Driver Dever is at the controls of J69/1 Class No. 68579.

The last 'up' train from Thaxted to Elsenham eases round the curve towards Cutler's Green behind Class J69/1 0-6-0T, No. 68579.

S. Moss Collection

On the final day, 13th September, enthusiasts and local people paid their last respects to the 'Gin & Toffee'. By evening several hundred people gathered at Elsenham to watch the departure of, or travel on, the last 'down' train. With Driver Dever and Fireman Agnew in charge, Class J69/1 locomotive No. 68579 was beautifully turned out, and decorated with laurel wreaths and a Union Flag. Over 400 passengers packed into the three ex-GER corridor coaches which were decorated for the occasion with streamers. Prior to departure, a black-draped coffin, bearing the inscription 'Died Waiting' was borne with great solemnity through the crowds on the platform to the guards van, where it was placed in the charge of Guard T. Buck for the journey to Thaxted.

It was an especially sad occasion for Guard Buck who, starting his railway career as a lad porter in 1906, had been promoted to guard on the light railway when it opened in 1913. Accompanying him on his last journey before retirement was Mr P. Reeve, who had been guard in charge of the first train to Thaxted on the official opening day, 31st March 1913.

With Cambridge District Operating Superintendent Mr J. W. Dedman and Commercial Superintendent Mr A. Johnson on board, the 'right away' was given, and exactly on time at 7.55 p.m. the train eased round the curve away from Elsenham into the gathering dusk, amidst the sound of exploding detonators and cheering. At each of the intermediate halts more passengers boarded to swell the complement on the already overcrowded train. All along the route people gathered to wave and cheer the 'Thaxted Flier' on its last journey, and at Thaxted a large crowd gathered to witness the arrival, supplementing the meagre light of the oil lamps with car headlights.

As the passengers alighted, the coffin was removed from the brake van. The last flashlight photographs were taken as No. 68579 was uncoupled, prior to taking water and running round the train. After the tanks were replenished, No. 68579 hauled the three coaches back to Elsenham before continuing its journey on to Bishop's Stortford. The coaching stock remained at Elsenham for some time before the footsteps were removed and the vehicles dispersed to other locations.

Thereafter, freight services continued to run on Monday, Wednesday and Friday only. No. 68579 was retained at Bishop's Stortford Shed to work these services, although on a few occasions a J15 Class 0-6-0 tender locomotive was substituted. The meagre goods traffic that remained after the closure of the line to passenger traffic gradually diminished and often the service ran on Wednesday only. The end was inevitable, and the Railway Executive withdrew the freight facilities from 1st June 1953.

The final chapter of the line's forty years of active life came with the removal of the track. Occasional trips with a J15 Class locomotive hauling engineers' wagons heralded the arrival of the removal contractors. Commencing at Thaxted, work proceeded quickly and within weeks the oxy-acetylene cutters had reduced trackwork into short lengths suitable for loading into the wagons, which were propelled to site each morning and removed each evening to Elsenham yard.

With the passage of time evidence of the light railway has disappeared, the trackbed reclaimed by the former landowners or their successors,

The last 'up' train waits at Thaxted Station as a coffin, draped in black and lettered 'DIED WAITING R.I.P.', is conveyed with great solemnity along the platform on 13th September 1952.

S. Moss Collection

The last passenger train from Elsenham to Thaxted. Class J69/1 0-6-0T, No. 68579, adorned with wreath and Union Flag, awaits departure at 7.55 p.m. on 13th September 1952.

Author's Collection

and ploughed in as extension to fields. On the few embankments and cuttings, grass and trees have obliterated the former route, although between Henham and Sibley's the trackbed has been used as an access road by the local farmer.

Positive evidence of the former light railway can be found at Thaxted, where the brick built engine shed, water tower and wooden station buildings are utilized by the present owner. At Elsenham, the curve of the Thaxted branch bay platform at the back of the 'up' platform can be traced, but the site of the track and run-round loop have succumbed to the plough. The embankment which carried the spur to the goods yard can be clearly traced from the site of the junction to the former level crossing, where a ramp in the road marks the route of the line.

Thaxted locomotive shed and water tank, on 8th March 1972. The former is now used as a garage.

G. Pember

The former station building at Thaxted, now in use as an office, on 8th March 1972.

G. Pember

The only bridge on the Elsenham & Thaxted Light Railway spanned Horham Lane (No. 2452), 4 miles and 70 chains from Elsenham, situated between Cutler's Green and Thaxted. It had a square span of 11 ft. 11 in. and skew span between abutments of 12 ft. 8 in.

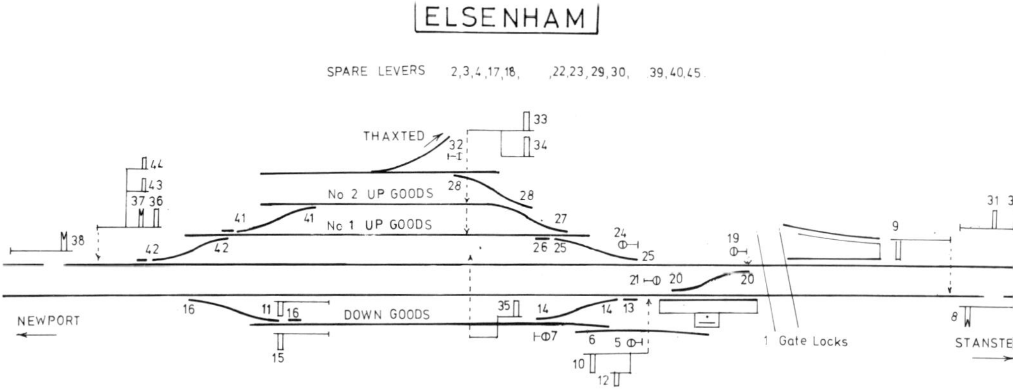

Elsenham Station, situated 35½ miles from Liverpool Street on the ex-GER main line to Cambridge, still retains a rural charm despite the new housing development which has sprung up on the west side of the line. The main line is served by staggered platforms, the 'down' platform north, and the 'up' platform south, of the bisecting level crossing. The gates and signals were controlled from the signal box situated on the 'down' platform, whilst the booking office and waiting shelter are on the 'up' side. From 11th December 1983, the signal box is scheduled for closure and all colour light signals protecting the level crossing will be operated from Cambridge power box.

Elsenham Station, looking north, showing the staggered main line platforms. The Thaxted branch train, in the charge of Class J69/1, No. 68530, is standing in the bay at the back of the 'up' platform, on 30th June 1951.

H. C. Casserley

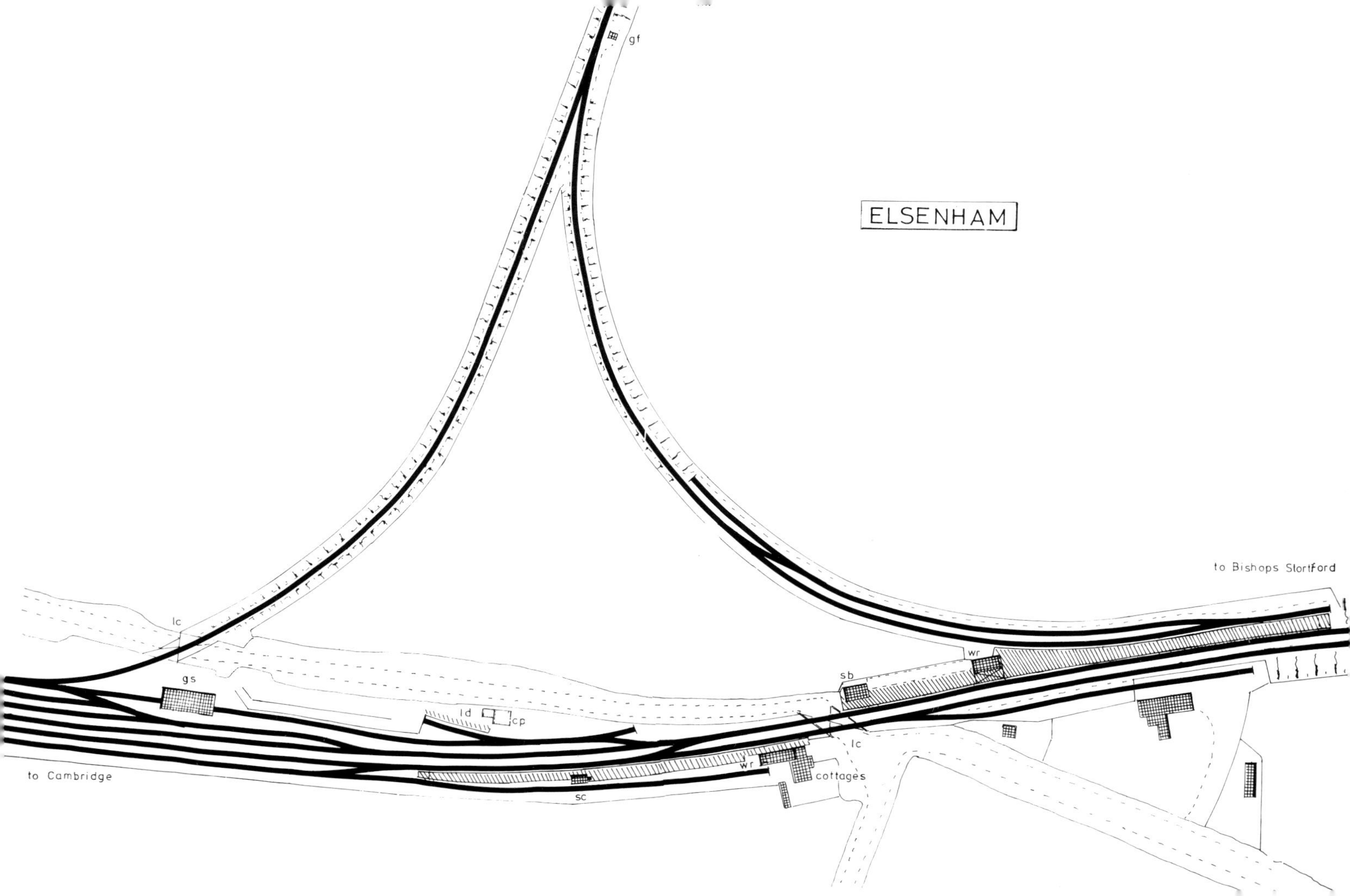
ELSENHAM
gf
lc
gs
ld
cp
sb
wr
lc
wr
cottages
sc
to Cambridge
to Bishops Stortford

A J20 Class 0-6-0 trundles past Elsenham with an 'up' freight, just as J68 Class No. 8645 prepares to run round its train in the Thaxted branch platform. Note the spare coach stabled in the siding in the middle background. The photograph was taken in 1948.

T. Middlemas

Arrival at Elsenham. Class J68 0-6-0T, No. 68645, stands in the bay platform at the junction station. Although the main line platform was of normal height, the Thaxted bay platform, like all the other branch stations, was 1 ft. in height.

D. Trevor Rowe

Class J69/1 0-6-0T, No. 68579, waits hopefully for passengers in the bay platform at Elsenham on 10th September 1952. Note the destination board, denoting 'Elsenham & Thaxted', on the side of brake third No. 62461.

S. C. Nash

Elsenham signal box on the 'down' main line platform, with its typical GER station nameboard which advised passengers 'Elsenham for Thaxted line', photographed on 6th August 1951.

J. F. Aylard

The Thaxted light railway made an almost triangular junction with the main line, but the only physical connection maintained was via the spur leading to the goods yard on the 'up' side, north of the station. The other spur, complete with run-round loop and short siding, served the passenger bay at the back of the 324ft. long 'up' main line platform. Although so nearly adjoining the main line, the track terminated at buffer stops at the London end of the platform.

Class J69/1, No. 68530, eases along the spur line, between the Thaxted branch and the goods yard, on 14th July 1951, before picking up wagons to form a mixed train.

LCGB/Ken Nunn Collection

Class J69/1 0-6-0T, No. 68530, with the morning freight train, stands on the spur connecting the goods yard with the branch at Elsenham, on 14th July 1951. The main branch line from the platform is in the foreground.

LCGB/Ken Nunn Collection

The locomotive and passenger coaches of the 11.50a.m. train from Thaxted, leaves the goods wagons for the goods yard at the shunter's cabin on the main single line at Elsenham, before proceeding to the station. The photograph was taken on 29th August 1952 and the locomotive is Class J68, No. 68645.

R. E. Vincent

From the platform, 200ft. in length and 1ft. in height, the light railway curved sharply away on an 8¾ chain curve in an easterly direction. Twenty chains from the buffer stops the 9½ chains left-hand curve connecting spur from the goods yard was joined. The junction was controlled by a small lever frame situated in a wooden hut standing on the south side of the line. The frame itself was locked and unlocked by Annett's key attached to the train staff.

Class J68 0-6-0T, No. 8645, waits to depart from Elsenham with the 1.43p.m. to Thaxted on 28th April 1951.

Ken Nunn

Class J69/1 0-6-0T, No. 68579, storms away from Elsenham, round the 8¾ chain radius right-hand curve, with the 6.24 p.m. to Thaxted on 10th September 1952. In the background is the waiting shelter, on the 'up' main line platform.

S. C. Nash

J67/2 Class 0-6-0T, No. 68609 climbing the 1 in 50 out of Elsenham with a two coach train to Thaxted in 1948. The connecting line from the goods yard is on the right.

Dr I. C. Allen

J68 Class 0-6-0T, No. 68645 approaches Elsenham, in 1952, with the branch train. The run-round loop is in the foreground. To the left is the booking office on the 'up' main line platform, and beyond, the signalbox on the 'down' main line platform.

T. Middlemas

A view from the branch train, hauled by Class J69/1 0-6-0T, No. 68530, leaving Elsenham and approaching the junction with the spur from the goods yard. On the right of the junction is the small hut containing the ground frame to work the points, which were released by Annett's key attached to the train staff. Beyond the junction the line climbs at 1 in 50 on a straight course towards Mill Road. The 18ft. wide formation of the railway is apparent, but it was never intended to lay double track.

H. C. Casserley.

The minute Mill Road Halt, 70 chains from Elsenham, facing west. The small waiting hut was transferred from Pidley-cum-Fenton siding on the Somersham to Ramsey East branch.

Lens of Sutton

The small halt at Mill Road (Henham), opened on 18th December 1922, with the hut, removed from Pidley-cum-Fenton siding, as passenger accommodation.

D. Trevor Rowe

J69/1 Class 0-6-0T, No. 68579 pulls into Mill Road Halt with the branch train on 11th September, 1952.

Dr. I. C. Allen

From the junction, the line continued on a straight course climbing at 1 in 50 before entering Mill Road Halt (70 chains from Elsenham), serving the western end of the village of Henham. The platform on the north side of the line consisted of a 25ft. strip of raised clinker with timber facing, 1ft. in height. A small hut, removed from Pidley-cum-Fenton Goods Station on the Somersham to Ramsey East line, served as a waiting-shelter, and a nameboard and two oil lamps completed the layout. On leaving the platform, Mill Road was crossed by an ungated level crossing, protected by

MILL ROAD HALT

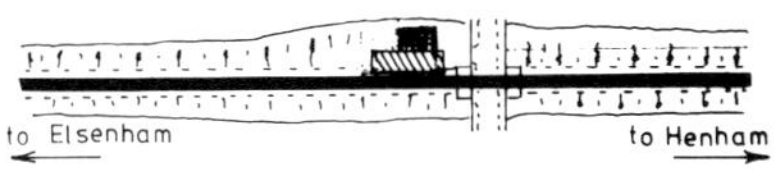

cattle guards, as were all other public road crossings on the branch. A sinuous stretch of line followed, climbing, initially, at 1 in 200 to a short level stretch before falling at 1 in 200 and 1 in 50. After another level section on a 30 chain left-hand curve, the line climbed again at 1 in 50 on a

HENHAM HALT

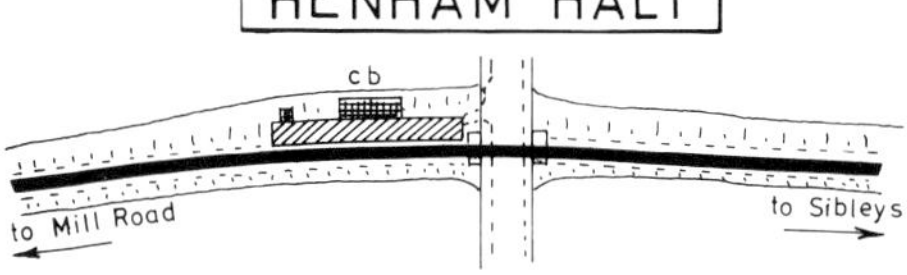

30 chain right-hand curve before entering Henham Halt (1 mile 55 chains from Elsenham), where the accommodation consisted of an old four wheel

A busy time at Henham Halt on 15th August 1936. J69/1 Class, No. 7193, waits for passengers to join the two coach branch train, using the steps provided especially for use at the low halts. This view is facing Elsenham.

T. Middlemas

Henham Halt, 1 mile 55 chains from Elsenham, facing Elsenham. The five compartment, four wheel coach body was added by the GER, to afford passengers shelter from the elements, soon after the line was opened to traffic. The brick-built structure on this remote halt was a gents' toilet.

Lens of Sutton

Henham Halt from the train; a view facing Thaxted. The gate at the end of the platform led to the road to Henham village one half mile to the left, and Woodend Green to the right. On 30th June 1951 the coach body looks the worse for wear.

H. C. Casserley

Class J69/1, No. 68579, stands at Henham Halt on the final day of passenger operation, 13th September 1952. Guard Butt is closing the door of third No. 61471, and the other vehicles are brake thirds, Nos. 62450 and 62461.

J. Watling Collection

coach body. Here, as at Mill Road, the platform, 100 ft. in length on the north side of the line, was of raised clinker and ashes, on which stood the usual two oil lamps and nameboard. The road to Henham village and the hamlet of Woodend Green was crossed immediately on leaving the platform. Continuing the climb at 1 in 50, before easing to 1 in 200, the light railway then entered another straight section on the level, near the 2¼ mile post. The collar work was not over, however, for this was followed by further stretches of 1 in 270, 1 in 50 and 1 in 60 round 20 chain radius right and left-hand curves, to the summit of the line 407 ft. above sea level near the 2¾ mile post. Along this section of line three further ungated level crossings were passed before the line entered Sibley's for Chickney

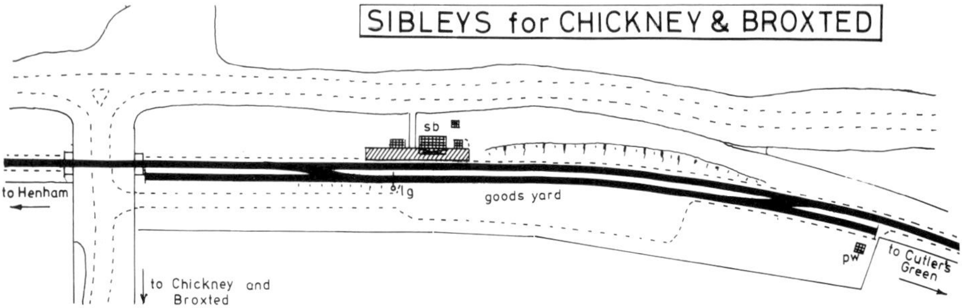

& Broxted Station, 2 miles 76 chains from Elsenham. Traffic for the last-named places was never very remunerative, for the hamlet of Chickney and the village of Broxted were 2 miles and 2½ miles away to the south. Over the last quarter mile before the station the railway ran parallel to the road and was only separated by a wooden fence. Sibley's was the only intermediate station boasting a goods loop, 325 ft. in length, and two short sidings, 155 ft. and 100 ft. long, the points of which were controlled by Hodgson's key which was kept with the train staff. The buildings on the 100 ft. long platform were of wooden construction and included a disused van body, which served as a parcels store. Platform illumination, during the hours of darkness, was provided by two post-mounted and two wall-mounted oil lamps.

Sibley's for Chickney & Broxted Station, viewed from the west, on 1st April 1913, with cattle guards and fencing installed to stop animals trespassing on the track. The goods yard gate is to the right of the picture.

Sibley's (for Chickney & Broxted) Station, facing Thaxted. Note the ornate oil lamps and the point lever released by Hodgson's key which was attached to the train staff. Shunting could be carried out by using a tow rope at this station.

Lens of Sutton

Sibley's (for Chickney & Broxted) Station, 2 miles 76 chains from Elsenham. The platform, of raised clinker and ashes, was 1 ft. high and 100 ft. long. The van body was for storage of parcels, whilst the main building housed the waiting-room and staff accommodation; the station being staffed by one porter. The goods siding loop and yard are in the foreground.

Sibley's (for Chickney & Broxted) Station, from the train, on 30th June 1951. The van body was used for storage of parcels and packages. The hamlet of Chickney and the village of Broxted were, respectively, two miles and two and a half miles south of the railway, and never generated much traffic for the line.

H. C. Casserley

'Buckjumper' 0-6-0T, No. 68579, pauses at Sibley's with an 'up' working, on 13th September 1952, as enthusiasts look out from every vantage point on the train.

D. Trevor Rowe

The line left Sibley's on a 25 chain right-handed curve, falling at 1 in 50 to cross the valley of a small stream. It was in this valley, during World War II, that a line of wagons was dumped to act as an anti-tank line. Once across the culvert the branch continued on a straight course in an easterly direction past the hamlet of Chaureth, or Cherry Green, rising, initially, at 1 in 50 and then falling and rising at 1 in 100 with intermediate level stretches. From the 4¼ mile post the line descended at 1 in 50 to Cutler's

An impeccable Cutler's Green Halt, complete with nameboard, three post oil lamps, a row of fire buckets and a platform seat. The view is taken facing Thaxted, and the rather exposed location, with only a footpath access from Cutler's Green village half a mile to the north, led the GER to later provide a coach body as a passenger waiting-room.

Cutler's Green Halt, in 1913, just after the opening of the line. Note the absence of covered accommodation for passengers. Thc halt had no road access, only a footpath across fields to the village.

British Rail

The remote Cutler's Green Halt, facing Thaxted. The platform, like other stations on the branch, was raised clinker and ashes with timber facing 1 ft. in height and 100 ft. long.

Cutler's Green Halt, facing Elsenham. The coach body was added by the GER, soon after the line opened, to give passengers waiting accommodation.

Lens of Sutton

Cutler's Green Halt, on 30th June 1951, looking towards Elsenham. The halt had no road access and could only be approached by a footpath.

H. C. Casserley

Green Halt, 4 miles 50 chains from Elsenham. The halt had a low platform, 100 ft. in length, with a coach body serving as a waiting-room. Two oil lamps, a row of fire buckets and a nameboard completed the scene.

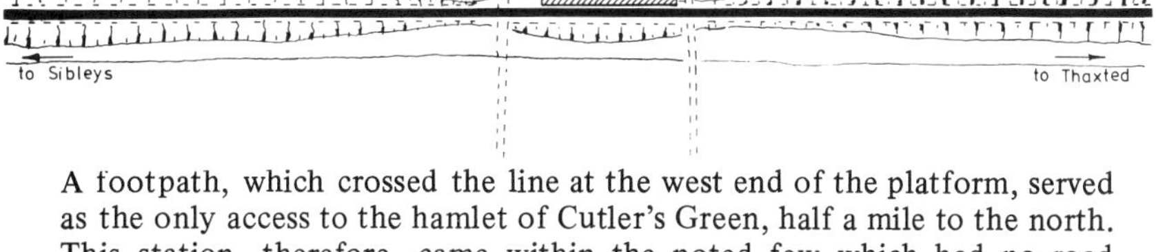

A footpath, which crossed the line at the west end of the platform, served as the only access to the hamlet of Cutler's Green, half a mile to the north. This station, therefore, came within the noted few which had no road access whatsoever. Beyond the halt an occupational crossing was passed as the line descended, initially, at 1 in 180 over Horham Lane underbridge (No. 2452) at 4 miles 70 chains, and then at 1 in 50. A horseshoe bend of 20 chains right-hand, followed by a 10 chain left-hand curve, brought the light railway on a falling gradient of 1 in 260 into the terminus at Thaxted, 5 miles 41 chains from Elsenham.

Thaxted Station soon after opening in 1913.

A view facing the buffer stops, of Thaxted Station buildings in close up. The notice boards retained 'LNER' until the closure of the line.

A close up of Thaxted Station buildings, viewed facing Elsenham, including the old four wheel coach body used as a parcels store. The cattle dock is at a higher level, whilst a 16 ton all-steel open wagon stands in the loading dock.

Thaxted Station. The coach then used as waiting accommodation was a GER four wheel suburban third, dating from 1882–1885. Similar bodies were provided at Henham and Cutler's Green halts.

Lens of Sutton

Thaxted Station, from the train, in 1952. The scene is little changed from the day the line was opened in 1913. The only immediate visible alteration is the LNER notice board showing a British Railways poster.

Thaxted platform, on 30th June 1951, with two of the ex-GER corridor coaches alongside. The lack of passengers is all too evident. For economy reasons the station was located three quarters of a mile away from the town on the opposite side of the Chelmer Valley, a factor which weighed heavily against potential traffic and which led to ultimate closure.

S. C. Nash

Thaxted Station and yard. From left to right are the back goods road, 500 ft. long, goods and coal siding, 390 ft. long, main single line terminating in the locomotive shed, passenger platform loop and loading dock siding. The three ex-GER bogie corridor coaches are at the platform. To the right are the loading and cattle docks.

Thaxted Station, on 30th June 1951, with ex-GER No. E62450 corridor brake third at the platform. Beyond can be seen the locomotive shed and the station exit.

H. C. Casserley

J69/1 Class 0-6-0T, No. 68579 waits at Thaxted with the branch train on 11th September 1952.

Dr. I. C. Allen

Class J68 0-6-0T, No. 8645, departs from Thaxted with a train for Elsenham in 1951. The loading gauge spans the entrance to Thaxted goods yard.

The station had one platform 100 ft. in length on the south side of the line, with a small office building and a van body serving the requirements of the passenger and parcels traffic respectively. At the west end of the platform, raised on a higher level, was the cattle pen and loading dock which served little purpose in the last few years of the line's existence. The passenger station actually stood on the run-round loop with the main line continuing on to terminate in the brick-built engine shed which was large enough to accommodate the branch locomotive. Alongside stood the well house and water tank. Below this was the accommodation for footplate staff. The platform road continued on a rising gradient to form a 60 ft. long siding where a coal wagon was accommodated to facilitate coaling of

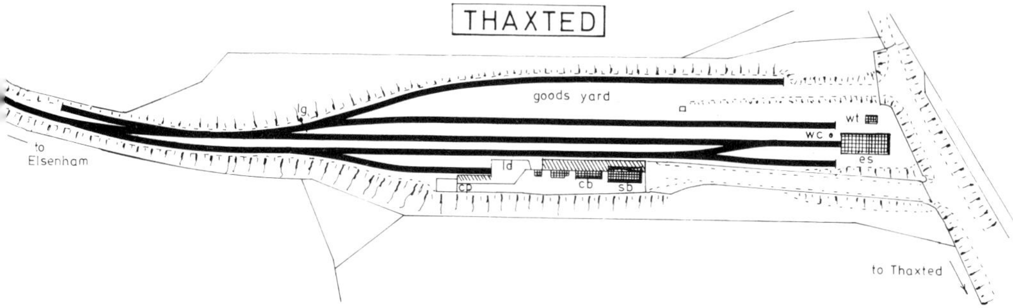

the locomotive. To the north of the main line was the goods yard and its two sidings, 390 ft. and 500 ft. long. Access to the goods yard for road transport was afforded by a gate at the east end of the yard. The points at the terminus were all controlled by Hodgson's key attached to the train staff. The inconvenient site of Thaxted Station, high on a hill almost a mile from the town and at the end of a blind lane, led to considerable loss of traffic.

Thaxted Station, facing the buffer stops. Two of the ex-GER corridor bogie brake thirds stand at the platform on 30th June 1951. Class J69/1, No. 68530, stands by the shed, whilst the goods yard sidings are devoid of traffic; an all too evident feature after World War II.

H. C. Casserley

Elsenham locomotive shed, just large enough to hold an 0-6-0T engine, and adjacent water tower with mess room below. On 30th June 1951 Class J69/1 0-6-0T, No. 68530 is taking water from the crane. The water for locomotives was obtained from the crane, fed from the adjacent tank. The water from the well was pumped into the storage tank by means of a water raising cock fitted to the locomotive, and all engines working the Thaxted branch had to be fitted with this equipment.

H. C. Casserley

The approach road to Thaxted Station, and the locomotive shed and water tower, pictured on 27th March 1937. Two private owner wagons, and a wagon owned by the LNER, stand in the coal siding, whilst locomotive coal supplies were obtained from an LMS 5 plank open wagon. A novel sleeper stop block is provided to stop this wagon from accidently running down the grade into the platform road. Thaxted town was three quarters of a mile from the station, and can be seen on the horizon, beyond the windmill.

There were no signals on the branch, and although mile posts were sited on the 'down' or north side of the line, no gradient posts were erected.

The speed limit was fixed by virtue of Light Railway Standard to 25 m.p.h., although tender locomotives running tender first were limited to 15 m.p.h. The exception to this rule was the stipulated 10 m.p.h. over the five ungated public level crossings, imposed within 200 yards each side of the crossings. A board with a figure 10 painted thereon was erected at such points to call the driver's attention to the limit. The 10 m.p.h. limit was also imposed on curves with a radius of 9 chains or less.

Permanent Way

The original track of the Thaxted Light Railway consisted of second-hand bull head steel rail, weighing 78lb. per yard (originally weighing 85lb. per yard). The rails were laid in lengths of 30ft. in chairs of cast iron weighing 43lb. each, secured to sleepers by two oak trenails and two wrought iron spikes. The fishplates joining the rails weighed 28½ lb. per pair and were secured by 4⅞ in. steel bolts. The rails were laid on sleepers of creosoted timber 8ft. 6in. by 10in. by 5in. Eleven sleepers were placed under each rail length and were laid on ballast of ashes and clinker. The ballast was 1ft. in depth below the track with drainage carried out by side ditches and drain pipes. The width of the formation was 18ft. but was wider at stations.

Soon after the Grouping in 1923 the LNER replaced the existing permanent way with 85 and 90lb. per yard rails in 30ft. lengths. By the outbreak of World War II these rails had been replaced by 45ft. length track, and these remained in use until the closure of the branch. The ashes used for the ballasting of the track were supplied from the various locomotive depots on the GER system, and when supplies were not available wagon loads were obtained from Tate & Lyle's sugar refinery at Silvertown and British Sugar Corporation factories at Felstead and Ely.

The maintenance of the line was covered by a permanent way gang based at Elsenham, initially consisting of 1 ganger and 4 platelayers. After World War II the maintenance was carried out by a gang of three men based at the junction, who as well as working on the branch, spent some time on the main line.

Signalling

ELSENHAM AND THAXTED Light Railway.

Stations and Signal Boxes: Stations.	Signal Boxes.	Telephones shown thus: ●—●	Description of Block System in operation.	Distance from Signal Box next above: Miles.	Chains.	Open: Week-days.	Sundays.	Refuge Sidings: Down.	Up.	Whether Switch provided.	Remarks.
Elsenham	......	●	Staff only.	...	...	Continuously from 2.0 a.m. Mons.	Until 6.0 a.m.	...	...	...	
Henham (Halt)*	......			1	64	For running of trains shown in Working Time Tables, and for trains specially advised.	......	...	...	...	No Signals or Signal Boxes are [illegible], and the distances given are from [illegible]
Sibleys for Chickney and Broxted	......	●		1	20	do.	....	...		...	The special Regulations for working this [illegible] Railway are contained in the Appendix.
Cutlers Green * (Halt)	......			1	55	do.	....	...	...		*Trains call only when required to take up or set down Passengers.
Thaxted	......	●		...	70	do.	... ...	...	...	...	

From GER Working Timetable : 1922

LIST OF SIGNAL BOXES, ADDITIONAL RUNNING LINES, LOOPS AND REFUGE SIDINGS

ELSENHAM AND THAXTED LIGHT RAILWAY

One Engine in Steam	Elsenham Station	...	...	...	...	...	...	..	...	Continuously	
	Mill Rd., Henham (Halt)	1	101	...	...	...	..	..	...	... ...	No signal boxes.
	Henham (Halt)	...	1451	...	...	.	...	...	...	... ...	
	Sibleys for Chickney and Broxted	1	446	...	..	...	...	...	...	... ...	
	Cutlers Green (Halt) ...	1	1211	...	...	...	...	...	...	... ...	
	Thaxted	...	1536	...	...	...	...	...	...	... ...	

K 97

From BR (ER) Working Timetable : 1950

The railway can be counted amongst the very few operating without semaphore signalling, it being worked on the 'train staff without ticket' principle, with one engine in steam or two coupled together. The points leading to and from sidings at Elsenham, Sibley's and Thaxted were normally kept locked and set for the main single line. When shunting was carried out, the Hodgson's patent hand bolt point locks were released by the keys, one, painted red, locking and unlocking the points on the main single line, and the other, painted blue, locking and unlocking the points in the siding leading to the main line. The keys, except when required for use, were kept on the branch locomotive in the custody of the engine driver. The points in the single line near Elsenham Station, dividing the entrance to the goods yard and passenger station, were worked from a ground frame situated in a wooden hut on the south side of the single line, and controlled by Annett's key attached to the train staff.

The train staff, round in shape, painted green and lettered 'Elsenham – Thaxted', was kept, when not in use, in the custody of the foreman in charge at Thaxted Station. At the public level crossing over the Thaxted line leading to the goods yard at Elsenham, the gates across the railway were kept locked, and were only unlocked and opened for the passage of a locomotive or train. A member of the station staff at Elsenham was responsible for opening and shutting the gates and ensuring that the gate lamp was illuminated during the hours of darkness, or during fog or falling snow.

Line No. 97—ELSENHAM TO THAXTED

ELSENHAM AND THAXTED LIGHT RAILWAY

The points in the Single Line near Elsenham Station, dividing the entrance to the Goods Yard and the Passenger Station, are worked from a ground frame, which is controlled by Annett's Key attached to the Train Staff.

The points leading to and from the Single Line at Elsenham, Sibley's and Thaxted Stations are locked by Hodgson's locks, two keys being provided ; one painted red, locks and unlocks the points in the Main Single Line, and the other painted blue, locks and unlocks the points in the siding leading to the Main Single Line. The keys must be kept on the engine in the custody of the Driver, except when required for use.

Where gates are not provided at public road level crossings, aboard with the figure **10** on it is erected 200 yards on each side of the level crossing, and the speed of trains must not exceed **10** miles an hour when approaching within a distance of 200 yards of such level crossings.

Public Road Level Crossings not provided with gates are situated as under :—

Between Elsenham and Henham Halt.

One, provided with cattle guards, about 1 mile from Elsenham.
One, provided with cattle guards, at Henham Halt, about 1¾ miles from Elsenham.

Between Henham Halt and Sibley's Station.

One, provided with cattle guards, about ¼ mile from Henham Halt.
One, provided with cattle guards, about 1 mile from Henham Halt.
One, provided with cattle guards, at Sibley's Station.

At the public level crossing over the line leading to and from the Goods Yard at Elsenham, the gates are to be kept locked across the railway, and must only be unlocked and opened for the passage of a train over the crossing, and after the train has passed over the crossing, the man appointed for the duty must close and relock the gates across the railway. During darkness, or during fog or falling snow, the gate lamp must be lighted and placed on one of the gates at the public road level crossing near Elsenham Goods Yard. During fog or falling snow, a Fogman is to be provided about 200 yards on the Thaxted side of this crossing, and he must place one detonator on the rail, in order to denote to the Enginemen the vicinity of the level crossing.

The engine whistle must be sounded on approaching all public road level crossings.

An engine, train, or vehicle must not be allowed to stand foul of any of the public road level crossings.

Shunting must not be allowed to take place on the Main Single Line at any of the stations unless the Branch engine is at the station.

The use of a tow rope is authorised, when necessary, at Sibley's or Thaxted Station, and is to be carried in the Branch goods brake van for use as required.

An engine or vehicle (loaded or empty) having a greater weight than **16 tons** on any one pair of wheels must not be run on the Light Railway.

In the case of Mixed trains, one passenger vehicle is to be considered equal to one loaded wagon of goods.

During fog or falling snow, the man appointed to work the ground frame near Elsenham Station must place one detonator on the rail about 200 yards on the Thaxted side of the ground frame, for each approaching train.

Passenger train vehicles in use on the Light Railway are not to be allowed to come on to the Main Line at Elsenham Station unless the footboards of the vehicles have been removed.

Instructions for operating the branch.
LNER Appendix : 1947

During foggy weather, or falling snow, a fogman (platelayer) was positioned 200 yards on the Thaxted side of the level crossing, and instructed to place two detonators on the rail, 10 yards apart, to warn enginemen of the vicinity of the crossing. In these adverse weather conditions, it was also a requirement for the man appointed to work the ground frame near Elsenham to place two detonators on the rail, 200 yards on the Thaxted side of the ground frame, for each approaching train. Likewise, at Thaxted, the foreman in charge was instructed to place two detonators on the line 200 yards in advance of the terminus.

CHAPTER FOUR — Timetables and Traffic

Although the Thaxted Light Railway was built essentially to provide cheap and speedy transport for agricultural products, the GER provided a service of between three and seven passenger trains per day, during the 39 years the branch was open. The passenger service did little to attract an increase in the population as the figures below show, and the London commuter traffic arrived too late to make any impression.

Population	*1901*	*1911*	*1921*	*1931*	*1951*	*1961*
Elsenham	453	422	408	382	598	832
Henham	700	741	726	695	750	729
Chickney	20	32	33	37	31	32
Broxted	531	548	516	479	507	510
Thaxted	1,659	1,672	1,596	1,610	1,837	1,905
Total:	*3,363*	*3,415*	*3,279*	*3,203*	*3,723*	*4,008*

Light railway train services were noted for their infrequency and slowness, and the Thaxted line was no exception with the majority running as mixed trains, the 5½ mile journey occupying between 22 and 28 minutes. The initial weekday service announced by the GER, commencing on 1st April 1913, consisted of four 'up' and five 'down' trains with departures from Thaxted at 8.08a.m., 11.38a.m., 2.03p.m. mixed, and 5.06p.m.; and from Elsenham at 9.20a.m. mixed, 12.25p.m. mixed (Saturdays excepted), 12.33p.m. (Saturdays only), 3.00p.m., 5.40p.m. and 7.20p.m. The railway brought Thaxted within almost 1½ hours journey time of London. Passengers departing on the 8.08a.m. from Thaxted could arrive at Liverpool Street 1 hour 32 minutes later, with a return on the 4.30p.m. from Liverpool Street in a slightly faster time of 1 hour 31 minutes, both being accomplished by changing at Elsenham only. All trains were shown booked to stop, only if required, at Henham and Cutler's Green halts, on signal being given to the driver for passengers joining trains, and notice being given to the guard for those alighting.

By July 1915, the service was increased by one train in each direction with Thaxted departures at 8.15a.m., 11.02a.m., 12.09p.m., 2.17p.m. (Saturdays only), 2.28p.m. (Saturdays excepted) mixed, and 5.00p.m. 'Down' trains from Elsenham departed at 9.25a.m. mixed, 10.42a.m., 12.48p.m. mixed, 3.20p.m., 6.20p.m., and 8.07p.m. mixed. The balanced 'up' working was utilized by the daily goods train from Thaxted to Elsenham yard. In the May 1916 timetable the same number of trains ran in each direction with slight alteration in timings. Freight traffic from Thaxted was conveyed by the 2.11 p.m. (Saturdays only), or 2.28 p.m. (Saturdays excepted) mixed trains and the 6.50 p.m. goods, whilst in the 'down' direction three mixed trains at 9.05 a.m., 12.48 p.m., and 8.07 p.m. were considered sufficient to handle inward commodities. In addition, the 8.13 a.m. Thaxted to Elsenham passenger train was permitted to work one truck of cattle on Tuesdays and Thursdays if the truck was fitted with the Westinghouse brake.

The notice published in the Great Eastern Railway Public Timetable was evidence of the railway situation through World War I.

> 'During the continuance of the war, the train service is liable to be altered or cancelled without prior notice and the Great Eastern Railway Company hereby give notice that it will not be responsible for any loss damage or delay in consequence thereof.'

By January 1917, the weekday service consisted of four passenger, one mixed and one goods train in the 'up' direction, with departures from Thaxted at 8.13 a.m., 10.20 a.m., 12.02 p.m., 1.50 p.m. (Saturdays excepted), 2.08 p.m. (Saturdays only) and 5.40 p.m. The goods departed at 7.02 p.m., and with 10 minutes permitted for shunting at Sibley's, was allowed 37 minutes to Elsenham. 'Down' departures from the junction were 9.05 a.m., 11.00 a.m., 12.50 p.m., 2.32 p.m. (Saturdays excepted), 2.50 p.m. (Saturdays only), 6.32 p.m. and 8.00 p.m.

ELSENHAM AND THAXTED LIGHT RAILWAY.

Single Line.

Worked by Train Staff, without tickets. For regulations for working this Light Railway see Special Instruction No. 1045.

DOWN WEEK DAYS.

Miles from Elsenham M. C.	Station		1	2	3	4	5	6	7	8
			Mxd.	Pass.	Mxd.	Pass. NS	Pass. SO	Pass.	Pass.	Mxd.
			a.m.	a.m.	p.m.	p.m.	p.m.	p.m.	p.m.	p.m.
— —	Elsenham (S)	dep.	9 5	11 25	12 50	2 32	2 50	4 23	7 2	8 30
1 55	Henham Halt ...	„	*	*	*	*	*	*	*	*
2 76	Sibleys	arr.	9 17	11 36	1 2	2 43	3 1	4 34	7 13	8 42
		dep.	9 22	11 37	1 7	2 44	3 2	4 35	7 14	8 47
4 50	Cutlers'Grn.Halt ..		*	*	*	*	*	*	*	*
5 41	Thaxted (S)	arr.	9 32	11 46	1 17	2 53	3 11	4 44	7 23	8 57

UP WEEK DAYS.

Station		1	2	3	4	5	6	7	8
		Pass.	Pass.	Pass.	Mxd. NS	Mxd. SO	Pass.	Pass.	Gds.
		a.m.	a.m.	p.m.	p.m.	p.m.	p.m.	p.m.	p.m.
Thaxted .... (S)	dep.	8 10	10 46	12 2	1 50	2 8	3 47	5 55	7 32
Cutlers' Green Halt ...	„	*	*	*	*	*	*	*	—
Sibleys	arr.	8 20	10 56	12 12	2 0	2 18	3 57	6 5	7 44
	dep.	8 21	10 57	12 13	2 5	2 23	3 58	6 6	7 54
Henham Halt	„	*	*	*	*	*	*	*	....
Elsenham ...... (S)	arr.	8 33	11 9	12 25	2 17	2 35	4 10	6 18	8 9

=1 May work one truck of cattle to Elsenham on Tuesdays and Thursdays if the truck is fitted with Westinghouse brake pipes.

GER Working Timetable : 1920

ELSENHAM AND THAXTED LIGHT RAILWAY.

Single Line.

Worked by Train Staff, without tickets. For regulations for working this Light Railway see Special Instruction No. 1045.

DOWN WEEK DAYS.

Miles from Elsenham M. C.	Station		1	2	3	4	5	6	7	8	9
			Gds.	Mxd.	Pass.	Mxd.	Pass. NS	Pass. SO	Pass.	Pass.	Pass.
			a.m.	a.m.	a.m.	p.m.	p.m.	p.m.	p.m.	p.m.	p.m.
— —	Elsenham (S)	dep.	7 25	9 5	11 25	12 50	2 32	2 50	4 25	5 55	7 40
1 55	Henham Halt ...	„	.....	*	*	*	*	*	*	*	*
2 76	Sibleys	arr.	—	9 17	11 36	1 2	2 43	3 1	4 36	6 6	7 51
		dep.	.....	9 22	11 37	1 7	2 44	3 2	4 37	6 7	7 52
4 50	Cutlers'Grn.Halt	„	—	*	*	*	*	*	*	*	*
5 41	Thaxted (S)	arr.	7 50	9 32	11 46	1 17	2 53	3 11	4 46	6 16	8 1

1 To work Thaxted traffic only.

UP WEEK DAYS.

Station		1	2	3	4	5	6	7	8	9
		Gds.	Pass.	Mxd.	Pass.	Mxd. NS	Mxd. SO	Pass.	Pass.	Gds.
		a.m.	a.m.	a.m.	p.m.	p.m.	p.m.	p.m.	p.m.	p.m.
Thaxted .... (S)	dep.	5 50	8 10	10 40	12 12	1 50	2 5	3 47	5 20	6 35
Cutlers' Green Halt ...	„	.....	*	*	*	*	*	*	*	—
Sibleys	arr.	—	8 20	10 50	12 22	2 0	2 15	3 57	5 30	6 4[illegible]
	dep.	.....	8 21	10 57	12 23	2 5	2 20	3 58	5 31	6 5[illegible]
Henham Halt	„	—	*	*	*	*	*	*	*	....
Elsenham ...... (S)	arr.	6 27	8 33	11 9	12 35	2 17	2 32	4 10	5 43	7 12

1 To work coal empties and unimportant down road traffic, to go forward on 4.10 a.m. ex Temple Mills. Engine to perform station shunting at Elsenham.

=2 May work one truck of cattle to Elsenham on Tuesdays and Thursdays if the truck is fitted with Westinghouse brake pipes.

=8 To convey down road break goods to go forward on 6.10 p.m. goods ex Bishop's Stortford.

9 Not to work coal empties from Thaxted.

GER Working Timetable : 1921

E[illegible]SE[illegible]AM AND THAXTED
[illegible]GHT RAILWAY.

Singlo Line.

Work[illegible]d by T[illegible]in Staff, without tickets. For rogulations for working t[illegible]s Light Railway see Special Instruction No. 1045.

Miles from Els[illegible]	[illegible]OWN [illegible]EK DAYS.		1	2	3	4	5	6	7	8	9
			Gds.	Mxd.	Pass.	Mxd.	Pass.	Pass.	Pass.	Pass.	Pass.
							NS	SO			
M. C.			a.m.	a.m.	a.m.	p.m.	p.m.	p.m.	p.m.	p.m.	p.m.
— —	E[illegible]ham	dep.	7 25	9 5	11 25	12 50	2 32	2 50	4 25	5 55	7 3[illegible]
1 55	H[illegible]n Halt	„	.....	*	*	*	*	*	*	*	*
2 76	Si[illegible]	arr.	—	9 17	11 36	1 2	2 43	3 1	4 36	6 6	7 4[illegible]
		dep.	.....	9 22	11 37	1 7	2 44	3 2	4 37	6 7	7 5[illegible]
4 50	Cu[illegible]Grn.Halt	„	—	*	*	*	*	*	*	*	*
5 41	T[illegible]d	arr.	7 50	9 32	11 46	1 17	2 53	3 11	4 46	6 16	7 [illegible]

1 To w[illegible] Thaxted traffic only.
[illegible] From 2[illegible]h July to 16th September inclusive, to start at 2 58 p.m. [illegible]d run 8 minutes later.

[illegible] WE[illegible] DAY[illegible].		1	2	3	4	5	6	7	8	9
		Gds.	Pass.	Mxd.	Pass.	Mxd.	Mxd.	Pass.	Pass.	Gd[illegible]
						NS	SO			
		a.m.	a.m.	a.m.	p.m.	p.m.	p.m.	p.m.	p.m.	p.m.
Thaxted	dep.	5 50	8 10	10 40	12 12	1 50	2 5	3 47	5 20	6 [illegible]
Cutlers' [illegible]n Halt	„	.....	*	*	*	*	*	*	*	—
Sibleys	arr.	—	8 20	10 50	12 22	2 0	2 15	3 57	5 30	6 [illegible]
	dep.	.....	8 21	10 57	12 23	2 5	2 20	3 59	5 31	6 [illegible]
Henham [illegible]	„	—	*	*	*	*	*	*	*	....
Elsenh[illegible]	arr.	6 20	8 33	11 9	12 35	2 17	2 32	4 10	5 43	7 [illegible]

1 To w[illegible] coal empties and unimportant down road traffic, to go forward [illegible] 4.10 a.m. ex Temple Mills. Engine to perform station shunting [illegible] Elsenham.
[illegible] May wor[illegible] one truck of cattle to Elsenham on Tuesdays and Thu[illegible]s if the [illegible] is fitted with Westinghouse brake pipes.

GER Working Timetable : 1922

ELSENHAM AND THAXTED LIGHT RAILWAY.

Single Line.

Worked by Train Staff, without tickets. For regulations for working this Light Railway see Special Instruction No. 1045.

Miles from Elsenham.	DOWN WEEK DAYS.		1	2	3	4	5	6	7	8	9	10
			Gds.	Mxd.	Pass.	Mxd.	Pass.	Pass.		Pass.	Pass.	Pass.
							NS	SO				
M. C.			a.m.	a.m.	a.m.	p.m.	p.m.	p.m.		p.m.	p.m.	p.m.
— —	**Elsenham**	dep.	7 25	9 5	11 25	12 50	2 32	2 50	.....	4 25	5 55	7 38
— 70	Mill Road Halt	„	—	9 9	11 29	12 54	2 36	2 54	—	4 29	5 59	7 42
1 55	Henham Halt ...	„	.....	9 13	11 33	12 58	2 40	2 58	.....	4 33	6 3	7 46
2 76	Sibleys	arr.	—	9 18	11 37	1 3	2 44	3 2	—	4 37	6 7	7 50
		dep.	.....	9 23	11 38	1 8	2 45	3 3	.....	4 38	6 8	7 51
4 50	Cutlers'Grn.Halt	„	—	9 29	11 43	1 14	2 50	3 8	—	4 43	6 13	7 56
5 41	**Thaxted**	arr.	7 50	9 33	11 47	1 18	2 54	3 12	.....	4 47	6 17	8 0

1 To work Thaxted traffic only.

UP WEEK DAYS.		1	2	3	4	5	6	7	8	9	10
		Gds.	Pass.	Mxd.	Pass.	Mxd.	Mxd.	Pass.	Pass.	Mxd.	
						NS	SO				
		a.m.	a.m.	a.m.	p.m.	p.m.	p.m.	p.m.	p.m.	p.m.	
Thaxted	dep.	5 50	8 10	10 40	12 10	1 50	2 5	3 47	5 20	6 27	—
Cutlers' Green Halt ...	„	.....	8 14	10 44	12 14	1 54	2 9	3 51	5 24	6 31	.....
Sibleys	arr.	—	8 20	10 50	12 20	2 0	2 15	3 57	5 30	6 37	—
	dep.	.....	8 21	10 57	12 21	2 5	2 20	3 58	5 31	6 49	.....
Henham Halt	„	—	8 26	11 2	12 26	2 10	2 25	4 3	5 36	6 54	—
Mill Road Halt	„	.....	8 30	11 6	12 30	2 14	2 29	4 7	5 40	6 58	.....
Elsenham	arr.	6 20	8 34	11 10	12 34	2 18	2 33	4 11	5 44	7 4	—

1 To work coal empties and unimportant down road traffic. Engine to perform station shunting at Elsenham.
–2 May work one truck of cattle to Elsenham on Tuesdays and Thursdays if the truck is fitted with Westinghouse brake pipes.
–8 To convey down road brake goods to go forward on 6.10 p.m. goods ex Bishop's Stortford.
9 Not to work coal empties from Thaxted.

LNER Working Timetable for the branch : 1924

The end of hostilities brought about an easing of the service offered by the GER and by March 1920 the working timetable showed an increase to seven trains in each direction. The 'up' service from Thaxted consisted of 5 passenger, 1 mixed and 1 goods train each weekday, with departures at 8.10a.m., 10.46a.m., 12.02p.m., 1.50p.m. (Saturdays excepted), 2.00p.m. (Saturdays only), 3.47p.m., 5.55p.m. and 7.32p.m. goods. In the 'down' direction 4 passenger and 3 mixed trains departed Elsenham at 9.05a.m. mixed, 11.25a.m., 12.50p.m. mixed, 2.23p.m. (Saturdays excepted), 2.50p.m. (Saturdays only), 4.23p.m., 7.02p.m. and 8.30p.m. mixed. Passenger trains were allowed 23 minutes for the 5½ mile journey, mixed trains 27 minutes with 5 minutes allowed for shunting at Sibley's, and goods trains 37 minutes with 10 minutes allowed for shunting at Sibley's.

When the LNER took over the light railway from 1st January 1923, the new authority found the service of seven trains in each direction adequate. The July 1924 passenger timetable showed Thaxted departures at 8.10a.m., 10.40a.m., 12.10p.m., 1.50p.m. (Saturdays excepted), 2.05p.m. (Saturdays only), 3.47p.m., 5.20p.m. and 6.27p.m. Elsenham departures had changed little from the previous years except for an earlier last train in the evening. Trains departed at 9.05a.m., 11.25a.m., 12.50p.m., 2.32p.m. (Saturdays excepted), 2.50p.m. (Saturdays only), 4.25p.m., 5.55p.m. and 7.38p.m. Four years later the September 1928 timetable showed exactly the same services, except that the 6.27p.m. ran as a mixed train Mondays and Fridays, and passengers only on Saturdays.

As a result of the 1926 coal strike, passenger train services were reduced and, from 31st May, only the following trains ran: Elsenham to Thaxted; 9.10a.m., 11.25a.m., 12.50p.m., (Saturdays only), 2.50p.m. (Saturdays only), and 7.39p.m. Thaxted to Elsenham; 8.10a.m., 10.40a.m., 12.10p.m., (Saturdays only), 2.05p.m., (Saturdays only) and 6.27p.m. During the later General Strike, services were withdrawn.

The timetable from 1st October 1934 continued to show 7 trains in each direction along the branch. Passenger trains by now were allowed 24 minutes for the 5½ mile journey whilst mixed trains were allowed 40 minutes. Mixed trains departed Thaxted at 10.40a.m. and 6.27p.m. (Saturdays excepted), and Elsenham at 11.24a.m. All others ran as passenger services. The fastest 'down' timing from London to Thaxted was 1 hour 30 minutes by the 1.19p.m. (Saturdays only) and 6.30p.m. from Liverpool Street, whilst the fastest 'up' journey was 1 hour 35 minutes by the 8.10a.m. from Thaxted, all journeys accomplished by one change of train at Elsenham.

ELSENHAM AND THAXTED LIGHT RAILWAY.

Single Line.

Worked by Train Staff, without tickets. For regulations for working this Light Railway see Appendix.

Miles from Elsenham (M.)	(C.)	DOWN WEEK DAYS.		1	2	3	4	5	6	7	8	9	10
				Gds.	Mxd.	Pass.	Mxd.	Pass. NS	Pass. SO		Pass.	Pass. •	Pass.
				a.m.	a.m.	a.m.	p.m.	p.m.	p.m.		p.m.	p.m.	p.m.
—	—	**Elsenham** Ⓢ	dep.	7 25	9 19	11 25	12 50	2 32	2 50	.....	4 25	5 55	7 38
—	70	Mill Road Halt	„	—	9 23	11 29	12 54	2 36	2 54	—	4 29	5 59	7 42
1	55	Henham Halt ...	„	.....	9 27	11 33	12 58	2 40	2 58	.....	4 33	6 3	7 46
2	76	Sibleys	arr.	—	9 32	11 37	1 3	2 44	3 2	—	4 37	6 7	7 50
			dep.	.....	9 37	11 38	1 8	2 45	3 3	.....	4 38	6 8	7 51
4	50	Cutlers'Grn.Halt	„	—	9 43	11 43	1 14	2 50	3 8	—	4 43	6 13	7 56
5	41	**Thaxted** Ⓢ	arr.	7 50	9 47	11 47	1 18	2 54	3 12	.....	4 47	6 17	8 0

1 To work Thaxted traffic only.

UP WEEK DAYS.		1	2	3	4	5	6	7	8	9	10
		Gds.	Pass.	Mxd.	Pass.	Mxd. NS	Mxd. SO	Pass.	Pass.	Mxd. SO	Mxd. NS
		a.m.	a.m.	a.m.	p.m.	p.m.	p.m.	p.m.	p.m.	p.m.	p.m.
Thaxted .... Ⓢ	dep.	5 50	8 10	10 40	12 10	1 50	2 5	3 47	5 20	6 27	6 27
Cutlers' Green Halt ...	„	.....	8 14	10 44	12 14	1 54	2 9	3 51	5 24	6 31	6 31
Sibleys	arr.	—	8 20	10 50	12 20	2 0	2 15	3 57	5 30	6 37	6 37
	dep.	.....	8 21	10 57	12 21	2 5	2 20	3 58	5 31	6 38	6 49
Henham Halt	„	—	8 26	11 2	12 26	2 10	2 25	4 3	5 36	6 43	6 54
Mill Road Halt	„	.....	8 30	11 6	12 30	2 14	2 29	4 7	5 40	6 47	6 58
Elsenham Ⓢ	arr.	6 20	8 34	11 10	12 34	2 18	2 33	4 11	5 44	6 53	7 4

1 To work coal empties and unimportant down road traffic. Engine to perform station shunting at Elsenham.

=2 May work one truck of cattle to Elsenham on Tuesdays and Thursdays if the truck is fitted with Westinghouse brake pipes.

=8 To convey down road brake goods to go forward on 6.5 p.m. goods ex Bishop's Stortford.

=9 and 10 Not to work coal empties from Thaxted.

LNER Working Timetable : 1928

ELSENHAM AND THAXTED LIGHT RAILWAY.

SINGLE LINE.

Worked by Train Staff without tickets. For regulations for working this Light Railway see "Appendix."

Miles from Elsenham (M.)	(C.)	DOWN WEEK DAYS.		1	2	3	4	5	6
						Gds			
						p.m.			
—	—	**Elsenham** .... Ⓢ	dep.	.....	.....	1 30	.....	.....	.....
2	76	Sibleys	arr.	—	—	*	—	—	—
			dep.	.....	.....		.....	.....	.....
5	41	**Thaxted** ...... Ⓢ	arr.	—	—	2 0	—	—	—

3 Engine to work 2.52 p.m. (SO) 3.57 p.m. (SX) Thaxted to Elsenham.

UP WEEK DAYS.		1	2	3	4	5	6	7
				Gds.				
				a.m.				
Thaxted ...... Ⓢ	dep.	.....	.....	9 25	.....	.....	.....	.....
Sibleys	arr.	—	—	*	—	—	--	—
	dep.	.....	.....	—	.....	.....	.....	.....
Elsenham ... Ⓢ	arr.	—	—	9 50	—	—	—	—

3 Engine to perform shunting at Elsenham and work trip to Bishop's Stortford with Braintree branch traffic as necessary.

LNER Freight Working Timetable : 1944

The summer 1939 timetable showed Thaxted departures at 6a.m. goods, 8.15a.m., 12.13p.m. (Saturdays excepted), 12.17p.m. (Saturdays only) mixed, 1.45p.m. mixed, 3.25p.m., 5.19p.m., 6.23p.m. (Saturdays only) mixed and 6.34p.m. (Saturdays excepted) mixed. The morning goods also conveyed coal empties and unimportant goods traffic, with the engine later performing shunting duties at Elsenham, whilst the 8.15a.m. passenger departure was allowed to work one wagon of cattle to Elsenham on Tuesdays and Thursdays. The last mixed train of the day was prohibited from working coal empties from Thaxted. In the 'down' direction, departures from Elsenham were at 7.38a.m. goods, 9.19a.m. mixed, 12.50p.m. (Saturdays excepted) mixed, 12.55p.m. (Saturdays only) mixed, 2.24p.m. (Saturdays only) or 2.26p.m. (Saturdays excepted) mixed, 4.23p.m., 5.53p.m. and 7.34p.m. The 7.38a.m. goods also worked Thaxted parcels traffic and newspapers off the 5.56a.m. from Liverpool Street, whilst the 2.26p.m. mixed, if required to shunt at Sibley's, was allowed an extra 11 minutes on the journey, giving an arrival time at Thaxted of 3.10p.m.

J67/2 Class 0-6-0T, No. 68609, leaves Cutler's Green Halt with the 4p.m. Thaxted to Elsenham train on 18th August 1951.

J. F. Aylard

J67/2 Class 0-6-0T, No. 68609, hauls the 1.43p.m. (SO) train from Elsenham to Thaxted, between Henham and Sibley's, on 18th August 1951. The switchback nature of the line can be seen to the left of the picture where the gradient alters sharply.

J. F. Aylard

The two coach 11.50a.m. Thaxted to Elsenham train, hauled by J67/2 Class 0-6-0T, No. 68609, drifts down the 1 in 50 gradient towards Elsenham on 18th August 1951.
J. F. Aylard

J69/1 Class 0-6-0T, No. 68530, slows for Henham Halt with the 4p.m. Thaxted to Elsenham train on 6th August 1951. The second coach is on the ungated level crossing.
J. F. Aylard

When World War II was but a few months old, the service was cut back drastically, with the 1940 passenger timetable showing only two mixed trains in each direction. Compared with earlier years the fastest journey to and from London was taking 1 hour 42 minutes on the 7.41 a.m. from Thaxted and 3.55p.m. from Liverpool Street. By October 1942, the service reverted to three trains in each direction, with departures from Thaxted at 7.42a.m., 2.52p.m. (Saturdays only), 3.57p.m. (Saturdays excepted and 5.25p.m. Elsenham departures were 8.45a.m., 5.05p.m., 7.45p.m. (Saturdays excepted) and 7.55p.m. (Saturdays only). All ran as mixed trains with timings varying from 21 to 23 minutes for the 5½ mile journey. These continued until 1945.

ELSENHAM AND THAXTED LIGHT RAILWAY

Single Line.

Worked by Train Staff without ticket. For regulations for working see "Appendix"

DOWN **WEEKDAYS**

Miles from Elsenham M. C.	No.	2	4	6	8	10
	Description	Mxd	Mxd	Mxd	Mxd	Mxd
	Class					
			SO	SX		
		am	PM	PM	PM	PM
	Elsenham (S)	8 45	1 57	2 32	5 5	7 45
70	Mill Road Halt	8 49	2 1	2 35	5 9	7 49
1 55	Henham Halt	8 53	2 5	2 40	5 13	7 53
2 76	Sibley's	8 58	2 10	2 45	5 18	7 58
	Sibley's	8 59	2 11	2 46	5 19	7 59
4 50	Cutler's Green Halt	9 5	2 17	2 52	5 25	8 5
5 41	**Thaxted** (S)	9 8	2 20	2 55	5 28	8 8

Passenger trains are worked on the " **Conductor-Guard** " principle.

Sec K

ELSENHAM AND THAXTED LIGHT RAILWAY

Single Line.

Worked by Train Staff without tickets. For regulations for working see "Appendix"

WEEKDAYS **UP**

Miles from Thaxted M. C.	No.	3	5	7	10	13
	Description	Mxd	Mxd	Mxd	Mxd	Mxd
	Class					
				SO	SX	
		am	am	PM	PM	PM
	Thaxted (S)	7 41	10 0	2 52	3 57	5 50
71	Cutler's Green Halt	7 45	10 4	2 56	4 1	5 54
2 45	Sibley's	7 51	10 10	3 2	4 7	5 59
	Sibley's	7 52	10 11	3 4	4 8	6 5
3 66	Henham Halt	7 57	10 16	3 9	4 13	6 10
4 51	Mill Road Halt	8 1	10 20	3 13	4 17	6 14
5 41	**Elsenham** (S)	8 5	10 24	3 17	4 21	6 19

Passenger trains are worked on the " **Conductor-Guard** " principle.

LNER Working Timetable : May 1946

ELSENHAM AND THAXTED LIGHT RAILWAY

Single Line.

Worked by Train Staff without ticket. For regulations for working see "Appendix"

DOWN **WEEKDAYS**

Miles from Elsenham M. C.	No.	2	3	4	6	8	10	12
	Description	Mxd	E & V	Mxd	Mxd	Mxd	Mxd	Mxd
	Class							
				SO	SX		SX	
		am	am	PM	PM	PM	PM	PM
	Elsenham (S)	8 35	*11 20*	1 55	2 28	5 0	6 42	7 55
70	Mill Road Halt	8 39		1 59	2 32	5 4	6 46	7 59
1 55	Henham Halt	8 43		2 3	2 36	5 8	6 50	8 3
2 76	Sibley's	8 48		2 8	2 41	5 13	6 55	8 8
	Sibley's	8 49		2 9	2 42	5 14	6 56	8 9
4 50	Cutler's Green Halt	8 55		2 15	2 48	5 20	7 2	8 15
5 41	**Thaxted** (S)	8 58	*11 40*	2 18	2 51	5 23	7 5	8 18

Passenger trains are worked on the " **Conductor-Guard** " principle

Sec K

ELSENHAM AND THAXTED LIGHT RAILWAY

Single Line.

Worked by Train Staff without tickets. For regulations for working see "Appendix"

WEEKDAYS **UP**

Miles from Thaxted M. C.	No.	3	5	7	10	12	14
	Description	Mxd	Mxd	Mxd	Mxd	Mxd	Mxd
	Class						
							SX
		am	am	am	PM	PM	PM
	Thaxted (S)	7 36	10 0	11 50	4 0	5 50	7 23
71	Cutler's Green Halt	7 40	10 4	11 54	4 4	5 54	7 27
2 45	Sibley's	7 46	10 10	12 0	4 10	6 0	7 33
	Sibley's	7 47	10 11	12 5	4 11	6 5	7 34
3 66	Henham Halt	7 52	10 16	12 10	4 16	6 10	7 39
4 51	Mill Road Halt	7 56	10 20	12 14	4 20	6 14	7 43
5 41	**Elsenham** (S)	8 0	10 24	12 18	4 24	6 19	7 48

7 To Stansted arr. 1.0 p.m.

Passenger trains are worked on the " **Conductor-Guard** " principle.

Final LNER Working Timetable : October 1947

The lengthy span of time between the morning and early afternoon service did nothing to attract passengers to the railway, and the LNER made little attempt to restore services to their pre-war level. In 1946 the service was increased to four trains in each direction, with the additional 'up' train departing Thaxted 10a.m. and the 'down' train departing Elsenham at 1.57p.m. (Saturdays only), 2.32p.m. (Saturdays excepted), filling a much needed gap in the frequency. British Railways, however, did increase it in 1948 with five trains in each direction available to passengers. Contrary to expectation, services were not reduced as a result of the fuel crisis in March 1951. The final working timetable in 1952 showed six 'up' and five 'down' trains on Mondays to Fridays, and one less in each direction on Saturdays, with departures from Thaxted at 7.36a.m., 9.55 a.m., 11.50a.m., 4.00p.m., 5.45p.m. (Saturdays excepted), 6.00p.m. (Saturdays only) and 7.23p.m. (Saturdays excepted), and from Elsenham at 8.55a.m., 11.a.m. (goods), 1.43p.m. (Saturdays only), 2.28p.m. (Saturdays excepted), 5p.m., 6.24p.m. (Saturdays excepted) and 7.55 p.m. The 11.50a.m., 5.45p.m. (Saturdays excepted) and 6p.m. (Saturdays only) in the 'up' direction and the 8.55a.m. 'down' ran as mixed trains, and were allowed 5 or 6 minutes to shunt at Sibley's. The fastest journey time from London to Thaxted was now 1 hour 27 minutes on the 3.56p.m. from Liverpool Street which connected with the 5p.m. from Elsenham.

PASSENGER POINT-TO-POINT RUNNING TIMES

From	To	Distance M. C.	Pass to Pass	Pass to Stop	Start to Pass	Start to Stop	Remarks
ELSENHAM TO THAXTED (Single Line) (Mixed Trains)							
Elsenham (S)	Mill Rd. Halt	0 70	—	—	—	3	Worked on Conductor guard principle.
Mill Rd. Halt ..	Henham Halt	0 65	—	—	—	3	
Henham Halt	Sibleys ..	1 21	—	—	—	5	
Sibleys ..	Cutlers Gn.H.	1 54	—	—	—	5	
Cutlers Gn. H.	Thaxted (S)	0 71	—	—	—	3	
THAXTED TO ELSENHAM							
Thaxted (S)	Cutlers Gn.H.	0 71	—	—	—	3	Worked on Conductor guard principle.
Cutlers Gn. H.	Sibleys ..	1 54	—	—	—	6	
Sibleys ..	Henham Halt	1 21	—	—	—	4	
Henham Halt	Mill Rd. Halt	0 65	—	—	—	3	
Mill Rd. Halt ..	Elsenham (S)	0 70	—	—	—	4	

LNER point to point timings for passenger trains.

In the years before the advent of the railway to Thaxted, local people were reliant on local carriers for conveyance of their produce and goods to and from market. By 1906, George Coe was operating from Newbiggin Street every Thursday to White Lion Street, Bishopsgate, returning from London on Saturday. William Rogers took his waggon to Elsenham Station daily from the town at 7.40a.m. and 4.30p.m., whilst Dunmow was served by George Tyrell on Tuesdays, Thursdays and Saturdays.

ELSENHAM AND THAXTED LIGHT RAILWAY

Single Line.

Worked by Train Staff without ticket. For regulations for working see "Appendix"

DOWN WEEKDAYS

Miles from Elsenham	No.	1	2	3	4	5	6	7	8	9	10	11	12	13	14	15
	Class		B	K	B		B		B		B		B			
	Description		Mxd		Mxd		Mxd		Mxd		Mxd		Mxd			
					SO		SX				SX					
M. C.			am	am	PM		PM		PM		PM		PM			
	Elsenham (S)		8 55	11 0	1 43		2 28		5 0		6 24		7 55			
70	Mill Road Halt		8 59		1 47		2 32		5 4		6 28		7 59			
1 55	Henham Halt		9 3		1 51		2 36		5 8		6 32		8 3			
2 76	Sibley's		9 8		1 56		2 41		5 13		6 37		8 8			
	Sibley's		9 14		1 57		2 42		5 14		6 38		8 9			
4 50	Cutler's Green Halt		9 20		2 3		2 48		5 20		6 44		8 15			
5 41	Thaxted (S)		9 23	11 20	2 6		2 51		5 23		6 47		8 18			

Passenger trains are worked on the " Conductor-Guard " principle

ELSENHAM AND THAXTED LIGHT RAILWAY

Single Line.

Worked by Train Staff without tickets. For regulations for working see "Appendix"

WEEKDAYS **UP**

Miles from Thaxted	No.	1	2	3	4	5	6	7	8	9	10	11	12	13	14	15
	Class			B		B		B			B	B	B		B	
	Description			Mxd		Mxd		Mxd			Mxd	Mxd	Mxd		Mxd	
												SX	SO		SX	
M. C.				am		am		am			PM	PM	PM		PM	
	Thaxted (S)			7 36		9 55		11 50			4 0	5 45	6 0		7 23	
71	Cutler's Green Halt			7 40		9 59		11 54			4 4	5 49	6 4		7 27	
2 45	Sibley's			7 46		10 5		12 0			4 10	5 55	6 10		7 33	
	Sibley's			7 47		10 6		12 5			4 11	6 0	6 15		7 34	
3 66	Henham Halt			7 52		10 11		12 10			4 16	6 5	6 20		7 39	
4 51	Mill Road Halt			7 56		10 15		12 14			4 20	6 9	6 24		7 43	
5 41	Elsenham (S)			8 0		10 19		12 18			4 24	6 14	6 29		7 48	

7 To Stansted arr. 12.52 p.m.

Passenger trains are worked on the " Conductor-Guard " principle.

BR (ER) Working Timetable : 1950

K 5

ELSENHAM AND THAXTED LIGHT RAILWAY

Single Line.

Worked by Train Staff without ticket. For regulations for working see "Appendix"

DOWN WEEKDAYS

Miles from Elsenham	No.	1	2	3	4	5	6	7	8	9	10	11	12	13	14	15
	Class		B	K	B		B		B		B		B			
	Description		Mxd		Mxd		Mxd		Mxd		Mxd		Mxd			
					SO		SX				SX					
M. C.			am	am	PM		PM		PM		PM		PM			
	Elsenham (S)		8 55	11 0	1 43		2 28		5 0		6 24		7 55			
70	Mill Road Halt		8 59		1 47		2 32		5 4		6 28		7 59			
1 55	Henham Halt		9 3		1 51		2 36		5 8		6 32		8 3			
2 76	Sibley's		9 8		1 56		2 41		5 13		6 37		8 8			
	Sibley's		9 14		1 57		2 42		5 14		6 38		8 9			
4 50	Cutler's Green Halt		9 20		2 3		2 48		5 20		6 44		8 15			
5 41	Thaxted (S)		9 23	11 20	2 6		2 51		5 23		6 47		8 18			

Passenger trains are worked on the " Conductor-Guard " principle

ELSENHAM AND THAXTED LIGHT RAILWAY

Single Line.

Worked by Train Staff without tickets. For regulations for working see "Appendix"

WEEKDAYS **UP**

Miles from Thaxted	No.	1	2	3	4	5	6	7	8	9	10	11	12	13	14	15
	Class			B		B		B		B		B	B		B	
	Description			Mxd		Mxd		Mxd		Mxd		Mxd	Mxd		Mxd	
												SX	SO		SX	
M. C.				am		am		am		PM		PM	PM		PM	
	Thaxted (S)			7 36		9 55		11 50		4 0		5 45	6 0		7 23	
71	Cutler's Green Halt			7 40		9 59		11 54		4 4		5 49	6 4		7 27	
2 45	Sibley's			7 46		10 5		12 0		4 10		5 55	6 10		7 33	
	Sibley's			7 47		10 6		12 5		4 11		6 0	6 15		7 34	
3 66	Henham Halt			7 52		10 11		12 10		4 16		6 5	6 20		7 39	
4 51	Mill Road Halt			7 56		10 15		12 14		4 20		6 9	6 24		7 43	
5 41	Elsenham (S)			8 0		10 19		12 18		4 24		6 14	6 29		7 48	

Passenger trains are worked on the " Conductor-Guard " principle.

The final BR (ER) Working Timetable to show passenger services : June 1952

Freight carried on the Thaxted branch included barley, wheat, hay, straw and vegetables. The great increase in the production of sugar beet, in the late 1920s, found considerable tonnages of beet being despatched from Sibley's and Thaxted to the British Sugar Corporation factories at Felstead and Ely. Barley was initially sent to the maltings at Bishop's Stortford, Sawbridgeworth and Ware, but with the rationalization and closure of maltings it was later sent further afield to Bury St. Edmunds, Godmanchester and Scotland. In the initial years, milk was also despatched to Bishop's Stortford in the familiar 17 gallon churns, two loads being sent daily, the first by the early morning train and the second by the last 'up' service. This traffic ceased by the mid-1920s. Other exports from Thaxted included local confectionery, and toys from a Thaxted manufacturer which included almost life-size mechanical elephants and horses used in fairgrounds, which apparently moved into the goods vans or wagons under their own power.

By far the largest commodity received in the goods yards at Sibley's and Thaxted was coal and coke for domestic and horticultural consumption. Other imports included seed potatoes from Scotland, animal foodstuffs and fertilizers for local farms, agricultural machinery, and 'smalls' traffic for local shops and warehouses.

Livestock handled was two-way traffic, and cattle wagons were a common feature on the branch mixed trains until the late 1940s. Outgoing cattle were regularly sent to Bishop's Stortford market on Thursdays, Waltham Cross for Waltham Abbey on Tuesdays, as well as Hertford and Cambridge. Although livestock was handled, the area served by the branch was essentially arable farming and, therefore, crops provided the greater proportion of goods receipts.

No mechanical aid was available for lifting items into or out of wagons at either Thaxted or Sibley's, although Elsenham was host to a 15cwt. fixed crane, an 8 ton cart weighbridge and a 1 ton 2cwt. capacity weighing machine. Cartage in the area was performed by an agent.

Shunting was not allowed to take place on the main single line at any of the branch stations unless the branch engine was at the station. The use of a tow rope, which allowed the shunting of vehicles from an adjacent road, was authorized at both Sibley's and Thaxted, and when not in use was normally kept in the custody of the guard and carried in the branch goods brake van.

In 1919, the GER appendix to the working timetable showed that the length of goods trains was not to exceed 14 wagons of mineral traffic, 20 wagons of goods traffic or 30 empty wagons. Later, a length limit of 28 wagons was imposed and in LNER days the J69 Class locomotives were allowed to haul 11 heavy, 19 goods and 22 empties, and the J15 Class, 12 heavy, 21 goods and 24 empties, although it is doubtful if trains of this length were ever conveyed. On mixed trains a passenger coach was equal to one loaded goods wagon.

The 8.55 a.m. mixed train climbs the 1 in 50 away from Elsenham, hauled by Class J69/1 0-6-0T, No. 68530, on 14th July 1951.

LCGB/Ken Nunn Collection

The morning freight shunt from the main line goods yard at Elsenham, approaches the junction points of the spur and the main single branch east of Elsenham Station, on 14th July 1951. It is hauled by 0-6-0T, Class J69/1, No. 68530.

LCGB/Ken Nunn Collection

A line up of GER personnel, at Thaxted, on the day of the official opening. They are, from left to right, unknown porter, Foreman in charge Woodley of Thaxted, Station Master H. Butters of Elsenham, who was responsible for the operation of the light railway, and Percy Reeve, Conductor Guard of Thaxted.

Conductor Guard, Percy Reeve, who worked on the first official and public train across the branch on 31st March and 1st April 1913. This photograph was taken just prior to his retirement.

Staff

Supervision of the light railway throughout its forty years operation came under the station master at Elsenham, and Mr H. W. Butters, who was in charge of the junction station in 1913, was the first recipient of the post, for which he received a higher grade.

The number of people manning the line was kept to a minimum. Of the twelve employed, five were motive power men, two drivers, two firemen and a cleaner (alternating with a coalman). The traffic staff totalled four, with a foreman in charge at Thaxted, a porter at Sibley's and two conductor guards responsible for issuing tickets on the trains in addition to their regular duties. Percy Reeve and Tom Buck spent most of their railway careers as conductor guards on the Thaxted branch. The permanent way laid almost completely in ashes and clinker, and fencing and associated assets, were kept in order by three gangers.

Fares

Only third class accommodation was available on the Thaxted line services, and as booking offices were not provided at stations for reasons of economy, the guards collected all the fares on the train. This applied equally to journeys originating at Elsenham, for the booking office never handled Thaxted bookings. There were no through fares to the branch stations, and all passengers were required to re-book on the train. Only single tickets were issued, of the bell-punch type, roughly printed on white paper and bearing the legend 'GER', later 'LNER' and 'British Railways (E)', similar to bus tickets. The guard cancelled them on issue with orthodox bell-punch.

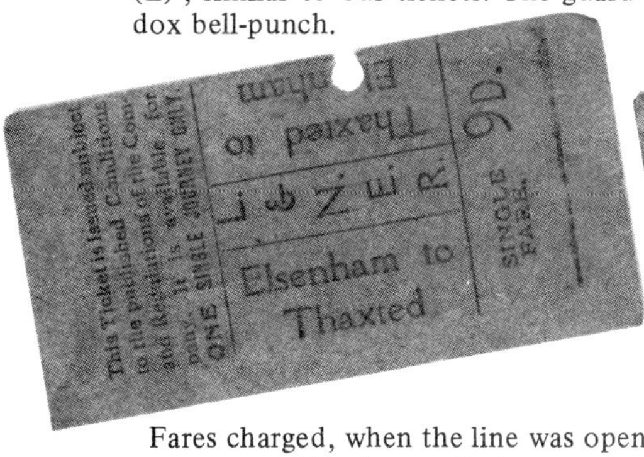

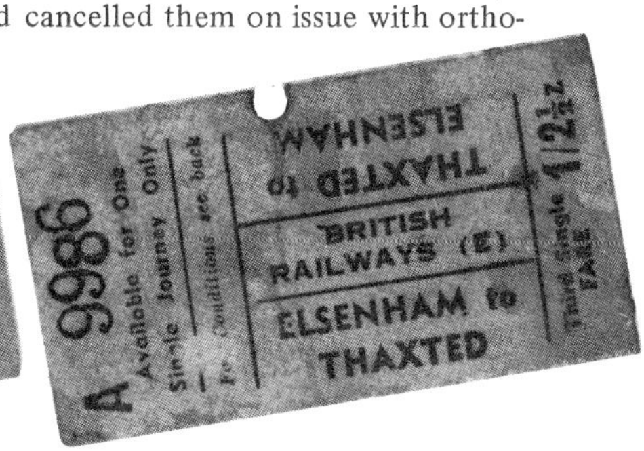

Fares charged, when the line was opened, were (single journey only):

Elsenham to Henham	2d
Elsenham to Sibley's	3d
Elsenham to Cutler's Green	5d
Elsenham to Thaxted	6d
Henham to Sibley's	1d
Henham to Cutler's Green	3d
Henham to Thaxted	4d
Sibley's to Cutler's Green	2d
Sibley's to Thaxted	3d
Cutler's Green to Thaxted	1d

The personal luggage allowance for each passenger was restricted to 60lb. Any items in excess of this weight, or any luggage conveyed on the light railway was charged at the following rates:

Luggage not exceeding 7lb. in weight	3d
7lb. and not exceeding 14lb. in weight	5d
14lb. and not exceeding 28lb. in weight	7d
28lb. and not exceeding 56lb. in weight	9d

By 1935 the fare from Elsenham to Thaxted was 9d, and when the line closed in 1952 the fare for the same journey was 1s 2½d. Fares from intermediate stations were increased in proportion.

Fares in operation when the line was closed were third class single only, as follows:

Elsenham to Mill Road	2d
Elsenham to Henham	4d
Elsenham to Sibley's	8d
Elsenham to Cutler's Green	11d
Elsenham to Thaxted	1/2½d
Mill Road Halt to Henham	2d
Mill Road Halt to Sibley's	6d
Mill Road Halt to Cutler's Green	9d
Mill Road Halt to Thaxted	1/-
Henham Halt to Sibley's	4d
Henham Halt to Cutler's Green	7d
Henham Halt to Thaxted	9d
Sibley's to Cutler's Green	4d
Sibley's to Thaxted	6½d
Cutler's Green to Thaxted	3½d

Class J67/2 0-6-0T, No. 68609 stands in the bay platform at Elsenham with the 5p.m. to Thaxted on 18th August 1951.

J. F. Aylard

J67/2 Class 0-6-0T, No. 68609, stands at Thaxted with the 5 p.m. from Elsenham on 18th August 1951.

J. F. Aylard

CHAPTER FIVE — Locomotives and Rolling Stock

The light construction of the Thaxted Light Railway, with its steep gradients and numerous curves, and the imposed 14 tons (later 16 tons) maximum axle loading, severely restricted the selection of locomotives available to work the services. The GER, however, possessed the sturdy R24 Class 0-6-0 tank locomotives with axle loading within these limits, and from the day of the official opening until closure the 'buckjumpers', as they were nicknamed, handled most of the traffic. Originally designed by J. Holden and built at Stratford Works between 1890 and 1904, the locomotives, fitted with Westinghouse brake for passenger work, gained fame on the 'Jazz' suburban services from Liverpool Street to Enfield Town and Chingford. Most depots throughout the GE system had an allocation of the class, and it was from Cambridge Motive Power Depot that the Thaxted branch locomotives were supplied.

The locomotive allocated to the light railway usually arrived on a Monday, changing over with the locomotive that had previously worked the line. The new locomotive then worked the services for two or three weeks, receiving a boiler washout and tube cleaning on Sundays when no trains ran. No repairs were carried out at Thaxted, and if the locomotive required maintenance it was returned to Cambridge.

The short wheelbase of the R24 Class was ideal for the line and, as far as can be ascertained, no attempt was made to remove the leading coupling rods as on the Kelvedon to Tollesbury Light Railway, to make them into 2-4-0Ts. The LNER, after 1923, classified the class to J67 and J69 with sub-sections, and it was usual for a J69/1 Class locomotive to work the Thaxted services.

The following locomotives were regularly used on the light railway services, and at other times performed shunting pilot duties at Cambridge.

GER No.	*LNER No. (1924)*	*LNER No. (1946)*	*BR No.*	*Condemned*
162	7162	8609	68609	September 1962
168	7168	8615		October 1940
169	7169	8616	68616	November 1958
193	7193	8600	68600	September 1962
196	7196	8603	68603	March 1958
271	7271	8579	68579	January 1960
353	7353	8530	68530	February 1961

No. 68579 hauled the last passenger trains on the line, and thereafter the thrice weekly goods service from Bishop's Stortford, with occasional substitution by J15 Class 0-6-0s.

Holden's GER R24R Class, LNER J69/1, 0-6-0T, No. 68579, stands at Thaxted on the final day of passenger service, 13th September 1952. No. 68579 hauled the last passenger train on the branch, and was then used occasionally on the goods working which ran until 1st June 1953.

Class J69/1 0-6-0T, No. 68579, stands at Thaxted, with brake thirds Nos. 62450 and 62461 on 10th September 1952, three days before the withdrawal of passenger traffic.

S. C. Nash

In the 1920s one of Holden's T18 Class 0-6-0Ts (LNER J66) was also utilized on the Thaxted service during a period when she was allocated to the Cambridge district. Dating from 1886, the class was initially only fitted with hand brakes but No. 294, when built in July 1887, received the Westinghouse brake for passenger work. This locomotive subsequently spent time, between 1926 and 1929, at the Essex shed as LNER No. 7294 before the Westinghouse brake was removed in October 1930, and she reverted to shunting duties, being fitted with steam brake only.

GER No.	*LNER No. (1924)*	*LNER No. (1946)*	*BR No.*	*Condemned*
294	7294	–	–	July 1937

Another class to be associated with the 'Gin and Toffee' line was the GER C72 Class (LNER J68), 0-6-0 tank locomotives introduced by A. J. Hill, and built at Stratford Works between 1912 and 1914. The locomotives, easily distinguished from the R24 Class by their cab with high roof, side windows, and large square, instead of round, front and rear spectacles, represented the final stage of the development of the original Holden 0-6-0 tank engines dating from 1886. The class did not appear on the Elsenham & Thaxted line until after 1935, when a locomotive displaced from the North East London Suburban services was sent to Cambridge. The following worked on the branch:

GER No.	*LNER No. (1924)*	*LNER No. (1946)*	*BR No.*	*Condemned*
49	7049	8645	68645	November 1959

With blower on, Class J68, No. 68645, prepares to depart Thaxted with the two coach branch train to Elsenham in 1951. No. 68645 was regularly used on the branch for fifteen years, along with J67 and J69 Class locomotives.

D. Trevor Rowe

Ex-GER 'buckjumper' Class J68 0-6-0T, LNER No. 8645, stands in the bay platform at Elsenham, in 1948. The main line is in the background and the run-round loop line in the foreground. The J68 could be distinguished from the J67 and J69s by the window in the cab sides, and the large square, instead of round, driver's spectacle window.

When the branch closed No. 68645 was initially reallocated to Norwich.
The LNER route availability allowed the following classes between Elsenham and Thaxted:

Tender: E4, J15, J21
Tank: F3, F4, F5, F7, J62, J63, J65 to J70, Y1, Y3, Y5, Y6 and Y10.

whilst British Railways graded the line to route availability 3 (RA3), although double-heading was prohibited.

The only other 'regular' to penetrate to Thaxted was the GER Y14 Class (LNER J15), designed by T. W. Worsdell, and introduced in 1883. Such was the success of the design that building continued until 1913. All but 19 of the class of 272 0-6-0 tender locomotives were built at Stratford, and the others by Sharp Stewart & Co. On most occasions their visits were on engineering trains or out-of-course freight trains, whilst one was in attendance during the latter days of the construction of the line. There were no turntables on the branch, and the class was restricted to 15 m.p.h. when running tender first. Members of the class which worked on the line after nationalization included Nos. 65356, 65391, 65406, 65438, 65445, 65461 and 65475.

Principle dimensions of Locomotives

Class	GER R24 LNER J67 0-6-0T	GER R24R LNER J69 0-6-0T	GER C72 LNER J68 0-6-0T	GER Y14 LNER J15 0-6-0	GER T18 LNER J66 0-6-0T
Cylinders 2 inside	16½ x 22	16½ x 22	16½ x 22	17½ x 24	16½ x 22
Motion			All: Stephenson with slide valves		
Boiler max. dia.	4ft. 2in.	4ft. 2in.	4ft. 2in.	4ft. 4in.	4ft. 2in.
Barrel length	9ft. 1in.	9ft. 1in.	9ft. 1in.	10ft. 0in.	9ft. 1in.
Firebox	4ft. 6in.	5ft. $2^{1}/_{16}$in.	5ft. $2^{1}/_{16}$in.	6ft. 0in.	4ft. 6in.
Heating firebox	78.0sq. ft.	86.77sq. ft.	86.77sq. ft.	105.5sq. ft.	78.0sq. ft.
Surface tubes	227 x $1^{5}/_{8}$in. 909.40sq. ft.	227 x $1^{5}/_{8}$in. 909.40sq. ft.	227 x $1^{5}/_{8}$in. 909.40sq. ft.	242 x $1^{5}/_{8}$in. 1,063.8 sq. ft.	227 x $1^{5}/_{8}$in. 909.40sq. ft.
Firebox grate area	12.4sq. ft.	14.5sq. ft.	14.5sq.ft.	17.9sq.ft.	12.4sq.ft.
Boiler pressure	160 p.s.i.	180 p.s.i.	180 p.s.i.	160 p.s.i.	160. p.s.i.
Coupled wheels	4ft. 0in.	4ft. 0in.	4ft. 0in.	4ft. 11in.	4ft. 0in.
Tractive effort	16,970lb.	19,091lb.	19,091lb.	16,942lb.	16,970lb.
Length over buffers	27ft. 8in.	27ft. 8in.	27ft. 8in.	–	28ft. 2½in.
Wheelbase	13ft. 10in.	13ft. 10in.	13ft. 10in.	16ft. 1in.	13ft. 4in.
Tender	–	–	–	12ft. 0in.	–
Weight in working order (Locomotive)	40ton	42ton 9cwt	42ton 9cwt	37ton 2cwt	40ton 6cwt
Weight in working order (Tender)	–	–	–	30ton 13cwt	–
Max. axle load	14ton	15ton 2cwt	15ton 2cwt	13ton 10cwt	15ton 1cwt
Water capacity	1,000 gall.	1,200 gall.	1,200 gall.	2,640 gall.	1,000 gall.
Coal capacity	2ton 5cwt	2ton 10cwt	2ton 10cwt	5ton	2ton 5cwt

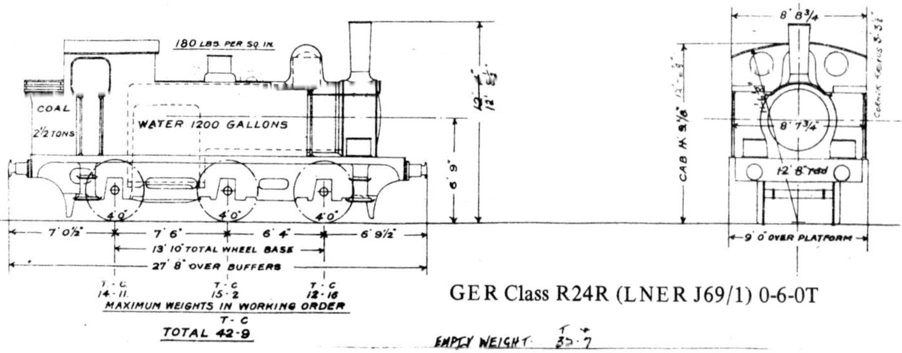

GER Class R24R (LNER J69/1) 0-6-0T

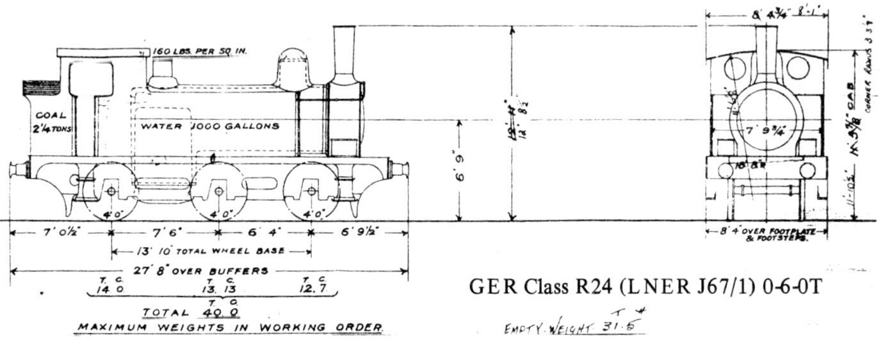

GER Class R24 (LNER J67/1) 0-6-0T

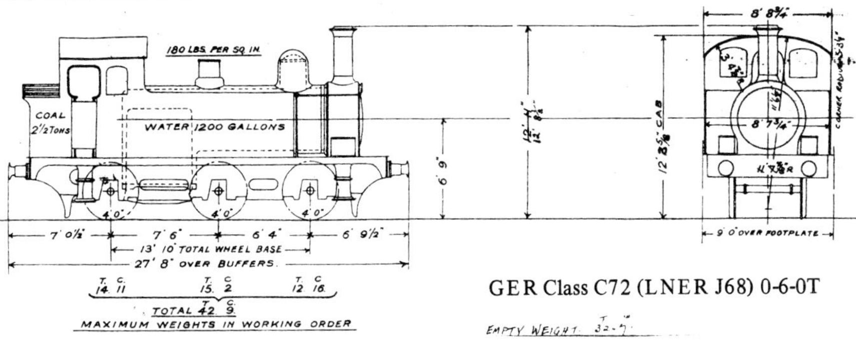

GER Class C72 (LNER J68) 0-6-0T

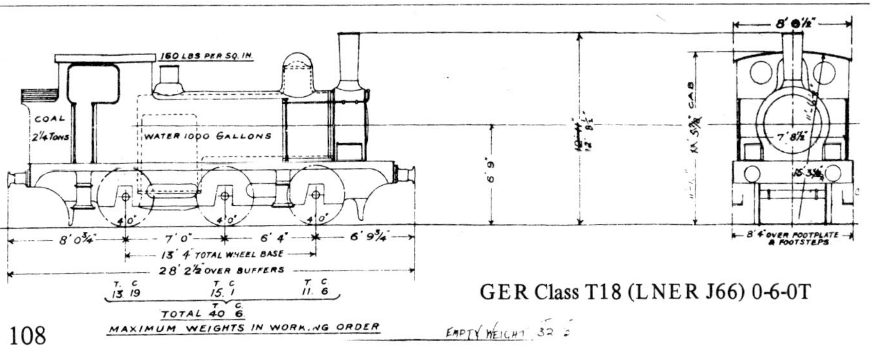

GER Class T18 (LNER J66) 0-6-0T

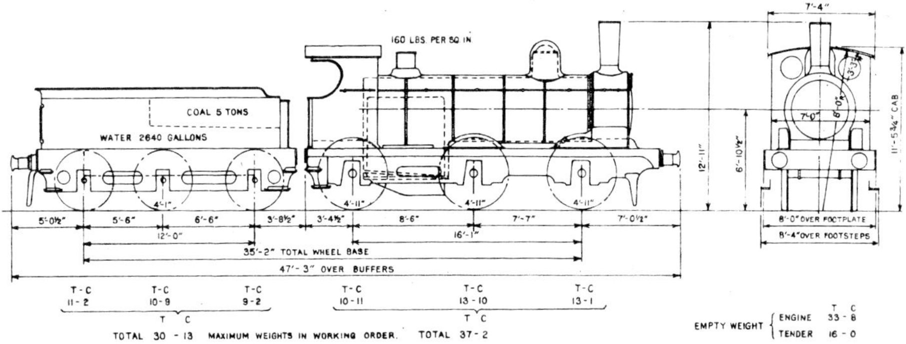

GER Class Y14 (LNER J15) 0-6-0

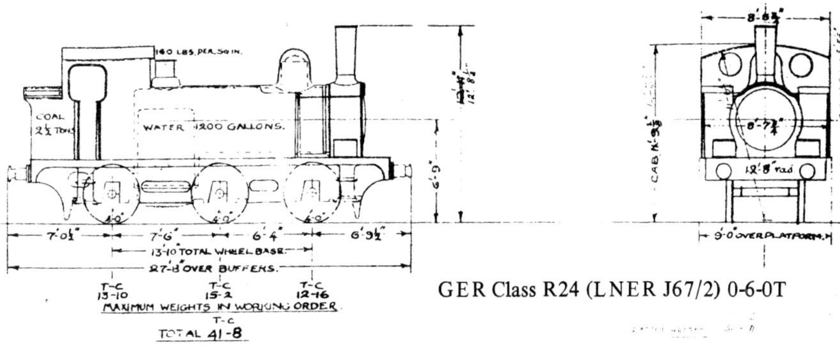

GER Class R24 (LNER J67/2) 0-6-0T

Thaxted Shed was a sub-shed of Cambridge Motive Power Depot which always supplied locomotives to the line. In BR days the code '31A' was given to Cambridge Shed, and branch locomotives duly carried this shed plate on the smokebox door.

Two sets of footplate staff were stationed at Thaxted during the time the line was open for traffic, the early turn signing on around 4.50a.m., whilst the second set relieved these men around 1.20p.m. The early turn men prepared the locomotive whilst the late turn disposed of the locomotive and raised water for the locomotive water storage tank. The footplate crews were supplemented by a cleaner (alternating with a coalman), who was booked on night duty to coal and water the locomotive for duty on the following day.

The locomotive foreman, at Thaxted, or as he was later called, driver in charge, received a half-day's extra pay per week for administrative duties, which included the submission of drivers' tickets and coal and oil returns to the District Motive Power Office at Cambridge. Thaxted drivers signed the route knowledge sheets to Elsenham only, but after World War II, they signed to Bishop's Stortford and Audley End, so that intermediate yard shunting, between turns, could be carried out by the branch engine at Newport and Stansted. Some Cambridge men also signed route knowledge sheets for the branch.

THAXTED DEPOT.

No. 1.

arr		dep.
a.m.		a.m.
	On Duty	4 50
	Loco'	5 35 L
	Thaxted	5 50 G
6 20	Elsenham	7 25 G
7 50	Thaxted	8 10
8 34	Elsenham	9 19
9 47	Thaxted	10 40
11 10	Elsenham	11 25
		p.m.
11 47	Thaxted	12 10
p.m.		
12 34	Elsenham	12 50
1 18	Thaxted	1 50 SX 2 5 SO
SX 2 18 SO 2 33	Elsenham	2 32 SX 2 50 SO
SX 2 54 SO 3 12	Thaxted	3 47
4 11	Elsenham	4 25
4 47	Thaxted	5 20
5 44	Elsenham	5 55
6 17	Thaxted	6 27
7 4	Elsenham	7 38
8 0	Thaxted	L
	Loco'	

Men change at Thaxted 1.18 p.m.

Second set water raising Thaxted until 9.30 p.m.

Locomotive and enginemen's diagram for Thaxted Depot, 13th July 1925.

In GER days, drivers were strict with the firemen and cleaners, especially if the branch locomotive was not spotlessly clean. A common test was to wipe a clean rag along the footplate, on the inside of the framing and the wheels, to make sure the cleaning had not been skimped. During the coal shortage in the 1920s and early 1930s, the cleaner, or coalman, was delegated to make briquettes from coal and cement to supplement the meagre coal supply, and cut up old sleepers for firelighters to light up the fire in the firebox.

Another aspect of this rural depot was boiler washing and tube cleaning. As no facilities were to hand, a boiler washer and fitter travelled from Cambridge to carry out these tasks. Later, boiler washing and tube cleaning was carried out by footplate staff, and for this operation the senior fireman was paid four hours Sunday rate for the work.

Some motive power staff were characters, and an amusing incident can be related of an accident which happened at Thaxted in the late 1920s. Whilst shunting a coal wagon in the goods yard, the fireman who was driving at the time failed to stop the locomotive pushing a loaded coal wagon through the buffer stops, demolishing the feed pipe to the water crane by the engine shed. With water gushing everywhere but none available for locomotive use, it was realized the engine would soon run short of water. Fortunately it was still on the rails, so a rapid run was made to Elsenham before reversing and continuing to Bishop's Stortford for water. Thereafter, until the feed pipe was repaired, the locomotive had to travel the ten miles to and from the Hertfordshire town for replenishment, before returning to Thaxted.

Motive power facilities at Thaxted, included a brick-built engine shed, 45 ft. 9 in. long by 22 ft. 6 in. wide, just large enough to accommodate one of the 0-6-0 tank locomotives. Originally doors were fitted, but these were removed in LNER days. Water was obtained from a water crane, fed from the adjacent tank raised aloft the pump house, the latter also being used as a mess room for the footplate staff. The water from the well was pumped

Class J69/1, No. 68530, gets up steam outside Thaxted Engine Shed.

Photomatic

Thaxted brick-built engine shed with accommodation for one 'buckjumper' J69/1 Class locomotive. No. 68579 awaits it next turn of duty on 10th September 1952.

S. C. Nash

Thaxted Locomotive Shed, on 30th June 1951, with Class J69/1, No. 68530 raising steam for her next trip to Elsenham. The water tank is to the left, and the raised locomotive coal siding on the right. Note the piles of ash which have been removed from the firebox.

H. C. Casserley

Class J69, No. 68609, stands outside Thaxted Shed on 23rd August 1952.

John H. Meredith

into the storage tank by means of a water-raising cock fitted to the locomotive, and all locomotives working the branch were fitted with this component. The water was considered hard for locomotive boilers, and molasses, and later chemical briquettes, were added to soften the water before topping up the side tanks. It was customary to top up the side tanks after each round trip to Elsenham, but coaling of the locomotive was carried out by the cleaner or coalman on night duty, from a wagon in the adjacent coal road. If the bunker required replenishment during the day, the fireman was responsible.

The headcode carried by the branch trains in GER days was a red disc with white outer rim, under the chimney during daylight, and a red head lamp under the chimney during darkness or fog and falling snow. After the Grouping, the LNER standard stopping passenger train code of a white headlamp, lit after dark or during fog or falling snow, or a disc under the chimney, was used on the Thaxted Light Railway trains, and remained in use until the withdrawal of passenger services. Freight trains on the branch carried the appropriate class headcode. The engine whistlecode, used at Elsenham from the branch to and from Elsenham Station via the goods yard, was three distinct sounds. In addition, the whistle was sounded on the approach to all ungated level crossings.

In the event of a mishap or breakdown, the light railway was covered by the Cambridge Motive Power Depot steam breakdown crane, latterly using a 45 ton capacity crane.

Coaching Stock

The GER, anticipating the probable passenger revenue, initially provided five coaches for their new light railway. As with vehicles originally provided for the Kelvedon & Tollesbury line, the three, six wheel six compartment thirds, and two, six wheel three compartment brake thirds, all built in 1891/2 for main line service, were chosen at random from the existing fleet.

Conversion work was carried out at Stratford Works early in 1913. The third class coaches had the compartment partitions removed, and a central gangway provided with a door at each end of the vehicle, opening out on to a drop-plate to enable the guard to walk through to adjacent vehicles to issue tickets. Tramcar type seats were fitted and four doors on each side of the vehicle blanked off, leaving only the end doors available for passenger access. The brake thirds received similar treatment, but in their case the central gangway was provided with a door to the guard's compartment. Two doors on each side were blanked off leaving only the end doors available for passengers.

To compensate for the low station platforms, the 3 ft. 6½in. Mansell wooden centre wheels, originally fitted, were replaced by wheels 2 ft. 9in. in diameter, whilst the headstock had to be modified to maintain buffer and drawbar level. For the convenience of passengers, outside steps were also provided, but as these fouled the main line loading gauge, they had to be removed before the vehicles returned to shops for maintenance. Lighting was by incandescent gas, and all vehicles were fitted with Westinghouse brakes.

Two of the original GER six wheel coaches stand at Thaxted. The first vehicle is a brake third and the other an ordinary third. These vehicles were originally built in 1891/2 for main line service, and were converted for use on the Thaxted Light Railway in 1913. During conversion the original 3ft. 6½in. wheels were replaced by wheels of 2ft. 9in. diameter, whilst the headstock was modified to maintain buffer and drawbar level. Even so, the vehicle was still above the 1ft. high platform and passengers boarding and alighting had to use the steps provided.

J. Watling Collection

J69/1 Class, No. 7193, stands at Thaxted, on 15th August 1936, with two of the original six wheel coaches supplied to the line. The leading vehicle is third No. 60866, followed by brake third No. 62913.

T. Middlemas

The five coaches proved more than adequate for the requirements of branch traffic. Usually only two vehicles, a third and brake third, were used for normal services, except on Thursdays when extra passengers travelled to Bishop's Stortford market, and the train was strengthened accordingly. By the early 1930s, it became evident to the railway authorities that with the gradual loss of traffic to the roads, the policy of working one third and one brake third together, with a similar formation as spare vehicles, covered all contingencies. Thus a third open became surplus to requirements, so when, in August 1932, No. 60879 became due for shopping, it was withdrawn from traffic. The remaining vehicles survived World War II, by which time they were in poor condition, and then open third No. 60866 and brake third No. 62913 were withdrawn from service on 21st June 1947. Both survived for a further 17 years as service vehicles without being renumbered. No. 60866 was finally broken up at Norwich Victoria on 14th March 1964, and No. 62913 suffered a similar fate at Cambridge later in the year. The last two coaches, third No. 60900 and brake third No. 62908 remained in service until 14th February 1948, by which time the ex-GER bogie vehicles had arrived to take their place. Both vehicles were broken up at Stratford on 10th April 1948.

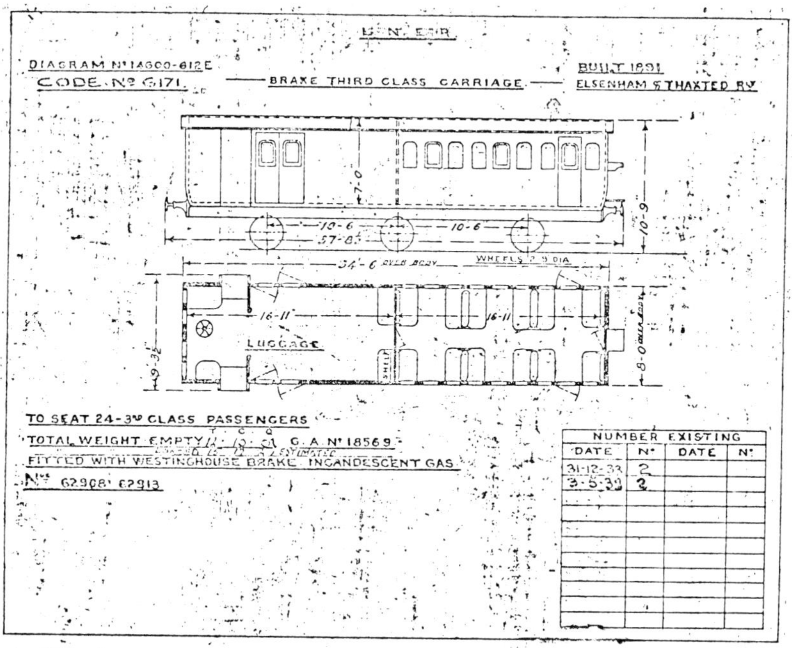

A GER six wheel brake third (diagram 612). Two vehicles, Nos. 94 and 253 were converted for use on the Light Railway.

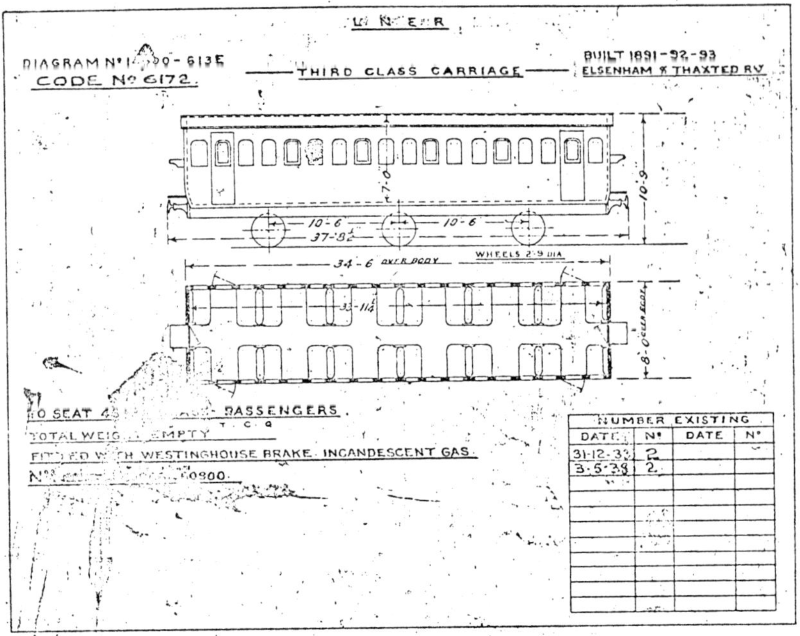

A six wheel full third (GER diagram 613). Three vehicles, Nos. 43, 97 and 439 were converted for use on the Thaxted line.

Brake third:

Diagram	*GER No.*	*LNER No.*	*Built*	*Withdrawn*	*Broken up*
612	94	62908	2/91	14.2.48	10.4.48
612	253	62913	2/91	21.6.47	1964

Third:

Diagram	*GER No.*	*LNER No.*	*Built*	*Withdrawn*	*Broken up*
613	43	60866	2/92	21.6.47	March 1964
613	97	60879	7/91	13.8.32	
613	439	60900	4/92	14.2.48	April 1948

Principle dimensions:

Length over buffers	37 ft. 8½in
Length over body	34 ft. 6 in.
Height	10 ft. 9 in.
Max. Width	8 ft. 0 in.
Wheelbase	21 ft. 0 in.

Seating: third class coach – 48 passengers; third class brake – 24 passengers;
Total weight empty – 12ton 10cwt.

The GER later provided a sixth vehicle for use on the light railway; luggage van No. 9. Originally built for the Wisbech & Upwell Tramway in September 1884, the vehicle's usefulness was limited owing to lack of guard's accommodation, and in 1903 it was replaced by a former suburban brake third which was converted to a full brake for service at Wisbech. After some months in store, No. 9 was transferred to the Downham–Stoke Ferry branch where it provided additional luggage accommodation. As parcels traffic increased on the Norfolk branch, its usefulness was again considered inadequate, and it was often replaced by an ordinary covered van. On the opening of the Thaxted line it was thought the van might serve some useful purpose in providing additional luggage accommodation. No. 9 was not transferred to the Elsenham–Thaxted line, however, until 23rd December 1913, where it was occasionally utilized as a general parcels and milk van when the normal brake was full. The van was withdrawn on 28th December 1929 without being renumbered by the LNER, and sent to Stratford for further use as an internal service vehicle, stock No. EX044, where it is believed to have survived until the mid-1950s.

Principle dimensions:

Length over buffers	15ft. 6in.	Width over body	7ft. 7in.
Length over body	12ft. 0in.	Wheelbase	6ft. 0in.
Height	10ft. 2in.	Total weight, empty	4ton 2cwt. 3qtrs

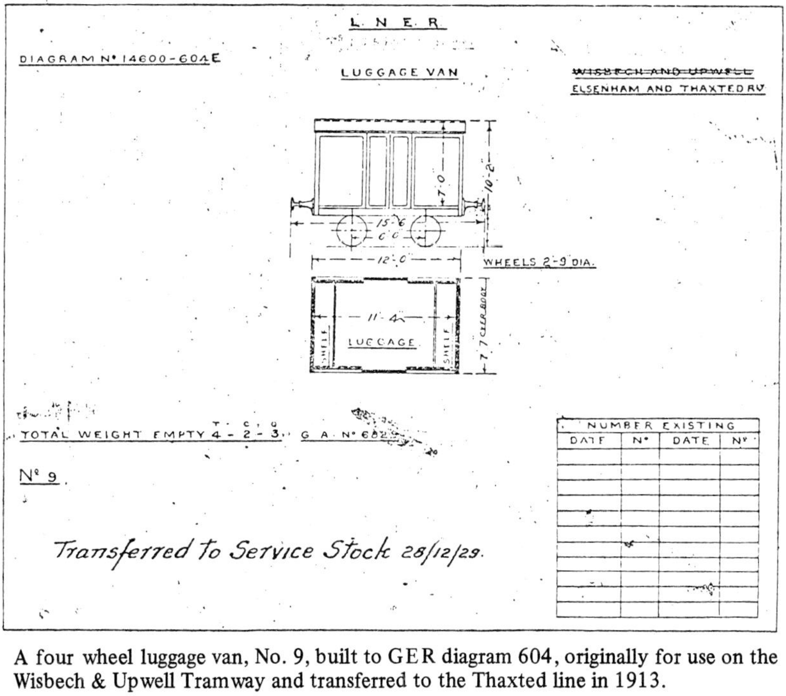

A four wheel luggage van, No. 9, built to GER diagram 604, originally for use on the Wisbech & Upwell Tramway and transferred to the Thaxted line in 1913.

The three bogie corridor coaches transferred to the line in 1947/48 had a chequered history before working out their days in the relative calm of the Thaxted line. The first of the trio, LNER No. 61471, was built by the GER as brake No. 369 in March 1914. Later, in World War I, it was converted into a Ward Car for No. 36 ambulance train. After hostilities, it was returned to the GER where it was rebuilt as an open third corridor coach, renumbered 649, and returned to normal main line service in March 1923. The other two vehicles came to the Elsenham to Thaxted line as corridor brake thirds. LNER No. 62450 was built as GER No. 415 and entered service as a brake and Infections Car for No. 28 ambulance train. On return from war service it was converted to a corridor brake third, and returned to traffic in July 1923. Both the above vehicles had 50 ft. bodies, but LNER No. 62461, with a 54 ft. body, was also built by the GER, as their No. 419, as a Pharmacy Car for No. 61 ambulance train. It was converted to a corridor brake third and returned to traffic in September 1924. All vehicles were fitted with electric lighting and Westinghouse and vacuum brakes when they entered the Thaxted service. In addition, all tables and lavatories were removed during the preliminary conversion carried out at Stratford.

J69 Class 0-6-0T, No. 68609, awaits departure at Thaxted with bogie coaches Nos. E62450 and E62461 on 23rd August 1952.

John H. Meredith

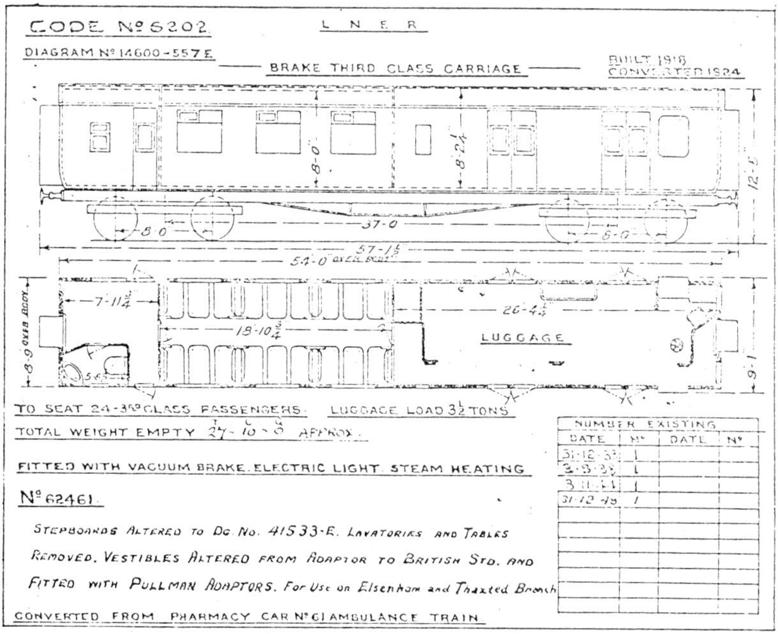

GER diagram 557; 57ft. brake third No. 62461

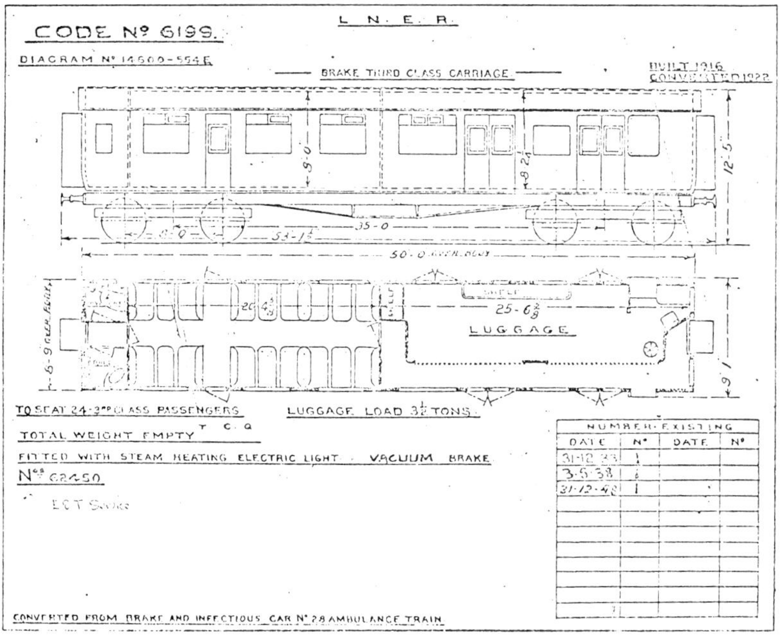

GER diagram 554; 53ft. brake third No. 62450

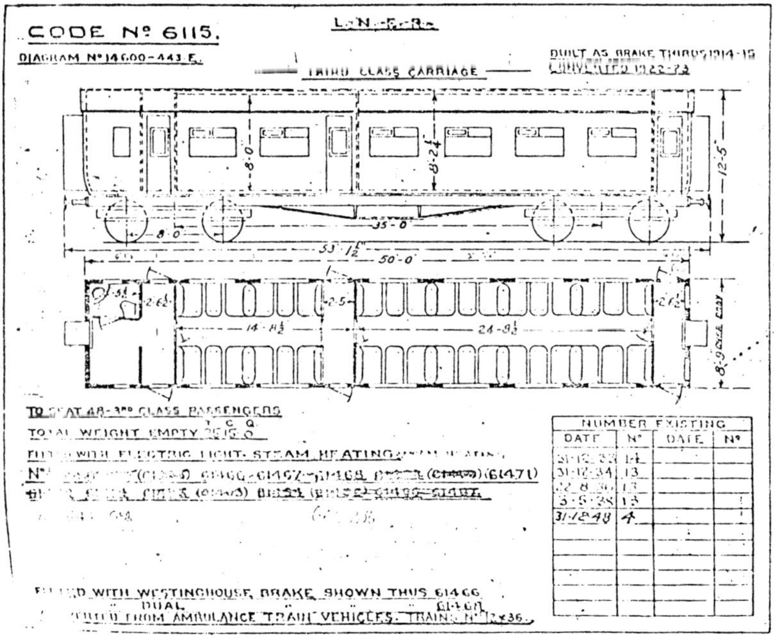

GER diagram 443; 53ft. third No. 61471

Two of the three coaches were utilized for normal daily services, with the third vehicle rarely being pressed into service, and usually standing spare at Elsenham. For the duration of their stay, Nos. 61471 and 62461 were painted in a dark brown livery, but No. 62450 sported a curious khaki green paintwork. As with the six wheel vehicles, side steps were again fitted to the vehicles for the convenience of passengers boarding and alighting at the low platforms, and these had to be removed before the vehicles travelled on the main line to and from shops. The small white destination boards bearing the legend 'Elsenham & Thaxted' in black lettering continued to be carried on the sides of these vehicles.

The three bogie corridor coaches, transferred to the Thaxted Light Railway in 1947/8, stand at Thaxted in September 1952. These vehicles, brake third No. 62461 to Diagram 557, No. 62450 to Diagram 554 and third No. 61471 to Diagram 443 had chequered histories before working out their days in the relative calm of the light railway. Note the steps on the side of the vehicles. ▶

J. Watling Collection

Thaxted Station, facing Elsenham, in 1952. The full complement of the passenger coaching stock used on the branch stands at the platform, two brake thirds and the full third, all ex-GER corridor stock. The open nature of the surrounding countryside is evident, with no other buildings in close proximity.

Ex-GER brake thirds, Nos. 62450 and 62461 stand at the platform at Thaxted, on 10th September 1952, whilst in the background Class J69/1, No. 68579, waits by the engine shed.

S. C. Nash

Detail of the centre doorway and destination board of third open coach, No. 61471, on the Elsenham & Thaxted branch on 29th August 1952.

R. E. Vincent

A passenger alights, from the train at Cutlers Green Halt, by using the side steps on the coach to reach the low platform only 1 ft. in height.

Lens of Sutton

Henham Halt, complete with the old coach body for passenger accommodation, seat and gents' toilet, in 1951.

D. Trevor Rowe

After the withdrawal of passenger services No. 61471 and 62461 were returned to Stratford and are believed to have been broken up soon after No. 62450 became a mobile office, renumbered into the service fleet as DE320639, and was finally condemned on 18th October 1958. Of the survivors, it is interesting to note that two of the original six wheel vehicles used on the line outlived their replacements by six years.

Diagram	*GER No.*	*LNER No.*	*Built*	*Withdrawn*
443	649	61471	3/14	
554	415	62450	1916	18.10.58 (Mobile office) (DE320639)
557	419	62461	1918	

Principle dimensions:

Coach No.	61471 Open third	62450 Brake third	62461 Brake third
Length over buffers	53ft. 1½in.	53ft. 1½in.	57ft. 1½in.
Length over body	50ft. 0in.	50ft. 0in.	54ft. 0in.
Max. height	12ft. 5in.	12ft. 5in.	12ft. 5in.
Width over body	8ft. 9in.	9ft. 1in.	9ft. 1in.
Wheelbase	43ft. 0in.	43ft. 0in.	45ft. 0in.
Seating	48	24	24
Total weight, empty	25ton 15cwt	27½ton	27½ton
Luggage		3½ton	3½ton

A variety of non-passenger carrying stock was used on the Thaxted Light Railway, ranging from fitted vans for perishable produce, fruit and flowers; cattle wagons, horse-boxes, carriage wagons and the occasional milk van. There were no restrictions in force to limit GER wagon types, although the majority utilized on goods services were 5 plank or high sided opens for general merchandise, and covered vans for grain and perishable traffic. Coal traffic for domestic use was usually handled in merchants' wagons or private owner colliery wagons, whilst locomotive supplies came in railway-owned wagons.